Teamster Power

Farrell Dobbs

MONAD PRESS, NEW YORK

First Edition, 1973

Published by Monad Press
for the Anchor Foundation, Inc.

Distributed by
Pathfinder Press, Inc.
410 West Street
New York, N. Y. 10014

Library of Congress Catalog Card Number 73-78115
Manufactured in the United States of America

To the main army of the over-the-road campaign, the rank-and-file Teamsters of Omaha and Sioux City.

Left to right: Dick Sodenberg, Louis Miller, and Malcolm Love carrying the first banners ever used by General Drivers Local 554 of Omaha-Council Bluffs.

Contents

List of Illustrations

Acknowledgments

As the author, I assume sole responsibility for this work. In doing so, however, I wish to thank various individuals for valuable help they have given.

Marvel Scholl, my closest companion, cooperated on a day-to-day basis in carrying through the project. She contributed recollections of events, of the people involved, and of the general conditions that prevailed during the period discussed. Parts of this information have been quoted directly from memoranda she compiled. Sharon Lee Finer typed the entire manuscript. Her accuracy, combined with prompt, efficient attention to all details, served constantly as an inspiration for me to keep plowing ahead.

As participants in the events described, Harry DeBoer, Jack Maloney, and Ray Rainbolt checked each chapter as it was prepared. In this way they were able to help assure that the story would be accurate. Louis Miller gave factual information about the Omaha strikes, including his recollections, which are quoted in the text. Albert S. Parker provided a key issue of the strike bulletin published by the Omaha Teamsters, the *Farmer-Labor Press*. Max Geldman extended full cooperation in the preparation of the chapter on the Federal Workers Section. George Novack, following through after the others had played their respective parts, edited the manuscript as a whole.

Information has been drawn from tape recordings and written matter left by V. R. Dunne and Carl Skoglund, who are now dead. Material from my files, assembled during the days when I was a Teamster official, has been used for reference and quotation. Issues of *The Organizer* and the *Northwest Organizer*, which served as organs of the Minneapolis General Drivers Union, have been drawn upon for verification of facts and events. Bound volumes of the Trotskyist weeklies *The Militant* and the *Socialist Appeal* have been similarly used. In addition information has been taken from the *Minneapolis Labor Review*, official organ of the AFL Central Labor Union; also from issues of the Minneapolis and St. Paul daily papers.

Members of Minneapolis Local 544's Executive Board at a session shortly after the murder of Pat Corcoran. Left to right: Farrell Dobbs, Grant Dunne, Carl Skoglund, V. R. Dunne, Miles Dunne, Jack Smith, William Brown, Nick Wagner. Although not then a board member, V. R. Dunne often attended its meetings in an advisory capacity.

A meeting of Local 544 job stewards.

Introduction

The Teamsters union is the largest and probably the most powerful labor organization in the United States. How did it acquire that power? That is the central theme of this book.

The rise of the truck drivers began in the early 1930s. During 1934 workers across the country were stirred by a series of dramatic strikes in Minneapolis, Minnesota. This struggle drew nationwide attention because of its unique features, even though only a single local union was involved. The union was General Drivers Local 574 of the International Brotherhood of Teamsters, an American Federation of Labor affiliate.

In a previous book (*Teamster Rebellion* [Monad Press, 1972]) I have written an extensive account of the 1934 Minneapolis strikes. The following synopsis of the story is intended simply to acquaint the reader with the background against which events described in the present volume were to unfold.

Like other AFL units, Local 574 had long been characterized by conservative policies and an obsolete craft union structure embracing few members. By 1934, however, it was drawing broad layers of workers into a militant fight against the general trucking employers of the city. The change resulted from an internal transformation the union was undergoing during the heat of battle. A new, militant leadership was gradually gaining control and proving its competence in the eyes of rank-and-file members who wanted to use the union's power in defense of their class interests.

Throughout the country labor militancy was on the rise under the pressures of severe economic depression. Millions upon millions were unemployed nationally. Workers lucky enough to have jobs had to get by as best they could on what were usually starvation wages. In Minneapolis, trucking companies paid as little as ten dollars and rarely above eighteen dollars for a work week ranging from fifty-four to ninety hours. It was not unusual for employed workers to need supplementary public assistance in order to support a family. Under these conditions the workers strongly desired a change for the better and they were ready to fight to bring it about.

Politically this mood was expressed in Minnesota through growing support to the Farmer-Labor Party, a statewide movement based upon an alliance of trade unions and farmers' organizations. In national politics the FLP tended to support the "New Deal" policies of Democratic President Franklin D. Roosevelt. Within the state, however, it contended for public office against both the Democrats and Republicans. Its political strength was reflected in the election in 1930 and again in 1932 of Floyd B. Olson, the FLP candidate for governor.

Although Olson sought to project a prolabor image, his basic objective was to advance his personal political career. For that reason he acted in a way calculated to assure the ruling class that he could be trusted to follow capitalist ground rules in exercising governmental authority. As a result, his performance in public office fell far short of the hopes and expectations of the working people who had elected him.

Parallel with their political support to the FLP, the workers were ready to join trade unions to fight for better wages and job conditions. At hand for the purpose in Minneapolis was only a small AFL movement consisting of a few local unions, which were little more than skeleton organizations. All were craft formations, restricted essentially to skilled or semiskilled workers.

A conservative officialdom sat astride this setup, seeking to win favor among the bosses through "statesmanlike" collaboration with them. This centered on efforts to create special job opportunities for relatively privileged categories of labor. Toward that end a few companies had been coaxed into hiring only AFL members; in return these firms were promised the patronage of organized labor as "fair" employers. Meanwhile, the needs of the bulk of the city's workers were ignored.

The AFL's "statesmanlike" approach was coldly received by the main sections of the ruling class. Anti-union policies were rigorously pushed by the major employer organization, the Citizens Alliance, which was dominated by the wealthiest, most powerful local capitalists. Faced with such strong opposition, the craft unions had been able to induce few companies to deal with them. This not only left them weak in numbers; they were more or less impotent, as shown by the fact that not a single strike had been won in the city for many years.

The conservative AFL officials had neither the desire nor the capacity to reverse this situation by organizing a militant

struggle against the bosses. Instead they looked to Governor
Olson for leadership in a "safe and sane" course intended to
gradually strengthen the trade union movement with the cooperation of "fair" employers.

In that setting, a plan of action was developed by members
of the Communist League of America (the organizational form
of the Trotskyist movement at that time). They aimed to provide the fighting leadership needed and wanted by workers
in the trucking industry. First, however, they had to battle
their way into Local 574, which had jurisdiction over the coal
yards in which they were employed. Steps could then be taken
to convert the union into an instrument capable of serving the
workers' needs. Policies based on revolutionary class consciousness could be introduced. Rank-and-file militancy could be
channeled into a showdown fight with the trucking employers.
Conservative union officials who failed to meet the test of battle
would begin to lose influence over the membership; and the
Trotskyist militants could gradually develop and consolidate
their role as the real leaders of the local.

Hundreds of unorganized workers in the coal industry were
ready for unionization. Yet they were not welcomed into Local
574 because the business agent wanted to protect a little job
trust he had set up through a closed shop contract with one
coal firm. To cope with this problem the Trotskyists formed
a voluntary organizing committee in the open-shop coal yards,
the object being to mobilize mass pressure for admission into
the union.

Support for that objective soon developed within Local 574's
executive board. A minority of the board favored the idea of
broadening the union membership and waging a struggle for
union recognition throughout the industry. After a time the
executive board was forced to reverse its exclusionist policy.
An official union compaign was then launched throughout the
coal industry and before long the yards were quite solidly
organized.

Demands for a working agreement were drawn up for submission to the coal employers. They refused to negotiate and
the industry was struck in February 1934. The strike had several characteristics which were new to the Minneapolis labor
movement. Instead of being half-heartedly conducted as a piece-
meal action, it involved all the workers in all the coal yards.
Picketing, which had been planned in advance, was conducted
militantly and effectively under the direct leadership of the
voluntary organizing committee. In the process rank-and-file
initiative and ingenuity were given free play with salutary

results. On the first morning of the walkout the industry was tightly shut down and it was kept that way.

After a three-day tieup during a severe cold wave the employers made a settlement with the union. Despite inept handling of the negotiations by the official leadership, Local 574 had scored a victory. Union recognition—the key issue of the strike—was extended indirectly in the form of an employer stipulation with the Labor Board, a governmental agency set up by Roosevelt. Signing of the stipulation was made contingent upon the outcome of a representation election conducted by the Board, which the union won. Gains were also registered concerning wages and job conditions.

Most important of all, it had been shown that a strike could be won. That imbued workers throughout the general trucking industry with a new sense of hope in the union. The stage was thus set for a wider and deeper struggle.

By this time the voluntary organizing committee had gained enough support in the union's expanded ranks to force through a decision giving it official status. With the help of sympathizers on Local 574's executive board, the Trotskyist-led committee was able to set into motion a new, big organizing drive. Members were taken in from all sectors of the trucking industry, except in limited areas where other Teamster locals had jurisdiction over a specific sub-craft. Local 574 also passed beyond the IBT norm of confining its membership more or less to truck drivers and helpers. Wherever possible workers whose jobs were in any way related to trucking—in shipping rooms, warehouses, etc.—were brought into the local. A shift was being made from the narrow craft form toward the broader industrial form of organization.

New members began flocking into the union by the hundreds. At a series of democratically conducted meetings the workers wrote their own ticket in shaping demands upon the employers. This helped to make the membership an integral part of the fight for a progressive union policy. It also gave fresh impetus to the organizing committee's efforts to establish rank-and-file control over all the union's affairs.

In the process, reinforcements came forward to strengthen the work of the organizing committee. Day by day the committee gained in leadership influence. Weaknesses stemming from incompetence within Local 574's officialdom were thereby being offset as the union prepared for a showdown with the general trucking employers.

At mid-April the membership drive culminated in a mass rally held in a downtown theater. Public notice was given there of the union's demands for a working agreement with the employers. The membership voted to strike if the demands were rejected. A large strike committee was elected to make the necessary plans for a walkout. The committee was also empowered to set a deadline for an employer response to the union's demands.

Parallel with these actions, steps were taken to put Governor Olson on record as sympathetic to the workers' cause. He was reluctant to take such a public stand, hoping instead to maintain an "impartial" posture. As a Farmer-Laborite, however, he could not ignore the wishes of the labor movement, which was putting considerable pressure on him to speak up. So he sent a letter to Local 574's mass rally counseling the workers to "band together for your own protection and welfare." That didn't make him a trustworthy ally. Yet it did make more difficult any attempt on his part to intervene against the union during the impending conflict.

All sectors of the AFL officialdom in the city were drawn into formal support of Local 574's demands. This put them under obligation to help the local win its fight; it also served as a means to parry moves they were to make later on. Cooperative relations were developed with organizations of the unemployed in what proved to be a successful effort to mobilize jobless workers as fighting allies of the union. An auxiliary was formed among women in Local 574 families to draw them into active support of the struggle. Collaboration was also established with farmers in the area.

Meantime, the employers persisted in their refusal to deal with the union. They denounced the workers' demands as a "Communist plot" to take over the city by imposing union control over all businesses. The Citizens Alliance announced steps to obtain cooperation from the mayor of Minneapolis and the city police in the event of a strike. The Alliance laid plans to reinforce the police with a large number of special deputies. Professional strikebreakers were also lined up for use against the union.

Local 574 in turn set up a big strike headquarters. It contained a commissary for feeding the strikers, an improvised hospital to care for union casualties, and a repair shop to service cars used by cruising picket squads. Plans for the picketing were carefully drawn, and the necessary command structure was devised. Convinced by such measures that the union meant business, the workers moved into action with high morale.

A strike against the general trucking employers began on

May 16, 1934. Massive picket detachments quickly put a stop
to all attempts at scab operations, demonstrating that Local
574 had become a power to be reckoned with. Then after four
days of relative quiet the bosses opened a campaign of violence
against the union. As they announced plans to begin operating
trucks, police and hired thugs launched brutal attacks on peaceful pickets. The workers fought back with grim determination,
doing the best they could barehanded.

After that the angry strikers equipped themselves with clubs
to defend their picket lines. On two successive days they fought
off assaults by large bodies of police and special deputies.
Scores were injured on both sides and two deputies were killed
during the bitter fighting in Minneapolis's market-place area.
The union came out victorious; not a single truck had been
moved.

After the second day of fighting a truce was arranged. Negotiations finally began, with Governor Olson acting as an
intermediary between the union and the employers. A settlement
resulted in which the general trucking employers agreed to
recognize the union in the indirect form of a Labor Board
consent order. Olson assured the union that the recognition
clause covered all its members, including inside workers on
jobs related to trucking. Wage increases given by employers
in an effort to prevent unionization were to remain intact;
further pay hikes were to be decided by negotiation or arbitration after the strike. The settlement terms were accepted by
the union membership and the victorious strikers returned
to their jobs after a ten-day walkout.

Shortly thereafter the Citizens Alliance launched a campaign
designed to repudiate the strike settlement. Trying to split the
union, the employers said they would deal with it concerning
only drivers, helpers, and platform workers; they flatly refused
to do any bargaining concerning inside workers. At the same
time they began a selective process of cutting wages and firing
union members. Their actions could have only one meaning.
They were deliberately forcing another strike, hoping that next
time they could crush the union. That intent was made doubly
clear when riot guns — murderous weapons using large scatter
shot — were issued to the city police.

Faced with these provocations, Local 574 again girded for
battle. In doing so it took an unprecedented step. A powerful
new weapon was created through publication of an official
union organ, *The Organizer*, which appeared daily during
the ensuing conflict. The paper served effectively to refute the
bosses' lies; it gave all workers the facts about the controversy

and thereby helped greatly to mobilize support for the local.

One aspect of the labor mobilization took the form of a massive protest demonstration against the Citizens Alliance. Among the thousands who participated were members of other trade unions, unemployed workers, small farmers from the vicinity, and college students. All were united around the slogan: "Make Minneapolis a Union Town."

At this point Daniel J. Tobin, general president of the International Brotherhood of Teamsters, launched a red-baiting attack on Local 574 through editorials in the official IBT magazine. He centered his fire on Trotskyist militants in the local. They were accused of "creating distrust, discontent, bloodshed and rebellion." The Minneapolis labor movement was urged to "get busy and stifle such radicals." Tobin's diatribe was gleefully reprinted by the trucking bosses through a paid ad in the capitalist press, and they became even more adamant toward the union.

Tobin's onslaught provoked an indignant reaction among rank-and-file unionists. They looked upon the Trotskyists as honest, competent, fighting leaders whose qualities had been proven in battle. Since the local's internal affairs were now being conducted on a democratic basis, they felt that Tobin was actually hitting at the aims and aspirations of the union membership as a whole. This opinion was clearly demonstrated at a July 16 membership meeting where Local 574 decided by unanimous vote to resume the strike against the trucking companies. A passage in the strike call stated:

"We say plainly to D. J. Tobin: If you can't act like a Union man, and help us, instead of helping the bosses, then at least have the decency to stand aside and let us fight our battle alone."

A broad strike committee was again elected by the membership and empowered to make all executive decisions during the walkout. The official executive board was made an integral part of the larger body, although subordinate to it. In this way a highly effective leadership formation was created to guide the ranks in the coming showdown. The union could act as a solidly united force with a single purpose and a single policy.

As in May, hostilities began with an impressive demonstration of Local 574's strength. Trucking operations were quickly brought to a halt. Then on the fourth day of the strike, July 20, 1934, a large body of police using riot guns fired without warning on a peacefully conducted mass picket line. When it was over, sixty-seven pickets and bystanders lay wounded and two of them died later from their injuries. Most of the victims of the police riot had been shot in the back.

Waves of anger over this outrage swept through the city's working class. Sections of the middle class, horrified by the police violence, also gave support to the union. The strikers themselves, backed by a growing mass of sympathizers, continued their peaceful picketing in defiance of the murderous cops. Although a few trucks were moved under armed convoy, the tie-up remained basically effective. Riot guns had failed to break the strike; in fact it had gained new vigor.

In this tense situation federal mediators on the scene came forward with a proposal for settlement of the dispute. They called for recognition of the union wherever it could win a representation election conducted by the Labor Board. On the issue of hourly wages the union demanded 55 cents for truck drivers and 45 cents for helpers and inside workers; this was reduced by the mediators to 52 1/2 cents and 42 1/2 cents for the respective categories. Governor Olson then endorsed the proposal and called upon the union and the employers to accept it; if this were not done, he announced, he would declare martial law and impose a strike settlement on the mediators' terms. In this difficult situation Local 574 decided it was advisable to accept the proposed settlement; however, the arrogant employers rejected it.

On July 26 Olson put the city under martial law and decreed that trucks could be operated only by firms which accepted the mediators' proposal. Soon, however, military permits for general trucking operations were being issued so loosely that the strike was endangered. Local 574 reacted by preparing to resume mass picketing in defiance of the military. Olson thereupon ordered his troops to seize the strike headquarters and arrest the union leaders. With the help of conservative AFL officials he then tried to induce the seemingly headless union to call off the strike.

His scheme didn't work. Militant picketing exploded upon the city, despite the presence of troops, and casualties among scab truck drivers mounted by the hour. Olson's action brought swift condemnation from the membership of AFL unions and the ranks of the Farmer-Labor Party. He found himself compelled to release those Local 574 leaders his soldiers had managed to arrest and return the strike headquarters to the union; he also felt it necessary to tighten up on the issuance of military permits for scab trucking.

After that the controversy settled into a war of attrition. The employers tried unsuccessfully to get a court injunction against

Olson so they could resume the use of police violence against the union. Then the federal mediators sought to induce Local 574 to accept a watered-down version of the terms they had proposed earlier for ending the strike. When that failed the bosses began to maneuver for a rigged Labor Board election in which scabs would be ruled the "eligible" employees. While all this was going on, Olson increased the granting of permits for scab trucking and he intensified military arrests of pickets.

By now the attrition was causing difficulties for Local 574. Things were getting rough for strikers whose families had fallen into dire economic need during the long conflict. Hard put itself in meeting strike expenses, the union could do little more than help them fight to get on public relief. As a result a few strikers were giving up the struggle and drifting back to work.

The wear and tear was not confined to the union alone. Employers, too, were feeling the effects of the lengthy struggle and they could not hold out indefinitely against the union. Matters had boiled down to a question of staying power, with both sides put to the test.

At this stage a new mediator arrived from Washington, D.C. He informed the strike leaders that he had convinced the head of the Citizens Alliance to call off the fight. At the union's request he put in writing an assurance that the employers would accept his proposal for a settlement. The terms called for a Labor Board election to determine union recognition, with voting confined to employees on company payrolls as of the day the strike began. Union representation was to include inside workers at the wholesale market firms, and a decision on wages was to be made through arbitration.

On August 21, 1934, the union membership voted to accept the new settlement proposal, and the strike ended. In the Labor Board elections the union won bargaining rights for a majority of those employed in the general trucking industry. The arbitration award set hourly wages at 52 1/2 cents for truck drivers and 42 1/2 cents for helpers and inside workers; a year later each category was to be increased another 2 1/2 cents an hour.

Basic to the whole struggle had been the winning of union recognition. With that accomplished any lag on other matters would be only limited and temporary. Now firmly established in the industry, the union was in a position to make steady advances. On balance, the workers had won a sweeping victory and Local 574 had emerged from the struggle as a major power in the Minnesota labor movement.

1. Frame-Up Attempt

The triumph of General Drivers Local 574 over the trucking employers came as a body blow to the Citizens Alliance. For years this capitalist organization had exercised a virtual dictatorship over Minneapolis. It controlled the city government, including the police department from behind the scenes. Its banker wing kept a tight grip on the public purse strings, and its capitalist advertisers dictated the editorial policies of the daily newspapers. These powers were used to maintain an open-shop paradise in which working people were ruthlessly exploited for the private profit of the employing class.

When the Teamster organizing drive was opened in the spring of 1934, the Citizens Alliance had countered with a mobilization of its own. A special membership campaign was launched in an effort to develop a solid front of all employers in the city. Funds were raised for a war chest. An "advisory committee" was created to set policy for the trucking bosses. If any firm hesitated to challenge the growing Teamster power, threats of financial reprisal were used to keep it lined up in the Alliance wolf pack.

Under a propaganda cover branding the unionization drive a "Communist plot," stool pigeons and agents provocateurs were planted in Local 574. Armed thugs and professional scabs were lined up for use against the workers. Although deputies mobilized during the May 1934 strike were certified by the authorities as "special police," they were to all intents and purposes a private army of the bosses. They were recruited mainly by the Citizens Alliance, which also played a key role in arming them and setting up a special headquarters for their use.

During the July-August strike the police were ordered to make a murderous assault on peaceful pickets with riot guns. Coping with the angry public reaction to this outrage was viewed by the Alliance leaders as simply a tactical problem. Efforts were made to counteract public condemnation of the cold-blooded deed by having civic organizations of the capitalists issue statements praising the "bravery" of the cops. After committing such brutal acts, the bosses then had the gall to demand that workers accused of "violence" during the struggle be denied their jobs.

None of these strikebreaking devices availed. Local 574 won the fight; a strong union emerged in the trucking industry, and the employers had to deal with it. This meant that the Citizens Alliance, already weakened by a major defeat, would now have to face a wider unionization trend among workers stimulated by the Teamster victory. The relationship of class forces had changed, and the Alliance leaders began to grope for new ways to combat the labor movement.

For openers they issued a fresh declaration of war, using Mayor A. G. Bainbridge as their mouthpiece. As the victorious strikers were returning to their jobs on August 22, 1934, the morning edition of the *Minneapolis Tribune* carried a statement by the mayor:

"Settlement of the strike should not be regarded as a victory for Communists. . . ." Bainbridge asserted. "I am serving notice here and now that our fight on Communism has just begun and I pledge myself to devote my time and effort to rid our city of those who defy law and order and who seek only to tear down our government. It will be a fight to the finish and I will not be satisfied until all those who foment unrest and hatred of legal authority are driven from our city. Let this serve as warning."

Pinpointing the central import of the mayor's declaration, Local 574 replied to him and the employers in its own newspaper, *The Organizer:*

"He [Bainbridge] means framing up every worker who fights for his rights. The Citizens Alliance, sore because they had to swallow the settlement, are planning to sic their bloodhound [Police Chief] Johannes onto some innocent individual workers and take it out of their hides. We warn all enemies of labor: Local 574 is going to take a hand in the fight against any kind of frame-up. Those who start this sort of business will be responsible for all the consequences."

A few weeks later another red-baiting attack on the labor movement was made obliquely. Early on the morning of October 16 vandals broke into the Workers Book Store, operated by the Communist Party in downtown Minneapolis. Furniture was overturned and smashed, pamphlets torn up and scattered on the floor. Scores of expensive volumes were

stolen, as was a small amount of cash in the store. A crude
sign left in the window proclaimed: "Modern Boston Tea Party.
No Reds Wanted in Minneapolis." The raiders then drove out
Wayzata Boulevard a few miles and made a bonfire of the
plundered literature. A second sign was left at the fire, saying:
"First Warning to Communists."

This act of vandalism was treated sympathetically in the
daily papers. The *Minneapolis Journal* went so far as to attribute it to "irate citizens angered by the activity of revolutionary forces in Minneapolis." Apparently it was thought that
such a propaganda twist could build up public support of
vigilante attacks on "reds." Behind that notion lay the assumption that the unpopularity of the Communist Party would
prevent significant protest from within the trade union movement. If that had proved to be the case, attacks of the kind
could gradually have been extended to include other victims.

The Communist Party, which had by then become completely
Stalinized, had itself been the author of its isolation from the
mass movement. A combination of ultraleft policies and blind
factionalism had caused the CP to Trotsky-bait the Local 574
strike leaders during the conflict with the employers. To the
embattled workers this seemed much like the red-baiting carried
on by the bosses, and the Stalinists came to be looked upon
as enemies of the union. Aware of this sentiment, the Citizens
Alliance policy makers were trying to exploit it to their advantage.

Once again, however, they had underestimated Local 574,
which had been the main victim of the Stalinists' unprincipled
factionalism. Through a statement printed in *The Organizer*
the union pointed out:

"There are many workers in this city who are out of sympathy with the Communist Party. But it would be a short-
sighted policy indeed to abstain for this reason from registering a vigorous protest against this vandalism. . . . If they
think they can get away with it, these vigilantes would like to
terrorize every worker, every liberal minded person in the
city. But they aren't going to get away with it. . . . If the
police will not stop the plundering of the workers by these
lawless vultures, the workers will."

On the heels of the vigilante episode a new plot was cooked
up, this time directly against Local 574. It stemmed from the
death of a special deputy, C. Arthur Lyman, during the May
1934 strike. Lyman was a wealthy lawyer who sat on the
board of directors of the Citizens Alliance. Since his death
the bosses had sought to picture him as a martyr "who fought

for his country abroad [in World War I], and who knew how to fight and die for the same principles at home." Now they had set out to find victims among the strikers who could be framed up on a charge of having killed Lyman; in the process they hoped to involve the strike leaders in an alleged conspiracy to commit murder. Their aim was not only to cripple the Teamster leadership; they plainly hoped to terrorize the entire AFL of the city and stem the developing trade union upsurge.

Word of the plot first reached Local 574 through an off-the-record tip from AFL officials sitting on the Hennepin County grand jury. They had been put on the jury because of their posture as "labor statesmen." Capitalism uses such types, wherever practical, to give labor token representation on public bodies. The aim is to create an impression that actions taken by these bodies have general working class approval.

It is a trick to entrap the trade unions in the mechanisms of capitalist rule so as to deceive workers about the antilabor character of governmental policies. The device is further intended to compromise the conservative wing of organized labor and use it to hamper working class efforts to fight off capitalist attacks.

In the Lyman case the grand jury had learned that murder charges were in preparation against Emanuel (Happy) Holstein, a Local 574 member who had served on the strike committee. Right then and there the union officials on the jury should have openly denounced the plot. Apparently feeling that such action would tarnish their image as "statesmen," they failed to do so. They did at least quietly inform Local 574 of what was in the wind, and that helped a good deal. The union was able to begin preparations to meet the impending attack.

Our informants also reported that the county prosecutor was floundering in uncertainty about the presentation of "evidence" against Holstein. His problem was understandable. Many strikers had doubtlessly wondered whether Lyman was one of the deputies they personally faced during the heavy fighting that took place in the marketplace area in May. There were also a few boasts on the subject, especially in taverns after a few convivial rounds. Considered soberly, however, no one could really know who struck this particular deputy.

For one thing it is highly unlikely that anyone on the union side knew that Lyman was among the deputies until his death was reported later in the newspapers. Teamsters and Citizens Alliance directors traveled in separate social circles and were not apt to be personally known to one another. Moreover, with a mass of pickets engaged in heated combat against a large body of police and deputies, personal features could not serve as marks of identity. The strikers wore union buttons, the cops were in uniform, and the deputies had special police badges pinned onto their civilian clothing. These were — and had to be — the ready means of distinguishing friend from foe in the fast-moving battle; opponents were not singled out as individuals. In such a situation it was preposterous to allege that a particular striker had clubbed a specific deputy.

These obvious facts were brushed aside by the employers. They were determined to use Lyman's death to pin a murder rap on the union by one means or another. So detectives were assigned to fabricate a case as best they could. When that had been done the county prosecutor was ordered into action. It was no doubt assumed that intensive propaganda could be used to paper over the big cracks in the "evidence."

Holstein was arrested on November 3 and held without charges. Local 574 immediately appealed to the whole labor movement for support against the frame-up. The appeal received a quick response. A broad trade union defense committee was formed at a big meeting of AFL officials. Simultaneously the Citizens Alliance plot was denounced in *Labor Review*, official organ of the Central Labor Union, a body composed of delegates from all AFL unions in the city.

"Organized labor is in an ugly mood at the attempted framing of Happy Holstein," the AFL paper declared. "Trade unionists have not forgotten how Henry Ness and John Belor, valiant members of Drivers 574, were slaughtered and more than 40 others shot in the back. That there has been no effort to apprehend or indict those big shot higher-ups responsible for giving the order for their slaying, while Happy Holstein, a humble worker, is being attempted to be framed, is convincing the workers more than ever that the so-called machinery of justice is the machinery of class justice and not of even-handed justice."

After about two weeks the defense committee obtained Holstein's release from jail through habeas corpus proceedings. He was then quickly rearrested, this time on a formal charge of having killed Lyman. Bail was set at $10,000. Placing its property under bond for the purpose, the Milk Drivers Union put up the bail and Happy was again released. The attempt to frame him finally ended when the grand jury voted a "no-bill" for lack of evidence.

In the meantime, a second intended victim, Phillip Scott,

had been arrested. He was a youth of nineteen who had been involved in the May strike. In preparing Phillip's defense the union lawyers learned from his mother that he had a history of emotional difficulties. While at school he had been kept in a special class under a doctor's care. Part of his emotional problem was a tendency to give answers calculated to satisfy anyone who questioned him.

Scott had been tricked into a drinking jag by a police detective. He was then thrown into jail, and a "confession" that he had clubbed Lyman to death was wormed out of him. On this basis the prosecutor designed a scenario intended to implicate the strike leadership. Phillip was put through the ordeal of a sensational trial, and in the end he was acquitted. With that the whole frame-up attempt fizzled out.

Having suffered yet another defeat, the bosses decided to lie back for the time being and watch for a new chance to throw a rabbit punch at the union.

2. Leadership Showdown

While fighting off the attempt to frame it on murder charges, Local 574 was also preparing to go forward in the general struggle against the trucking employers. An editorial in *The Organizer* set the tone for this perspective. After summing up gains made through the victorious strike struggles, the editorial added:

"A closer bond has been welded . . . [among] the men who produce for the profit of those who exploit them. As this bond grows closer, the degree of exploitation will lessen. The immediate task of the union is to consolidate its positions, gain new strength and prepare for the next step. . . . BUILD A BIGGER AND BETTER UNION!" (Emphasis in original.)

To implement these objectives it was necessary to resolve contradictions existing within Local 574's officialdom. Incompetents holding union office had to be removed. That could now be accomplished, thanks to the groundwork that had already been done. The Communist League had undertaken its campaign to win leadership recognition in the eyes of the union rank and file with clearly defined aims and carefully calculated tactics and timing.

From the outset the building of a broad left wing in the local was rooted in the programmatic concepts essential to a policy of militant struggle against the employers. Although this perspective entailed an ultimate clash with conservative union officials, their removal from office was not projected at the start as an immediate aim. That could have given the mistaken impression that the Trotskyist militants were interested primarily in winning union posts. To avoid such a misconception a flanking tactic was developed. Instead of calling for a quick formal change in the local's leadership, the incumbent officials were pressed to alter their policies to meet the workers' needs.

A program was advanced for the building of a strong organization capable of using its full power on behalf of all workers in the trucking industry. This outlook was counterposed to the then official policy of creating special opportunities for a relatively privileged few. The left-wing perspective got a widespread welcome from the workers. They were ready to mobilize and launch a fight to establish the union throughout the industry. It followed that the momentum developed through such a struggle would lead toward an ultimate showdown over the leadership question.

Initially the left wing had taken form around the voluntary organizing committee in the open-shop coal yards. The committee functioned both as a caucus of militant workers and as a union-building instrument. An unofficial, but nonetheless real, leadership component had thus come into being among a growing body of workers who had yet to fight their way into the union.

The main obstacle to full unionization of the coal industry was a clique organized by Cliff Hall, an apprentice bureaucrat with strong yearnings to win recognition as a "labor statesman." A member of the Milk Drivers Union, he had been hired by the executive board of Local 574 to serve as the local's business agent. He sat on the board as an ex-officio member and exercised control over a majority of that body.

A minority of two among the seven board members stood opposed to Hall. They were William S. Brown, the union president, and George Frosig, the vice president; both sympathized with the concept of building a bigger and stronger organization. With the help of mass pressure mobilized by the voluntary organizing committee, Brown and Frosig forced through a reversal in policy that brought the coal workers into the union.

During the ensuing coal strike the Hall clique was able to maintain official control. Yet with Brown's cooperation, as president of the local, the growing left wing inside the union could exert sufficient influence to make the picketing effective. This assured a partial union victory, despite bungled negotiation of settlement terms. This success, along with the general unionization campaign that followed, brought internal union developments to a new and higher plane. A situation of dual leadership authority began to take form.

The victorious coal workers had become a major component of the local. This strength was used to force through a decision upgrading the voluntary organizing committee to the status of an official union body. Workers pouring into the local from other sections of the trucking industry tended to emulate the veterans of the coal strike in looking to the now-official organizing committee for guidance. As a result the left wing gained steadily in size and influence.

Tactics inside the union on the leadership question were readjusted accordingly. On some matters the organizing committee simply by-passed the executive board; where this was not possible or advisable, it now had the strength to force the board into line on important issues. In every case, however, care was taken not to precipitate a premature leadership showdown over secondary matters. All tactical measures were shaped to conform with strategic objectives in the fight against the bosses.

When the May walkout took place a democratically elected strike committee exercised considerable power. This marked a further advance toward the left wing's aim of establishing rank-and-file control over all union affairs, even though the executive board's authority formally took priority over that of the strike committee.

After the strike another step was taken that intensified the development of dual leadership authority. Five left-wing leaders were officially added to the union's organizational staff. They were Grant, Miles, and V. R. (Ray) Dunne, Carl Skoglund and myself — all members of the Communist League. These five plus Bill Brown, the union president, were looked upon by most rank and filers as the real central leadership of the union.

When the bosses forced another strike upon the workers in July, Local 574 entered the most critical phase of the conflict. It had become imperative that all union matters be competently handled: policy decisions, picketing, negotiations — everything. Fortunately the local's internal situation had by then progressed to a point where the required measures could be taken.

The union elected a big strike committee, which was genuinely representative of the rank and file. This committee was given full executive authority in the strike, its powers explicitly superseding those of the executive board; the latter body was simply incorporated temporarily into the broad committee. This way the formal authority of incompetents on the executive board could be bypassed; this step minimized the danger of trouble from that quarter. With solid backing from the membership, the left wing had asserted full leadership responsibility for the duration of the struggle.

After the walkout ended, the strike committee was dissolved. Formal authority reverted back to the executive board where

Hall still controlled a narrow majority. Hoping to profit from post-strike weariness in the ranks, he launched a red-baiting attack on the Trotskyist militants as a cover for disruptive activities inside the organization. Encouragement from other conservative AFL officials emboldened the Hall clique; moreover they were obviously counting on help from Tobin, head of the International Brotherhood of Teamsters, who was in a position to put strong pressure on the local.

This situation could not be allowed to fester. Decisive action was required in the form of an open showdown over the leadership question. Having already gotten a bellyful of Hall and his kind, the union membership was ready for the step.

A decision was forced through to schedule a new election of union officers. Brown was reelected president of the local and Frosig was returned to the vice presidency, both having been on the progressive side all the way. An incumbent trustee, Moe Hork, who had broken off his earlier collaboration with Hall and performed well during the strike, was also reelected. The remaining posts were won by Trotskyist militants: Grant Dunne, recording secretary; F. Dobbs, secretary-treasurer; Ray Dunne and Harry DeBoer, trustees.

Neither Miles Dunne nor Carl Skoglund, who had been among the central leaders of the strikes, ran for office. Miles had been assigned to help a Teamster local in Fargo, North Dakota. Carl had a citizenship problem which made it inadvisable for him to be a candidate at that time.

Under IBT procedures the seven officers who had been elected constituted the executive board of the local. As its first official act the new board summarily fired Hall. Since his IBT membership was in the Milk Drivers Union, Hall's dismissal as business agent removed him entirely from the Local 574 scene. With the general housecleaning thus completed, the local was able to present a solid front against the bosses. Its power could be fully mobilized to defend and advance the workers' interests; and at the head of the struggle would stand battle-tested militants who were united around a common program.

The new, homogeneous leadership functioned as a team. No one strutted around as a star performer or tried to be a dictator. Genuinely collective effort prevailed, within a division of labor designed according to the union's needs, and the contributions of each individual were valued. Measures were initiated to gradually broaden the leadership team by educating outstanding militants in the ranks. In this way an expanding formation of secondary leaders was built up; they in turn helped to knit close relations between the leadership and the membership. Out of this process came a oneness which enabled the union to go forward as an effective combat force.

Traditional AFL "business agent" concepts were scrapped, as were other bureaucratic notions about "running" a union instead of leading it. The executive board members acted collectively as the central leadership of the local. In that capacity they did not presume to hand down orders to the rank and file; they gave overall guidance to the work of protecting and strengthening the organization, making executive decisions as needed to fulfill that responsibility.

A staff of full-time organizers was set up, composed of union officers and members who had played outstanding roles in the strikes. Their tasks in the main were to settle job grievances, recruit new members, handle negotiations with employers, and play a leading role in any walkouts that were called. Across an eighteen-month period the staff was built up to fourteen members. Included were Ray, Miles, and Grant Dunne, Carl Skoglund, Bill Brown, Harry DeBoer, George Frosig, Ray Rainbolt, Kelly Postal, Jack Maloney, Emil Hansen, Clarence Hamel, Happy Holstein. I was assigned to function as staff director.

On the question of staff wages the union leadership junked the outrageous bureaucratic practice of conniving to draw salaries comparable to those received by corporation executives. Staff pay was supposed to be twenty-six dollars a week, the going wage for truck drivers at the time; as new wage increases were won for the workers, the staff would then get a similar raise. For an extended period, however, the staff received at most twenty dollars a week, sometimes less. That resulted from money problems confronting the local in the aftermath of the long struggle against the bosses. In grappling with these problems the staff sought to lead by example, subordinating personal needs to union requirements at that difficult time. In various ways of their own, the union members reacted to the example by responding in kind.

Whether an elected officer or an apprentice organizer, all on the union staff got the same pay. None had to be hired in order to serve the union; they would do that in any case as best they could. It was a matter of making it possible for a given number of individuals to devote their entire time to organizational work. On that premise maximum effort was expected from each person; any variations in the services rendered would then result simply from differences in individual experience and ability.

Neither union post nor individual talent had any bearing

on the rate of pay. All staff members shared common subsistence problems and all received comparable wages, special
adjustments being made only where a given individual had
exceptional family responsibilities. In this, as in every other
respect, there was only one class of citizenship in the local;
it was shared equally by elected officers, full-time organizers,
and rank-and-file members.

To round out the organizational machinery a job steward
system was established. Union members at each company
selected a representative to fill the post. As would be expected,
those chosen as stewards had played prominent roles during
the strikes. In effect, the broad strike committee was being
transformed into a permanent union body with vital functions.

As direct union representatives on the job, it was the stewards'
duty to defend the rights of union members; to see that working agreements with the employers were enforced; to bring all
workers on the job into the union; and to insist that they keep
themselves in good standing. Regular meetings of the steward
body were held, with the union staff participating in the discussions. These sessions became a key part of the organizational mechanism because of the vital functions performed by
the stewards. They were to a large extent the eyes, ears, and
nerve center of the union.

Provisions for a closed-shop contract, entailing compulsory
union membership and dues payments, had been included
among Local 574's prestrike demands. This had been done
at the insistence of Hall, who took the bureaucratic view on
the question. That view sees the closed shop as a liberating
instrument—for the bureaucrats, that is, not the workers. It
enables officials sitting on top of a union to more or less freely
ignore or go against the wishes of the rank and file. No matter how dissatisfied this may make the workers, dues must
still be paid, and the bureaucrats continue to have a union
treasury at their disposal.

A different view on the same question arises when workers
are inspired by the union. They develop a healthy resentment
against freeloaders on the job and look for ways of forcing
them at least to contribute financially to the cause. That leads
them to favor putting a clause in the agreement with the employer making payment of union dues compulsory. It follows
from this that the closed-shop question is a tactical matter;
one to be decided according to the total complex of factors
in a given situation.

In Local 574's case, Hall's closed-shop demand was un-
realistic; as events proved, it took a bitter struggle to win

even the simplest form of union recognition. Yet with other, more complex factors in the internal union situation taking precedence, it was unwise to oppose Hall on the closed-shop matter. The issue was simply allowed to die a natural death during the fight with the bosses.

Now that the employers had been defeated and the local was firmly rooted in the trucking industry, the rank and file strongly favored compulsory union membership and dues payments. The problem was one of finding a way to apply the desired compulsion. Key steps toward that end had been taken in setting up the union staff and organizing the steward system. A further measure was then devised which came to be known as a "fink drive."

Drives of this kind took place periodically. They were conducted by mobilizing the entire union staff and a substantial number of volunteer union activists who took off from work for the purpose. A dragnet was formed to comb the city. Trucks were stopped on the streets; a check was made of loading docks, shipping rooms, warehouses, etc.; back dues were collected from delinquent members, and new members were signed up. Through this overall combination of measures the local was able to maintain a rather tight union shop.

Parallel with these steps, methods were devised to broaden the local's scope and streamline its structure. Full advantage was taken of the "general" charter it had received from the IBT. Workers whose jobs were by any plausible definition related to trucking were signed up as Local 574 reached into every quarter of the industry not explicitly covered by another IBT charter.

In its internal functioning the local held general meetings twice monthly which were open to all union members; these gatherings dealt primarily with broad and fundamental problems. To cope with matters arising from the diversified nature of the trucking industry, sub-sections were set up to handle matters peculiar to one or another part of the industry. This allowed the workers in each particular section to make decisions about their own unique problems. At the same time they had the advantage in dealing with the employers of solid backing from the union as a whole. From time to time one of the sections would find it necessary to call a strike in its sphere of the industry. As it turned out these fights were won without need of reinforcement through a general walkout by the union membership. But power of that kind was always there to be used if required.

Care was taken in systematizing the union machinery to

protect the democratic rights of the rank and file. Such concern, of course, came naturally from a leadership that strove consciously to involve the membership in every aspect of the local's activity. There was complete freedom of expression for all views. Policy matters were presented by the leadership in a reasoned way, and full discussion was encouraged so as to reach a clear understanding about the union's objectives. On all questions the general membership meeting had the final say; it was the supreme authority in the organization.

New by-laws were adopted by the local after they had been carefully thought out by the drafting committee and studied by the rank and file. Under the revised rules officers were elected for a one-year term. That procedure gave the membership a frequent opportunity to review their performance and decide whether they should be reelected or replaced. The election procedure began with nominations for office at a general membership meeting. A period of one month was then allowed for electioneering, during which opposition candidates were accorded equal rights with incumbents running for reelection. Voting then took place by secret ballot at the union hall, where polls were open for two days. The whole procedure was conducted by five election judges selected by the membership.

All in all, rank-and-file control over Local 574's affairs, including democratic selection of the leadership, had become a living reality. This was the mainspring of its strength.

3. Class-Struggle Policy

With the change in official leadership, efforts to construct an ever-stronger left wing took new forms within the local. It was no longer a matter of building a broad caucus around a militant program in order to displace misleaders sitting on top of the organization. Conscious revolutionists were now at the helm, and they enjoyed harmonious relations with the rank and file. As matters now stood the union itself had become a left-wing formation in the local labor movement and in the IBT. Internal differentiations had been reduced essentially to varying degrees of class consciousness. From this it followed that the next major task was to make the general membership more aware of the laws of class struggle.

Workers who have no radical background enter the trade unions steeped in misconceptions and prejudices that the capitalist rulers have inculcated into them since childhood. This was wholly true of Local 574 members. They began to learn class lessons only in the course of struggle against the employers.

Their strike experiences had taught them a good deal. Notions that workers have anything in common with bosses were undermined by harsh reality. Illusions about the police being "protectors of the people" began to be dispelled. Eyes were opened to the role of the capitalist government, as revealed in its methods of rule through deception and brutality. At the same time the workers were gaining confidence in their class power, having emerged victorious from their organized confrontation with the employers.

To intensify the learning process already so well started, the union leadership now initiated an educational program. Study courses open to all members were organized. The curriculum included economics, labor history and politics, public speaking, strike strategy, and union structure and tactics.

Wherever practical, officers' reports at membership meetings were given with a view toward making them instructive as well as factually informative. Articles of an educational nature were printed in the union paper. The themes varied from analysis of local problems to coverage of events and discussion of issues in the national and international labor movement.

These endeavors stood in marked contrast to the policies of bureaucratic union officials. Bureaucrats don't look upon the labor movement as a fighting instrument dedicated solely to the workers' interests; they tend rather to view trade unions as a base upon which to build personal careers as "labor statesmen."

Such ambitions cause them to seek collaborative relations with the ruling class. Toward that end the bureaucrats argue that, employers being the providers of jobs, labor and capital have common interests. They contend that exploiters of labor must make "fair" profits if they are to pay "fair" wages. Workers are told that they must take a "responsible" attitude so as to make the bosses feel that unions are a necessary part of their businesses. On every count the ruling class is given a big edge over the union rank and file.

In carrying out their class-collaborationist line, the union bureaucrats exercise tight control over negotiations with employers. They try to avoid strikes over working agreements if at all possible. When a walkout does take place, they usually leap at the first chance for a settlement.

Once a contract has been signed with an employer they consider all hostilities terminated. Membership attempts to take direct action where necessary to enforce the agreement are declared "unauthorized" and a violation of "solemn covenants." In fact the bureaucrats often gang up with the bosses to victimize rebel workers.

Local 574's leadership flatly repudiated the bankrupt line of the class collaborationists. There can be no such thing as an equitable class peace, the membership was taught. The law of the jungle prevails under capitalism. If the workers don't fight as a class to defend their interests, the bosses will gouge them. Reflecting these concepts, the preamble to the new by-laws adopted by the local stated:

"The working class whose life depends on the sale of labor and the employing class who live upon the labor of others, confront each other on the industrial field contending for the wealth created by those who toil. The drive for profit dominates the bosses' life. Low wages, long hours, the speed-up are weapons in the hands of the employer under the wage system. Striving always for a greater share of the wealth created by his labor, the worker must depend upon his organized strength. A militant policy backed by united action must be opposed to the program of the boss.

"The trade unions in the past have failed to fulfill their historic obligation. The masses of the workers are unorganized. The craft form has long been outmoded by gigantic capitalist expansion. Industrial unions are the order of the day.

"It is the natural right of all labor to own and enjoy the wealth created by it. Organized by industry and prepared for the gruelling daily struggle is the way in which lasting gains can be won by the workers as a class."

As these views set forth in the preamble affirm, there was no toying with reactionary ideas about stable class relations in the trucking industry. Stability was sought only for Local 574 itself, so that membership needs could better be served. Relations with the employers were shaped according to the realities of class struggle. The concepts involved are illustrated by the union's approach to the question of working agreements with the trucking companies.

It was recognized that contracts between unions and employers serve only to codify the relationship of class forces at a given juncture. More precisely, they merely record promises wrung from employers. If a union is poorly led, the bosses will violate their promises, undermine the contract in daily practice, and put the workers on the defensive. Conversely, a properly led union will strive to enforce the contract to the letter. It will also undertake to pass beyond the formal terms of agreement to the extent this may be practical in order to establish preconditions for improved written provisions when the contract comes up for renewal. In every case, either the unions will press for greater improvement in the workers' situation, or the employers will be able to concentrate on efforts to nullify gains the workers have made.

Another matter related to these basic considerations is the length of time working agreements are to remain in effect. Class-collaborationist union officials, who yearn for stable worker-employer relations, favor long term agreements. They want to keep the membership locked up in a given status-quo situation for the longest possible time. Militant union leaders, on the other hand, prefer relatively short term contracts, so that gains for the membership can be registered more frequently.

In Local 574's case the general practice was to limit agreements to a period of one year. This applied both to the nego-

tiation of renewal terms when the August 1934 strike settlement
expired later on and to the signing of contracts with companies
whose employees were newly organized.

On the question of making employers keep their promises,
the handling of grievances becomes vital. Here again class-
collaborationist policies entrap the workers. Union bureaucrats are quick to include a no-strike pledge in contract settlements and refer grievances to arbitration. The workers lose
because arbitration boards are rigged against them, the "impartial" board members invariably being "neutral" on the employers' side. Moreover, the bosses remain free to violate the
working agreement at will, as grievances pile up behind the
arbitration dam.

In a similar vein,˙ conservative union officials are prone
to make a general no-strike pledge when the capitalist government proclaims a "national emergency." They do so by
bureaucratic fiat, giving rank-and-file workers no voice in
the decision. Such "labor statesmanship" amounts to proclaim-
ing an overall "truce" between the workers and the bosses.
Actually no truce results at all. The capitalists simply use
their government to attack the trade union movement under
the guise of a "national emergency"; and the workers, deprived
in such a situation of their strike weapon, get it in the neck.

A development in the fall of 1934 involved this very issue.
In the name of "national recovery," President Franklin D.
Roosevelt asked labor to forgo its right to strike. Concerning
disputes with employers, he said, trade unions should accept
decisions by government boards as final and binding. William
Green, president of the AFL, was quick to second Roosevelt's
proposal and call upon the labor movement to put it into
practice. Local 574 gave both Roosevelt and Green its answer
through an editorial in *The Organizer*:

"*Labor cannot and will not give up the strike weapon.* Labor
has not in the past received any real benefits from the governmental boards and constituted authorities. What Labor has
received in union recognition, wage raises and betterment in
conditions of work, has been won *in spite of such boards.* . . .
The strike is the one weapon that the employers respect. . . .
Whether or not there is a period of industrial peace will depend upon the employers' reply to our demands." (Emphasis
in original.)

It did not follow from this position that Local 574 called
strikes lightly. There are always hardships involved for the
workers in such struggles. If the union moved blithely from
one walkout to the next, without careful regard of all factors

in the situation, it could easily wear out its fighting forces. The important thing is that a union stand ready and able to take strike action when required. In fact there are occasions where readiness to use the strike weapon can make its employment unnecessary.

Retention of the unqualified right to strike and readiness to use the weapon were central to the local's enforcement of the 1934 settlement with the trucking firms. Employer attempts to impose arbitration of workers' grievances were brushed aside. There had to be full and immediate compliance with the settlement terms — or else.

In carrying out this policy the union leadership did not merely sit back waiting for an occasional member to file a grievance. All workers were urged to demand their full rights on the job, to protest any denial of these rights and to stand in solidarity with fellow workers who ran into difficulties. Toward that end, an unusual provision was included in the by-laws when they were revised. New members entering the union were required to assume the following obligation:

"I do solemnly and sincerely pledge my word and honor that I will bear true allegiance to Local 574 and to the entire organized labor movement. I will obey the rules and regulations of my union. I will demand my full rights on my job in accordance with the union agreement under which I am working. I will not scab on my fellow workers in any industry or trade, and in the event of a strike by my union or any bonafide union, I will do all in my power to bring victory to the striking workers."

There was one important addition to the above obligation: when a meeting was called to take up grievances against the employer, the changed by-laws made compulsory the attendance of all union members working at the company involved.

Important though such provisions were, they served mainly as a means to educate the membership in basic union principles. Formal obligations and rules could not in themselves provide the dynamism needed to apply those principles in daily practice. For that purpose Local 574's fighting qualities had to be demonstrated anew in the changed situation after the July-August strike was settled. An opportunity to do so was speedily provided by the trucking companies.

Resisting adjustment to the new union presence in the industry, the employers tried in various ways to proceed as though nothing much had changed. Grievances involving discrimination against union members began to pile up. Theoretically, under the terms of the August settlement, these matters were to be adjusted by Roosevelt's Labor Board, but nothing was done by that body.

Notice was therefore served that failure of the Board to perform its agreed upon functions would lead to direct action by the union. The warning was ignored. A few companies were then struck — those guilty of the most flagrant violations — and they were compelled to settle all complaints. The whole industry got the message. After that only infrequent strike action was needed to enforce compliance with working agreements.

It was not only a matter of teaching the bosses a lesson. At the same time all union members received dramatic assurance that their grievances would get serious attention. Evidence was also given that the job stewards would be backed by the full union power. Unity of action was thus being forged between the executive board, organization staff, job stewards, and the rank and file to make the bosses toe the line.

The local was on the way to establishment of union control on the job. Moreover, it was to be the kind of control that always sought to help the workers and never to hurt them.

These progressive characteristics resulted from the class-struggle ideology that now predominated within Local 574. There were, of course, variations in the degree to which this ideology was grasped by different strata in the membership. Among the broadest layers class consciousness was developing only in the more elementary forms. There was an awakening realization of basic antagonisms in class interests between labor and capital. The need for working class unity was generally perceived, as was the necessity of using the union's power in aggressive defense of labor's interests.

A narrower but significant layer of the membership was learning political lessons from experiences in the class struggle. These workers were coming to understand some of the causes of class antagonisms between labor and capital. They were growing more perceptive about the class role of the bosses' government. The realization that class conflict under capitalism is an unending and complex process was permeating their consciousness.

Some of the more advanced workers gradually developed in their thinking to the point where they became receptive to revolutionary-socialist ideas. As a result they were recruited by ones and twos into the Trotskyist party, then called the Communist League.

In the revolutionary party — which represents the highest form of class consciousness within the labor movement — these

workers advanced further in their understanding of the class
struggle. They learned the necessity of the working class and
its allies orienting toward a fight for state power. It was
brought home to them that none of their basic problems could
be definitively solved until capitalism was abolished and society
reorganized on an enlightened socialist basis. They also began to learn about the program, strategy, and tactics required
to achieve that revolutionary goal.

It should be noted in passing that loyalty to a program does
not always lead automatically to full acceptance of the organizational responsibilities involved. There are cases where
organizational derelictions will occur on the part of otherwise
loyal individuals. Yet they will remain capable of important
contributions to the movement despite that weakness. An astute
leadership will keep the latter factor in mind and endeavor to
draw the given individuals into activity so far as possible.
Two examples within Local 574 will illustrate the point: they
concerned Bill Abar, a rank-and-file member, and Bill Brown,
president of the local.

Abar was a one-man army on a picket line, but he showed
little or no interest in routine union affairs. In a strike situation he was sure to be in the front row at membership meetings, eager for action. At other times, however, he was quite
consistently absent from meetings and correspondingly delinquent in paying his union dues. Although these derelictions
were regrettable, they were recognized as secondary in Abar's
case. The union staff used to take up a voluntary collection
to make sure that his dues obligations were met. This was
done out of respect for his qualities as a fighter and his re-
liability when a strike was on.

Brown, on the other hand, was fully active in the union. His
organizational shortcomings lay in a different quarter. He
considered himself a loyal Trotskyist and, politically, he was.
For his own reasons, however, he did not actually join the
Trotskyist party and give direct organizational help in building it. While this implied, if considered formally, that he should
be excluded from meetings of party members within Local
574, that was not done. He was invited to attend whenever
important matters related to union policy were to be taken up.

There were several reasons for this procedure. As a loyal
supporter of the party's class-struggle policy within the union,
Brown had earned the right to such respect and trust. He, in
turn, reciprocated by making useful contributions in discussions of policy matters. At the same time, such collective discussions broadened his own thinking beyond the ordinary,

more limited framework of formal union deliberations. This enabled him to act more effectively in helping to carry out the aims of the union leadership.

Policy discussions among the Trotskyists in Local 574 were basic to their functioning as an organized fraction of the party. Within the fraction, party comrades had equal voice and vote; this applied whether they were rank-and-file members, job stewards, organizers, or elected officers of the union. The procedure flowed from their common objectives as politically conscious militants. All sought to advance class-struggle perspectives among the workers generally and to help implement these perspectives in action. As for the differences in formal union status, these related primarily to the manner in which individual comrades contributed to the united effort.

Fractions of the kind functioned as a subdivision of a general membership branch embracing all party comrades in the city. Included in the branch were workers from various unions, along with students and intellectuals. Through their collective relationship—focused around political activity and socialist education—all were helped to broaden and deepen their revolutionary consciousness. This process was aided by party literature distributed nationally, especially the Trotskyist weekly paper *The Militant.*

Direct guidance and help from the party's national leadership was always available to members engaged in class-struggle activities. This was richly demonstrated during the critical July-August stage of Local 574's fight against the trucking bosses. Top leaders of the party came to Minneapolis to give on-the-spot aid to the embattled union. Their support included not only valuable political advice to the union leaders who were engaged in a complex struggle; they brought with them specialists to help in such vital matters as publishing *The Organizer*, mobilizing support among the unemployed, and handling legal problems.

Through its total efforts to reinforce the workers' struggles, the party was steadily winning new members. Its gains within Local 574 were only part of the development. The wider patterns of party growth were reflected in the statistics of the Minneapolis branch. In 1933 the branch had about forty members and close sympathizers; by the end of 1934 the figure had more than doubled to about 100.

Advances were also being made nationally, as symbolized by a particularly significant event. Late in 1934 the Communist League fused with the American Workers Party to establish a new organization called the Workers Party of the United

States. The fusion was based on common acceptance of the essential Trotskyist program.

Within the AWP were revolutionaries who had led a strike of auto workers at the Electric Auto-Lite plant in Toledo, Ohio. Their struggle had paralleled the Minneapolis strikes in both militancy and national significance. Now these revolutionary workers' leaders of Toledo and Minneapolis had come together in the same party. It was a good omen for the Trotskyist movement as it entered 1935 in the form of the Workers Party.

4. The Struggle Widens

Stimulated by the union victory in the trucking industry, workers throughout the city began to look toward unionization as a way to win a better life for themselves. Wherever a new fight developed, the rank and file sought to emulate Local 574's methods, especially in the formation of broad strike committees. Representatives of the General Drivers Union were usually invited to serve on these committees in order to advise the strikers on effective methods of struggle.

The opening skirmish in the widening conflict came in the fall of 1934 at the Arrowhead Steel Products Co. A majority of the plant's 200 employees joined Local 382 of the International Association of Machinists (IAM), AFL. The boss then locked them out and they promptly turned the lockout into a militant strike. At the strikers' request, Local 574 helped them organize the fight and it supported the picket line. After about two weeks the company agreed to deal with the union. A settlement was reached in which the workers got a raise in pay and the union became firmly established in the plant.

Local 382's success at Arrowhead gave impetus to an organizing drive it was conducting among mechanics in automobile sales agencies and repair shops. IAM Local 459 in St. Paul joined in the drive and over 2,000 mechanics were soon organized in the Twin Cities. In this case the battle was not to be won so easily. The Citizens Alliance took a hand in mobilizing the garage bosses against the workers and developing union-busting tactics. IAM officials, on the other hand, sought to go it alone, apparently hoping to impress the bosses with their "respectability" by keeping Local 574 out of the situation.

In order to present an image as "labor statesmen," the union leaders began by seeking a representation election through the Labor Board. The assumption seemed to be that a union victory in such an election would compel the bosses to come to terms with it; but things didn't work out quite that way.

Just before the scheduled election took place the Citizens Alliance made an attack on Herman Hussman, the business agent of Local 382. It took the form of court action to block the issuance of citizenship papers to Hussman, based on an attempt at character assassination. This anti-union ploy aroused general labor support to Herman's defense and in the end his papers were granted.

Despite the smear campaign, the IAM won the collective bargaining election. After that the garage bosses agreed to meet with union representatives, but they refused to make any concessions to the workers. In fact, they still contended that union recognition remained the primary issue. As a consequence the auto mechanics voted to strike all garages in the Twin Cities on January 3, 1935.

Picket lines were set up at the struck establishments, the strikers carrying banners pronouncing the firms "unfair to organized labor." The bosses weren't impressed by this tactic, nor were the scabs the Citizens Alliance helped to mobilize. Special company police were lined up in Minneapolis to protect strikebreakers, and some company officials themselves began to carry firearms. As day followed day with most garages still operating after a fashion, it became increasingly obvious that the strike was ineffective. Anxious and angry rank and filers began to put pressure on the union officials to seek competent aid, and Local 574 was finally afforded an opportunity to pitch in and help.

Ray Dunne was assigned to assist the St. Paul local. He promptly organized and led a large mobile force which swept from garage to garage clearing out the finks and closing the places down. This came as something of a shock to bosses and strikebreakers alike in St. Paul. They had simply watched from across the river as warfare raged in Minneapolis during 1934. The sudden impact of militant picketing close up threw them into consternation. Few attempts were made thereafter to reopen struck places. As a result the walkout remained relatively peaceful in that city until a settlement was reached.

In Minneapolis the situation was different. We were up against our old enemy, the Citizens Alliance, and the fight had to be organized accordingly. Jack Maloney and I were sent to help Local 382, along with George Dreon, who had served on our 1934 strike committee. The mechanics' committee made me tactical director of picketing operations. Maloney and Dreon were assigned to organize cruising picket squads along the lines developed earlier by Local 574.

Our first objective was to streamline the union's operational facilities. A commissary capable of serving hot food was set up in the headquarters. This made it possible for the strikers to eat regularly and at the same time to keep themselves available for duty. Since we intended to challenge the strong-arm tactics used by the bosses, emergency hospital facilities were also installed. A strike bulletin was printed to publicize the workers' cause. It came out in the form of a special edition of *Labor Review*, the Central Labor Union's official organ.

The policy of maintaining picket lines at all struck garages was continued in order to keep tabs on company activities. Wherever trouble developed, however, cruising picket squads were now rushed to the scene to present a strong union presence. Our object was to halt scab operations, and the strikers fought hard to attain that objective.

In the clashes that quickly developed, the bosses viciously confronted the strikers. At one garage a special cop shot three pickets: Claire Hogan, Burns Powers, and Everett Lindfors. The first two received leg wounds and the third was shot in the face.

At one of the major auto agencies, two of the head bosses did the shooting at the pickets. Bufort Eastman was hit in the thigh, H. W. Collins in the hand, and Louis LeMeaux in the leg. Refusing to be terrorized, the strikers disarmed the two gunmen and halted the scab operation that was going on. Police Chief Johannes, who had earned the name "Bloody Mike" in 1934, then moved in to attack the bosses' victims. He ordered the arrest of peaceful pickets for "disorderly conduct."

Despite the violence used against them, the strikers were effectively closing down the struck garages. Their position was further strengthened when, on January 16, the St. Paul garage owners made a settlement with Local 459. However, the Minneapolis bosses stubbornly resisted these pressures and continued to hold out against the union. This made especially acute a problem that had been caused by Herman Hussman, Local 382's business agent.

Hussman wanted to give the bosses a fight, but he was handicapped by his background training in AFL business agentry. This weakness caused him to keep a tight grip on negotiations, often meeting by himself with the federal mediator and the employers' committee. In the process he had developed a notion that one boss on the committee was friendly to the union. Although this "friend" was operating his garage with scabs, Herman insisted that the pickets leave him alone, lest he become antagonistic in the negotiations.

At the daily strike meetings Hussman made reports on his talks with the mediator and the bosses. As we listened to him each day it became increasingly clear that his "friend" was playing a con game against the union. The matter was discussed among the picket leaders and a decision was made that this particular boss needed a special goosing. Cruising picket squads paid a call at his garage, deliberately choosing a time when a negotiating session was in progress. They went through the place like a tornado, cleaning out all the finks. When the "friend" received a telephoned report of what had happened he went into a state of shock and called for adjournment of the negotiating session.

Hussman took the thing almost as hard as the boss had. He soon stormed into the union hall in a fit of rage. Pacing up and down, waving his arms in the air, he shouted, "Don't tell me this happened by mistake. There was a mastermind behind it." Finally he subsided, took a couple of aspirin and flopped down on one of the hospital cots to relax his taut nerves.

The goosing seemed to help. On January 19 the Minneapolis bosses signed an agreement with the union based on terms similar to those arrived at earlier in St. Paul. The workers received significant pay increases, job conditions were improved, and a steward system established to enforce the contract. Once again the Citizens Alliance had been whipped. A militant union had won recognition and was now firmly rooted in the garage industry.

While these actions were taking place in the Twin Cities, a significant battle had also developed in Fargo, North Dakota. Its origin dated back to September 1934. At that time the officers of General Drivers Local 173 in Fargo had put in a request for leadership guidance from the victorious Minneapolis Teamsters. Miles Dunne, who had visited the city a bit earlier and was familiar with the situation there, was sent to aid them. To indicate what he was walking into, a short background sketch is necessary.

Fargo, a city of less than 50,000, developed as a railroad and banking center based on the wheat economy of the region. There were also some foundries and food processing plants. Beyond that, employment was to be had mainly in printing, the building trades, and the distributive industries. The city's economic life was intertwined with that of the smaller adjacent community of Moorhead, Minnesota. The two towns were connected by a bridge across the Red River, which marks the boundary between Minnesota and North Dakota.

During the heyday of the Industrial Workers of the World there had been considerable union activity in and around this population center, and the boss class had become quite practiced in using vigilante methods to cope with it. In the 1920s the IWW declined, having been gravely crippled by repression during World War I; since then the Fargo labor movement had been weak, almost dormant. There were only a few AFL craft unions — all with small memberships. Workers put in long hours under bad conditions for low pay; many had no job at all in those depression times. Like toilers elsewhere in the region, they were stirred by news of the Teamsters' success in Minneapolis. As a result, the unions began to register gains in membership, especially Local 173 of the IBT.

At this point, Miles Dunne entered the scene. He first helped to launch an organizing drive in the milk industry, which processed raw milk for home distribution. The campaign was a quick success and demands were soon presented to the employers. When they refused to negotiate, a strike was called on November 3, 1934. The effectiveness of the walkout caught the bosses by surprise. At the end of the first day they asked for a truce and said they were ready to negotiate with the union. The workers agreed to this and ten days later a contract was signed providing for wage increases, regulation of hours, and better job conditions.

Local 173's success in the milk industry stimulated recruitment among freight haulers and in the coal yards. Also drawn in were workers engaged in cutting ice on the Red River, which their employers would sell the following summer. Employees on all these jobs were soon organized almost 100 percent. Demands were then served upon the bosses, who refused to negotiate. On January 22, 1935, the companies involved were struck. Ordinary picket lines, backed up by cruising squads, were established at each place of work. In no time at all, the strikers had the town sewed up tight.

Meanwhile the Fargo bosses had called upon the Citizens Alliance of Minneapolis to help them counteract the strategy and tactics introduced by Miles Dunne. This led to a mobilization of vigilantes akin to that used by the Citizens Alliance against Local 574 in May 1934. In the present case the American Legion was relied upon to recruit the private army desired by the ruling class. By the fifth day of the strike a force of about 300 had been built up and deputized by the city authorities to masquerade as "special police."

Armed with clubs, this repressive force attacked the union's picket lines on January 27. In the melee that followed, thirty-two strikers were arrested. They were officially charged with "rout," which the prosecutor later defined as "an action in the direction of a riot."

Shortly thereafter an assault was made on the union hall. At the time there were about seventy-five men on the premises, along with a score of women and children. A big force of deputies assembled in front of the building on First Avenue and—without warning—shot tear gas through the windows into Local 173's quarters on the second floor. As the tear-gas victims came down the stairs onto the street, they had to pass through a gauntlet of vigilantes, and several of the union men were beaten with clubs.

The union's books and records were seized as the deputies ransacked the headquarters. Seventy of the strikers who were in the hall were arrested on charges of "obstructing an officer." Other workers were picked up during the day, and by evening over ninety were in jail. One of them was Miles Dunne, who was charged with "inciting to riot."

When news of the assault reached Minneapolis, Jack Maloney and I were sent to help the Fargo strikers get themselves reorganized. The first task was to get Miles and the other union fighters out on bail. Bonds totalling almost $50,000 had been set for those arrested. To make things worse, the authorities ruled that only real estate within the city would be accepted as security for the bonds. That meant in effect that people wanting to help free the strikers would have to put up deeds to their homes as security. This made the prospects of quick action look rather gloomy.

Then aid was suddenly received from an unexpected quarter. It came from Mr. Ballew, an admirable old gentleman, whose full name I never learned. He adhered to civil libertarian principles; and he had the courage of his convictions. He also had large real-estate holdings in the city. Brushing aside the indignation his action caused among well-to-do acquaintances, he set out to demonstrate his angry disapproval of the way in which the bosses were violating the workers' democratic rights. Mr. Ballew put up his own property as security for bond, piece by piece as required, until all the strikers had been freed from jail.

Miles Dunne was among those released on bail, but with a proviso that he must leave the state. He simply went across the bridge to Moorhead, which is in Minnesota. This kept him available for consultation, even though it was no longer advisable for him to enter Fargo, where the action had to take place.

Our second major task was to help rally wide support for the strike. Twin projects were set into motion toward that end. Steps were taken to issue a printed strike bulletin setting forth the workers' cause. It would then be used as a means of building up a mass rally to protest against the violence of the ruling class.

At the outset we were unable to get the bulletin printed in Fargo. Not a single firm would accept the business. Even the officials of the AFL printers union refused to help. They timidly argued that publication of the projected bulletin "would antagonize the police." So William Cruden, president of Local 173, and I set out into North Dakota seeking a place that would do the work for us. We drove over fifty miles west of Fargo before we found a printer who would take the job.

"Where's your copy?" he asked.

"We'll write it for you now," we told him, "and we're in a hurry to get the job done."

He gave us pencils and some long sheets of paper used to pull galley proofs. We started to write. As soon as the first page of copy was ready we handed it to the printer, who ordered it set on the linotype machine. We kept writing and passing the copy to the linotype operator, page by page.

Finally he said, "You can quit now. You've got enough for the two-page tabloid you want."

We relaxed over our first meal of the day while the press work was done on the strike bulletin. Then we rushed back to Fargo with the bundles of the paper and received a jubilant greeting. The union had beaten the printing boycott. Now the strikers could get their side of the story out to the people of the city.

Meanwhile Jack Maloney and Austin Swalde, secretary-treasurer of Local 173, had been making preparations for the mass meeting. They had bludgeoned some of the AFL officials into helping them get a suitable hall. Bill Brown had agreed to come from Minneapolis to make the main speech. All it now took was use of a rubber stamp giving the time and place of the rally and the bulletin could be employed to help build a good turnout.

The meeting was a success. Attendance was large, with rank-and-file members present from most of the city's trade unions. Brown gave one of the fighting speeches for which he had become famous, and the workers loved it. They cheered him loudly. The strike continued thereafter with renewed vigor and the picket lines became larger.

As picketing activity resumed, preparations also began for

the upcoming trials of strikers who had been arrested. Local
574 took the initiative from Minneapolis in building a regional
defense movement in their behalf. Francis Heisler, a Chicago
labor lawyer and Trotskyist sympathizer, was retained as
chief counsel for the defendants. Two Fargo lawyers, Quenten
Burdick and Lee F. Brooks, collaborated with him. The trials
began February 13, 1935, before a prejudiced and hostile
judge by the name of Paulson. A packed jury sat in judgment
over the worker victims of the capitalist-engineered vigilante
attack.

Heisler was a battler and he went after States Attorney
Bergeson hammer and tongs. His slashing attack compelled
Bergeson to move for dismissal of cases involving workers
charged with "obstructing an officer" and with "rout." Judge
Paulson found it necessary to grant the motion.

Only sixteen of those arrested actually went to trial. Thirteen
rank-and-file unionists among them were accused of "rioting."
Cruden, Swalde, and a third officer of Local 173, Hugh
Hughes, were charged with "inciting to riot." All were convicted.
Each of the thirteen rank and filers received a two-month jail
sentence. Cruden, Swalde, and Hughes got six months each
at hard labor. All sixteen were released on bail pending an
appeal of the convictions.

While these events were transpiring, public meetings were held
from time to time in Moorhead, where Miles Dunne could
address the strikers and their sympathizers. His talks were
then featured in Local 173's paper. By this time the paper
was being printed in Fargo; mass pressure on officials of the
AFL printing unions induced them to help make that possible.
The union organ was now coming out weekly as the *Gate
City Labor Review.*

Its regular appearance served to promote mounting support
to the strike. Milk drivers in Local 173 put in all the time
they could on the picket lines. Help came from rank-and-file
printers and building trades workers. Faculty members and
students at an agricultural college in the city gave assistance.
Unemployed workers joined the picket lines in significant
numbers. Backing was received from the Farmers' Holiday
Association and the Farmers' Union. Militants among the
farmers put up signs along the roads leading into Fargo.
They read: "Scab Town. Stay Away. Don't Trade In It."

The boss class countered with a smear campaign against
the strike in the columns of the *Fargo Forum*, the local capitalist daily which had an extensive rural readership. Preachers
denounced Local 173 in their Sunday sermons. Using this

slander campaign for a cover, the trucking companies got anti-picketing injunctions from compliant judges in an effort to hamstring the union.

At this point, D. J. Tobin, head of the International Brotherhood of Teamsters, made his contribution. Toward the end of March he revoked the charter of Local 173 for alleged nonpayment of per capita taxes to the International. It was not enough for him that this criminal act purported to "outlaw" the strikers from the labor movement. He issued statements to the *Fargo Forum* — a capitalist newspaper — denouncing Miles Dunne and the officers of Local 173. At the same time he demanded that the local be expelled from the Fargo Trades and Labor Assembly, the central body of the city's AFL unions.

The strikers reacted to Tobin's attack with grim rage, as did many others in the local AFL movement. Delegates from the Teachers Union took the lead in opposing Tobin's efforts to have Local 173 expelled from the Trades and Labor Assembly. In the end, however, the conservative AFL business agents managed to carry out Tobin's dictate and oust the victimized IBT local from the Assembly.

Ironically enough, this blow came at a time when new developments were about to lend aid to the strikers' cause. Widespread expressions of resentment over the brutal tactics of the Fargo bosses were making it uncomfortable for members of the North Dakota legislature. Finally that body felt constrained to launch an investigation of the vigilante assault on the strike headquarters. This in turn put pressure on the state supreme court, as shown by its reversal later on of the guilty verdicts against Cruden, Swalde, and Hughes on charges of "inciting to riot."

Unfortunately, these developments came too late to have any real effect on the union's struggle. The strike had already been broken, thanks primarily to Tobin's stab in the back. As things now stood the workers in Local 173 could only strive to keep their union afloat and wait for a chance to renew the fight against the trucking bosses.

5. Broadening the Left Wing

Expansion of the labor upsurge opened the way to extend the left wing into wide trade union circles. Local 574 took the initiative in this step, which was welcomed and needed by many union militants. Diverse leadership problems had arisen as the tempo of unionization in the region gained momentum. Well-intentioned officials of new organizations usually lacked experience and as a rule they had only limited understanding of the class struggle. These handicaps could cause them to falter in times of crisis and make costly blunders. There were also various cases in which militant workers had difficulties with conservative officials sitting on top of existing unions that were experiencing new growth.

This general situation called for the development of organized cooperation among trade unionists who wanted to fight the bosses. Potential leaders needed help from skilled fighters so they could better qualify themselves to guide the workers in struggle. Collective discussion of problems and comparison of experiences was, therefore, on the order of the day. It was toward this end that Local 574 sought to bring together militants in both AFL and independent unions.

One of the main forces drawn into such collaboration was the Independent Union of All Workers (IUAW) in Austin, Minnesota. The union had established itself through a bitter struggle at the Hormel meat-packing plant in that town. Since the AFL was virtually nonexistent in the vicinity, it then proceeded to draw most of the town's other workers into its ranks. The IUAW also reached out to organize packinghouse workers elsewhere in Southern Minnesota. At the same time it established relations with other independent unions in the packinghouses of Northern Iowa.

The central leader of the IUAW was Frank Ellis, a man with considerable background experience in the IWW. Although not a Marxist, he had absorbed many class-struggle concepts, and he was every inch a fighter. He did all he could to teach the workers that they must rely entirely on their own strength, never putting their trust in any agent of the capitalist class. Ellis warned especially against thinking the workers could get any justice in the capitalist courts.

"No matter what the charge on which a worker is brought before a capitalist judge, it's a frame-up," he told young workers. "If you're caught stealing a church and the steeple is sticking out of your pocket, plead not guilty."

Among these young packinghouse workers was Joe Ollman. He progressed beyond Ellis in political consciousness to become a revolutionary socialist and a firm supporter of the Trotskyist movement. Joe played an outstanding role in left-wing activities of that period and later on he made important contributions to the building of the CIO packinghouse workers union.

Another ally drawn into the expanding left-wing movement was the Minnesota State Employees Association. With a Farmer-Labor governor in office who found it necessary to give at least verbal support to unionization drives, the organization was making significant headway among government employees throughout the state. Also noteworthy was the presence of quite a few radicals among these workers. One of them, Julius F. Emme, was the founding leader of the Association.

Emme, who had been a metal worker by trade, joined Machinists Local 459 in St. Paul around 1913. Many times after that he was arrested for his part in labor struggles, and he was looked upon as a left-wing leader in the trade unions. Having also entered the Socialist Party, he edited the *Minnesota Socialist* for a time prior to World War I. After the 1917 revolution in Russia he joined the Communist Party and remained a member until about 1925. Later he came to consider himself a Trotskyist, even though he did not formally join the revolutionary-socialist movement.

By 1928 Emme had become thoroughly blacklisted in the St. Paul metal industry, which caused him to go jobless until 1930. At that time he managed — through influence resulting from his role as one of the founders of the Farmer-Labor Party — to secure an appointment from Governor Olson as secretary of the State Industrial Commission. It was from the vantage point of this post that he had set out to organize the state employees. Then in 1935 he was fired by the commissioners for publicly criticizing a judge's conduct in a strike.

Although Emme died in October 1935 at the age of 56, he was able during the last months of his life to make some of his most important contributions to the movement.

Henry Schultz served as state organizer of the Minnesota State Employees Association. He was a railway brakeman by trade, but in those depression times his low seniority standing as a young worker afforded him little employment at the occupation. So in 1934 he pitched in to help Local 574 and played a prominent role in the July-August strike. His close association with the strike leaders also led him to join the Trotskyist movement. After the battle was won he continued to do what he could to help Local 574; however, the main portion of his time was now spent in organizing state employees.

Collaborators in left-wing activity were to be found in other quarters as well. They included various railroad and building-trades militants in Minneapolis, along with young veterans of the garage strike; workers with radical backgrounds in Duluth, Minnesota, and on the Mesabi iron range; and the young leaders of the Fargo strike.

A preliminary conference of left wingers was held in St. Paul in November 1934. Representatives came from about fifteen AFL and independent unions. All union officials in attendance were acting with the approval of their executive boards.

The Communist Party also turned up with all the people it could muster, hoping to capture the conference. Each individual Stalinist claimed to represent some paper organization, a gimmick they were good at inventing for such occasions. When speaking, they would begin, "In the name of 6,000 iron miners on the Mesabi range . . ." or with some equally fictitious claim of being a tribune for a large formation of workers. But their ploy didn't work. Too many were present who knew all about the unprincipled methods used by the Stalininsts, and they were firmly put in their place.

Getting down to serious business, the conference adopted a six-point program for the building of the left-wing movement. It included: recognition of class-struggle realities in all union activity; opposition to any and all forms of class collaboration with the bosses; working class solidarity and reciprocal aid in labor struggles; advocacy of the industrial form of union structure; organization of the unemployed with full trade union support; development of educational programs for the working class.

A period of contact work on the basis of these perspectives led to the convening of a larger left-wing gathering in Minneapolis on April 13, 1935. At that time a formal structure was initiated known as the Northwest Labor Unity Conference (NLUC). To rebut in advance charges of setting up a "dual federation," which could be expected from conservative AFL officials, the aims and functioning of the NLUC were carefully explained to the whole labor movement.

The new left-wing formation duplicated nothing, it was pointed out, and replaced nothing. It did nothing to disturb the existing unity of the movement. Organizational affiliation was not permitted; unionists could join the NLUC only as individuals. Its sole objective was to aid all workers' organizations in making labor unity more meaningful and productive. This key aim was pinpointed in its central slogan: "All workers into the unions. All unions into the struggle."

To carry forward the building of a left wing based on class-struggle perspectives, the conference selected a continuations committee. It included: Frank Ellis and Joe Voorhees of Austin; Milton Carlson and R. C. Sermon of Duluth; J. F. Emme and O. R. Votaw of St. Paul; William Cruden of Fargo; Ray Dunne, Carl Skoglund, and myself of Minneapolis.

Since class warfare leads to arrests and trials of workers on frame-up charges in capitalist courts, attention was given to the question of labor defense. Effective action required measures to cope with two problems that arose within the labor movement itself. One involved Stalinist factionalism in this sphere. The other had to do with the mishandling of cases by conservative labor lawyers.

Early in the 1920s, the then-healthy Communist Party launched a movement known as the International Labor Defense (ILD). It was developed under the guidance of James P. Cannon, who later became one of the founders and the principal leader of this country's Trotskyist movement. In keeping with correct principles, the ILD at that time functioned on a genuinely nonpartisan and nonfactional basis, standing ready to aid all class-war victims.

When the CP became infected with the virus of Stalinism, however, ILD policy was reversed. "Defense" activities were reduced to the small change of petty factional maneuvers. Victims caught in the toils of capitalist law were used in cynical ways to gain one or another form of partisan advantage for the CP itself. Political opponents of the Stalinists were usually refused any help at all. Worse than that, they were subjected to slander campaigns intended to hamper the promotion of support from other quarters.

The second problem was of a different nature. Difficulties arose with various individual lawyers, acting for a fee, who practiced class collaboration in the capitalist courts. Like the AFL bureaucrats who tried to build them up as "labor defenders," these worthies sought to curry favor with the ruling class.

Their college training had prepared them for this line of conduct. The "sanctity" of capitalist law had been drilled into them. They accepted as gospel the ruling class premise that lawyers are supposed to conduct themselves as "officers of the court." Conditioned mentally to argue either side of a case as chance might dictate, depending on who hired them, they were congenial toward opposing attorneys as fellow members of the legal fraternity. This not only led them to be chummy with government prosecutors; they tended to think in terms of making legal horse trades at the expense of their worker-clients. On the whole, such lawyers were not to be trusted as the defense arm of the labor movement.

Under the circumstances a new defense organization was urgently needed. Steps to meet that requirement had already been initiated by the now-expanded Trotskyist formation, the Workers Party. As a result, a structure of the kind desired had been brought into being nationally, known as the Non-Partisan Labor Defense (NPLD).

It dedicated itself to the support of any and all labor victims of capitalist injustice. Those who lent their names to the effort and contributed financial aid were in no way used for partisan political advantage. Moreover, solidarity was extended to defense efforts conducted by others, including those of the Communist Party. These policies were in keeping with the time-honored labor slogan, "An injury to one is an injury to all."

To achieve its aims the NPLD sought out competent lawyers who would fight for their clients. Funds were raised to provide bail, meet court costs, pay expenses attendant upon appeals of convictions to higher courts, and publicize the cases of those it represented. Attorneys of the kind who will really serve the workers' cause were usually obtained for a nominal fee or none at all. Ordinarily the cost of their services involved only their expenses in handling a case, especially where travel was necessary.

Understanding these to be the NPLD's attributes, the left-wing conference in Minneapolis voted to support the building of a regional branch of the defense movement. In fact it was this new unit, just coming into being, that arranged for Francis Heisler to defend the strikers victimized by the vigilante raids in Fargo.

The conference also took an important step concerning the labor press. Acute financial difficulties had made it necessary for Local 574 to suspend publication of its official organ,

The Organizer, in October 1934. Because of its great value in helping the union to grow in numbers and expand in influence, we had been looking for a chance to put the paper back into circulation. Then we learned that Julius Emme was also planning to start a union paper for state employees.

These mutual needs led us to bring the whole problem before the conference for consideration. A decision was made there to launch a publication forthwith on the basis of support from the entire left-wing movement. In effect this meant that Local 574's paper was to reappear, this time as the official organ of the Northwest Labor Unity Conference, under the name *Northwest Organizer*.

Weekly publication of the paper as a four-page tabloid began with the issue of April 16, 1935. It was printed by Argus press — the loyal friend of the union that had gotten out *The Organizer*, doing so in courageous defiance of heavy pressure from the Citizens Alliance during the July-August 1934 strike.

The layout for the *Northwest Organizer* was planned — and the contents of the first issue outlined — in a session at Emme's St. Paul living quarters, with Ray Dunne, Henry Schultz, and myself also present. For the first few weeks Henry and I got out the paper as best we could, with help from Ray on the editorial line. Later the editing was taken over by Carlos Hudson, a young Trotskyist intellectual with journalistic talent, who had helped out on the strike daily in 1934. He, of course, acted in consultation with the union leadership.

Marvel Scholl, who is married to me, made regular contributions to the paper, especially a column called "The National Picket Line," which became widely read for general labor news. Other regular features included "Bill Brown Says," containing barbed comments by the union president; and a lively column, "Keeping Step with 574," written by Miles Dunne. In harmony with its irreverent predecessor, *The Organizer*, the new paper carried a poem in its masthead, which read:

> When I ply my needle, trowel or pick,
> I'm a decent Sheeney, Wop or Mick,
> But when I strike, I'm a Bolshevik,
> I'm labor.

As things turned out, the decision to publish the *Northwest Organizer* was indeed timely. Local 574 was about to get the Fargo treatment from Tobin. Without the paper there is some doubt that the union could have weathered the storm that was soon to descend upon it.

6. Tobin Declares War

From the outset of the Trotskyist campaign in Local 574 it had been clear that a head-on clash with the president of the International Brotherhood of Teamsters was inevitable.

Tobin based his general line on collaboration with the ruling class, his execution of the policy taking some of the crudest forms. Organizationally he was a craft unionist of the old AFL school. Within the IBT he ran things with bureaucratic arbitrariness, giving short shrift to anyone who crossed him.

This put him squarely in opposition to the course now being followed in Local 574, whose general line was shaped in accordance with the realities of class struggle. Structurally the local was breaking away from the outmoded craft form and moving toward organization along industrial lines. No less important, rank-and-file democracy prevailed in its internal affairs.

Life itself had already clarified the fundamental difference between the two courses. In connection with the 1934 coal strike Tobin had sought to inject procedural obstructions that would have hamstrung the local, if he had gotten away with them. While the fight was raging in the market area during the May walkout, he ordered the union to seek arbitration of the dispute with the bosses, a piece of arrogance that the strikers ignored. Then in July, at a most critical point in the conflict with the Citizens Alliance, he publicly attacked Local 574. These episodes revealed that, if Tobin's line had been accepted, the local would still have been back where it was in 1933.

While standing up to Tobin whenever necessary in the interests of the struggle against the bosses, the Trotskyist leaders in the local had sought to minimize friction with him. This policy helped give us time to prepare for the collision that was bound to come.

During the strikes we had still been in the process of setting into motion forces that could be developed beyond his power to control. This aim had now been partially accomplished through the victory over the trucking companies. We had emerged from the fight with a body of seasoned troops capable of giving a good account of themselves. Yet we still needed a breather so that the union could recuperate from the wear and tear of the long battle. It would also help to have the widening class struggle in the region become more advanced before internal union trouble arose. For these reasons we were in no hurry for a showdown with the IBT dictator.

At the moment we were most vulnerable on the question of per capita taxes owed to the International. Unjust though Tobin's demands were in this regard — since he had acted to hurt the local instead of helping it — we acknowledged our debt and simply asked for time to clear it up. This was much like paying blackmail, but it was better than having trouble with him over such a matter.

In that period IBT locals were assessed per capita taxes of 30¢ on each monthly payment of membership dues and $1 on initiation fees for new members. Moreover, Tobin demanded that his tax come right off the top of dues collections. It meant taking a big bite out of Local 574's revenue from monthly dues of $1.60 and a post-strike initiation fee of $3. To make things worse, the local was saddled with heavy debts that had accrued during the long strike struggle.

Money was owed to doctors and hospitals for the care of wounded pickets. Grocers, butchers, and dairies had to be paid for supplies furnished on credit during the strikes. Debts of that kind amounted to over $10,000.

Funds were also needed for economic aid to injured members who had not yet been able to return to work. Freda Ness, whose husband Henry had been killed on Bloody Friday, and her four children had to have financial help. In fact these — not Tobin's taxes — were the obligations that we met right off the top of dues collections.

At the same time the union had to be kept in operation. Things like hall rent and other general expenses had to be paid. Even at an average weekly wage of about $18, it was not easy to provide funds for the necessary staff of organizers. To round out the picture of the local's financial bind it should be added that when I took office as secretary-treasurer the cash on hand was less than $800.

There were also exceptional problems concerning the raising of money through payment of membership dues. Although some 7,000 workers had signed up in Local 574 during the strikes, this figure had now dropped. A considerable number had come

from jobs clearly outside the local's jurisdiction, and they had
to be transferred to other AFL unions. This still left a few
thousand who properly belonged in the organization, but many
of them were experiencing personal difficulties. As a result
of these combined factors total monthly dues payments fell to
as low as 900 in the immediate aftermath of the strikes.

The workers' personal troubles were, of course, of an
economic nature. After going for weeks without pay, they had
fallen behind in house rent. Bills had accumulated for groceries, medical care, and other necessities. Most families were
in need of new clothing, especially with the children returning
to school after the summer vacation. In some cases these problems were aggravated because only part-time work was available. There were also instances where workers on seasonal
jobs had been temporarily laid off.

Now that the union had beaten the trucking bosses, the
workers felt that personal economic needs of such urgency
had to come first. Consequently they gave these matters a
certain priority for the time being over the payment of union
dues and certainly over Tobin's money demands upon the
local.

My records as secretary-treasurer show that Local 574 paid
Tobin about $3,500 in per capita taxes during 1934. This
figure stood in sharp contrast to the $400 he had received in
1933, which reflected the local's stagnant condition before the
big organizing drive got under way. As matters stood after
the strikes, however, we still owed him around $3,000 in back
taxes. Not wanting trouble on this score, we intended to pay
it. Our aim was to come as close as we could to keeping current per capita taxes paid and at the same time to gradually
whittle away at the back debt.

On October 20, 1934, I wrote to Thomas L. Hughes, general
secretary-treasurer of the IBT, who assisted Tobin in presiding
over the union from their ivory tower in Indianapolis, Indiana.
In the letter I informed him of our difficult situation and of
our intention to clear up the tax debt as soon as we could.
He sent a terse reply, saying that ". . . these matters must be
called to the attention of the General President, am referring
your letter to him and no doubt you will hear from President
Tobin, on this matter."

Weeks went by without any further word from Indianapolis.
This naturally made us suspicious that something was being
cooked up against the local, and we tried to take protective
measures. A letter was sent on December 3, 1934, to Emery
Nelson, secretary of the Teamsters Joint Council in Minneapolis.

The Council was a delegated body made up of the executive boards of the various IBT locals in the city. It was supposed to supervise the activities of these locals, acting in compliance with the "laws" laid down by Tobin and carrying out his specific directives.

After calling attention to our financial crisis, the letter to Nelson concluded: "We do not ask particularly for the donation of funds, but we do ask that the leaders of the Minneapolis labor movement sit down at a conference table with us where we will explain fully and without reservations the exact situation which now obtains and from this conference we will hope to obtain suggestions and influential support to help us solve our problem. . . . On this basis we ask that at the earliest possible date a joint meeting of the Executive Boards of the Teamsters Joint Council, the Central Labor Union and Local 574 be arranged."

The joint meeting of the three executive boards took place about a week later. Also present at the session was John Geary, an IBT vice president and general organizer for Tobin, who lived in St. Paul. Everyone agreed that we were entitled to sympathetic understanding of our problem. Yet there was a subtle differentiation of attitudes among those present. Some were genuinely responsive to the point of wondering out loud what might be done to help us. Others, however, reacted with nothing more than proper expressions of concern, behind which their real attitude lay concealed. In any case, we had gained a certain propaganda advantage for later use against Tobin. It was now a matter of record that he — not Local 574 — would be responsible for any split that might develop within the city's labor movement.

During the next few weeks we became heavily involved in supporting the strikes of garage workers in the Twin Cities and Teamsters in Fargo. At the same time tensions were mounting because of the trouble developing with the head of the IBT, which could be expected to break out into the open any day. It didn't help any that the Citizens Alliance had sniffed out this situation and was already looking for a chance to take another crack at Local 574.

Under these conditions tempers sometimes become short in the union staff and there was need of the homemade therapy we had spontaneously developed in the form of practical jokes. Both the temper ailment, and the treatment devised for release from the tensions that caused it, were reflected in an incident that took place one cold February day.

I sent Harry DeBoer to the bank to make a deposit for the

union. He soon returned, handed the money back to me, and said they refused to accept it. I blew my top over this petty capitalist maneuver against the union. "We'll see whether the hell they'll take it," I announced loudly, as I grabbed my overcoat and headed for the citadel of finance. When I got there the door was locked. Only then did the real score dawn on me. It was Washington's birthday, a legal holiday, and Harry had been sent to a closed bank. Wearing a sheepish grin I went back to the union hall where the staff was waiting to give me the horse laugh.

Before long Tobin's flunkies were maneuvering openly against us. John Geary tried to snatch ice and taxi drivers from Local 574 and put them into separate craft unions. Right wingers engineered the removal of Bill Brown from his post as organizer of the Teamsters Joint Council, a position he had held since 1932. This was done while Bill was sick and confined to bed.

Then the main blow fell. It came through an undated letter from the general secretary-treasurer of the IBT, which we received on April 15, 1935:

"Under instructions from the General Executive Board I am notifying you that . . . the charter of Local 574 is this day revoked. . . . " Hughes stated coldly. "Section 48 of the Constitution of the International reads as follows: 'No Local Union shall have any right to pay any bills before they pay the per capita tax due to the International Union each month'. . . . Local Union 574 owes the International now six months per capita tax. . . ."

Word of the charter revocation led immediately to the unseating of Local 574's delegates to the Teamsters Joint Council. The action was not only injurious to us, it hurt all Teamster locals. They should have been concentrating on a general organizing drive under the impetus of Local 574's victory in the trucking industry. Instead they were violating their own interests by letting Tobin use them in an internal union fight that could help only the bosses.

Ignoring the Council's action for the moment, we sent Hughes a prompt reply. He was reminded — for the record — of our earlier correspondence with him concerning our efforts to clear up the back debt on per capita taxes and his statement that we would hear from Tobin about the matter. "We have yet to hear from President Tobin," our letter pointed out, "and the subject was not brought up again by any of the International officers until the receipt of your letter informing us of the revocation of the charter." Our reply concluded with a formal appeal from the decision of the General Executive Board.

This action brought a direct response from the IBT president. On April 22, 1935, he addressed himself to me as secretary-treasurer of the local. After taking note of our tax delinquency and the provisions of the International constitution on the subject, Tobin read the riot act to us.

"You seek, as an excuse for your failure to comply with our laws," he went on, "the fact that you had a strike during which some of your members got into trouble, etc. We knew nothing about your strike except what we read in the papers. What we do know is that your strike was unauthorized and uncalled for and that conditions obtained during the strike which were in direct violation of our laws. . . . The pity of it is that the rank and file who are undoubtedly honest and sincere were led by officers such as you and your associates who have no regard for the laws of our organization or the laws of the organized Labor Movement. . . .

"When I say you, I mean, your local union, which local you and your associates claim to have represented. The tail does not wag the dog in this instance. . . . Better have no International Union than have one composed of organizations such as Local No. 574, because of the manner in which it has been conducted. Of course, your answer will be that you would not receive sanction of your strike. We have sanctioned or endorsed over fifty strikes within the last six months, but only in cases where they have lived to the law and were not acting in defiance of the principles of the trade union movement and where they were not pulling strikes for racketeering and propaganda purposes. . . ."

Tobin wound up his tirade with typical bureaucratic arrogance: "In view of the fact that you are now disassociated from the International Union, I now advise you that any further communications sent to the International Officers will not be answered."

The old tyrant really seemed to believe that he could conjure Local 574 out of existence by jerking a piece of paper off the wall in our headquarters. It would have been a neat trick, considering that the local had proven itself powerful enough to defeat the Citizens Alliance in a virtual civil war. Yet he had dealt us a treacherous blow that would be an aid to the bosses. Now we would have to guard constantly against getting knifed in the back as we continued the battle against the ruling class.

Our first step in mobilizing to fight off the new attack was
to call a general membership meeting. Word of the charter
revocation had spread swiftly, and Local 574 members turned
out in force to get the facts about the new threat to the union.
A reading of the letters from the top IBT officials brought
heated reactions. Tobin was roundly cursed by the workers,
who remembered well the foul blow he had struck at the local
when he attacked us publicly on the eve of the July-August
strike in 1934. Unanimous determination was expressed to
repulse the new assault. The executive board was given a vote
of confidence in its ability to give the necessary leadership
toward that end.

A footnote is in order concerning Stalinist policy in connection with this meeting. From 1928 to 1934 they had followed a sectarian, ultraleft course intended to split the labor
movement and reorganize it under Communist Party control.
This line, plus their blind factionalism toward the Trotskyists, had thrust them into isolation from the living class struggle in Minneapolis.

During 1935 they carried out one of the sudden switches
in policy for which Stalinism has long been notorious. Conditions of the class struggle in Minneapolis, or anywhere else
for that matter, had little or no bearing on their turn. It had
been dictated from the Kremlin after Hitler's seizure of power
in Germany, which raised a military threat to the Soviet Union.
Stalin had bureaucratically decided to seek "collective security"
through alliances with imperialist countries whose interests
conflicted with those of the German capitalists. Toward that
end he set out to use the parties of the Third International
as political pawns in Kremlin diplomacy. This led to the in-
famous "Popular Front" line of class collaboration in politics,
which the Communist Party is following to the present day.

The change in political line also brought an about-face in
Stalinist trade union policy. Previously they had made futile
attempts to build their own "red" labor federation. Now they
wanted at all costs to get back into the AFL; and to serve
that end, they suddenly became frenzied opponents of independent unionism, no matter what the reasons for its existence.

For the local Communist Party hacks the switch in line was
seen as a new opportunity to launch a factional attack on the
Trotskyist leaders of Local 574. In accordance with this aim,
they promptly undertook to twist the facts concerning the charter revocation. Their attack on us stressed the need for the
local to be part of the AFL. Reinstatement in the IBT was
impossible, they piously asserted, without paying Tobin the

per capita taxes he had coming. Implying dishonesty in the handling of union finances, they called for a large rank-and-file auditing committee to find out why the taxes had not been paid.

The Stalinists began to develop this line through a mimeographed leaflet distributed outside the hall where the charter revocation was reported to the union membership. Their action implied support of Tobin against the local. In a not very subtle manner they were saying that the only way for Local 574 to get back into the AFL was to remove its leaders. As most workers saw it, that goal put them in league with both Tobin and the Citizens Alliance in wanting the union beheaded.

Even though no one took the Stalinist claptrap seriously, Local 574 did have a vital decision to make as to its future course. The matter required careful thought in the light of existing objective conditions. Labor militancy was still on the rise nationally. Workers in basic industry were pouring into the AFL and bringing pressures for a change to the industrial form of organization in order to fight effectively against the monopoly corporations. But they faced an obstacle within the AFL hierarchy. Diehard craft unionists were maneuvering to prevent the workers from realizing their objectives.

As a result antagonisms had arisen between the rank and file and the AFL officialdom. This, in turn, was causing a progressive opposition to the old-line leaders to take form nationally. John L. Lewis, head of the United Mine Workers, was giving impetus to the trend by stepping forward as an advocate of industrial unionism. At that time, however, no one could be certain what course the developing conflict would take. It could result in an internal transformation of the federation, or it could lead to a split. Only further events would tell.

This meant that at this time Local 574 could find no significant force outside the AFL with which to ally itself. Nor could we plan to go it alone as an independent union, pending the outcome of the internal conflict developing within the existing labor federation. To do so would have thrown us out of harmony with the AFL movement in the city. Right-wing bureaucrats could then have succeeded in gradually thrusting the local into isolation from other organized workers and cutting it to pieces.

For these reasons the executive board decided to recommend a campaign for reinstatement into the IBT.

Broad support could be mobilized behind that objective because of the disruptive role played by Tobin. He was violating the spirit of solidarity forged during 1934, which had given new life to the city's trade union movement. On formal grounds of a piddling money question, he had expelled a local of some twenty years standing in the AFL, a local that had spearheaded the fight to make Minneapolis a union town. It was a self-evident act of spite against an organization that had transformed itself from the caricature of a union it had long been under the domination of the IBT head into a dynamic organization.

Despite Tobin, Local 574 had now become an effective fighting instrument. It was wholly representative of thousands of workers and fully capable of serving their interests. Moreover, its 1934 strikes had been endorsed by the entire AFL of the city, and all the workers knew that. Thus they would be quick to see through Tobin's claim that the strikes violated IBT "laws." It would become clear that he was actually demanding veto power over all Minneapolis labor.

In keeping with the demand for restoration of the IBT charter, the executive board proposed that the local continue to act as though it were still part of the AFL. The policy of expanding to the outer limits of IBT jurisdiction along industrial lines would, of course, be continued. But there would be no invasion of job categories specifically assigned to other AFL unions. Instead, we would aid these organizations in their struggles against the bosses.

Such measures of fraternal cooperation and our acts of solidarity in struggle would be in accord with the needs of the day. They would stand in marked contrast to Tobin's policies, which were relics of the past. As a result, workers throughout the city would feel they had a stake in the survival of Local 574.

When these policy recommendations were submitted to a general membership meeting of the union, a bit of an argument developed. It was not because anybody was inclined to capitulate to Tobin. Just the opposite. Some hot-headed but short-sighted workers wanted the local to forget the IBT altogether and go ahead entirely on its own as an independent union. They were motivated by a combination of bitter hatred for the Teamster boss and supreme confidence in the strength of their organization. Answers given by the leadership to such views helped to clarify the general picture of our situation, and the recommended course of action was approved.

Once again Local 574 was prepared to go into battle as a united force with a single policy.

7. The Opening Round

Even before Local 574's charter was revoked the Citizens Alliance had gotten wind of Tobin's imminent attack on us. Its strategists moved quickly to seek ruling class advantage from the IBT dictator's reactionary policy. A scheme was devised to draw conservative AFL officials into a united front with the bosses on a city-wide scale in opposition to left-wing trade unionists.

Toward that end a "public" body was projected. It was to be composed primarily of employers and AFL bureaucrats, with an added sprinkling of "neutrals," such as lawyers, preachers, and reformist politicians. These "civic-minded" individuals, all handpicked behind the workers' backs, were to sit in judgment over issues in dispute between workers and bosses. In short, they were to play a strikebreaking role.

To give their plot a deceptive coloration, the Alliance leaders resorted to another trick for which the ruling class is notorious. In naming their "public" body they tried to coopt an idea made popular by Local 574 during the 1934 struggle. They called it the "Committee of 100." That had been the designation of the broad formation elected within the union to lead the July-August strike. Now the bosses sought to use this honorable name to camouflage an anti-union setup through which they hoped to stem the mounting labor upsurge in the city.

Since early April the Alliance had been dangling its class-collaborationist bait before the AFL business agents, and some of them were nibbling at it. So we went after them in the first issue of the *Northwest Organizer*, which came out on April 16, 1935. Addressing ourselves to rank-and-file unionists throughout the city, we warned that the bosses aimed to divide labor's ranks into two factions. To do so, efforts were being made to whip up a lynch spirit against progressive trade unionists. The object was to weaken the workers' power and then launch a union-smashing campaign.

"If the labor leaders cannot see this for themselves," we urged, "it is up to the membership to show them where their interests lie."

In the same issue of the union paper, a report was given of the formation of the Northwest Labor Unity Conference. This vehicle for left-wing cooperation in the trade unions had become even more valuable in view of Tobin's attack on Local 574. During the crucial months immediately ahead it was to prove extremely useful in the fight for union democracy.

Since notice of the charter revocation had arrived only the day before the paper went to press, a big problem confronted us. We had to answer the attack, and the necessary work had to be done quickly. On top of that none of us had any journalistic know-how. We went ahead as best we could, and later on Marvel Scholl set down her recollections of our experience.

"Farrell brought Ray Dunne to our house for dinner," she wrote, "and afterwards we three — me on the old, old Smith portable we owned, with my then hunt, cuss and peck typing method — began to work. Page after page rolled out, as the two authors expanded points, added new ones, scratched out bad formulations, etc. When we had finished to all our satisfaction we had many pages of copy which were then rushed to Argus press.

"The next day mother took care of the kids so I could go with Farrell and Ray to the print shop. When we got there Ace Johnston, the linotype operator, handed us a sheaf of galley proofs containing our editorial statement. He remarked: 'There is enough in this one edit to fill your paper for three issues. You will have to cut it.'

"We went to a small coffee-and joint on the corner to do our job. After sweating blood over who knows how many cups of coffee, we finally managed to make the necessary cuts. We were learning the hard way how to make a certain amount of space suit what had to be said."

In the statement that emerged from the apprentice-labors Marvel described, we summarized the background factors involved in Tobin's revocation of Local 574's charter. It was pointed out that the gains for all Minneapolis workers implicit in the 1934 union victory were now put in jeopardy because the local could not pay its full tax tribute to Tobin. He had rewarded the workers for their splendid fight by giving the entire movement a stab in the back.

"The time has come for a showdown," we declared. "The International Unions must be shown that they are the servants of the workers and not their masters. Until this is done a real labor movement cannot be built."

Our declaration got a big response among the workers of

the city. They fully agreed that high-handed International officials had to be brought to book by the union rank and file. Many began to agitate for the return of all local charters to the AFL as a protest against Tobin's disruption of the movement, an act he had committed simply to maintain his bureaucratic rule over the Teamsters.

Although the spirit behind the idea was commendable, it was not a good tactic. Some local unions would have turned in their charters, but others would not have done so. A disadvantageous split could have developed as a result, and hardened within the movement — one of a far more serious nature than Tobin was able to precipitate on his own.

"It would be a mistake for the unions to cut themselves adrift from the unification made possible through the A. F. of L." the *Northwest Organizer* advised editorially. "The fight must be carried on in a different manner. First, and most essential, the bureaucracy, which sucks the life blood from the movement from the top, must be removed. To accomplish this the minor officials who hold office through subservience to the higher-ups, and who serve as their tools, must be replaced by real leaders who will serve the workers honestly. This can be accomplished in the elections held in the local unions. This new leadership, as it gains in numbers, will replace the petty bureaucrats in the central bodies and the state executive councils. From this point a real housecleaning can be accomplished which will completely rebuild the movement into a healthy and growing thing."

In keeping with this advice we submitted a written appeal to the Central Labor Union for support in our fight to gain readmission into the AFL. It was an extensive document that reviewed the problems faced by Local 574 in the aftermath of the 1934 strikes and gave the facts and figures concerning our per capita tax difficulties with Tobin. Our appeal concluded with a summary of the conflicting lines of policy involved in the dispute with the IBT head.

Tobin's line called for the payment of per capita taxes before any other bills were paid. Compliance with this demand, we pointed out, would have meant the local could have nothing more than a small office with a secretary in charge. The secretary could have done little more than collect dues from those who came to the office and forward the per capita tax to the International. This would have crippled the union, reducing it within a few weeks to its former impotent condition.

As against this bankrupt line, we counterposed the policy Local 574 was following. It was vital to check and finally defeat the bosses' plan of wholesale discriminations against union members. To do so we had set up a steward system and begun to build a well-knit staff of active organizers. There were still wounded pickets and their families to be cared for. Unpaid strike bills for doctors, hospitals, and food had to be settled. A suitable union hall had to be maintained. While meeting these imperative needs, we intended to pay the International every cent we could without crippling the local, and we expected to clear up the entire tax debt within a reasonable period of time.

This appeal for help in regaining our IBT charter coincided with a demand from Tobin that Local 574's delegates be unseated by the Central Labor Union (CLU). Right wingers in the central body wanted to comply with his demand, but they were in a minority. Most of the delegates from local unions, either expressing their own sentiments or reflecting pressures from rank-and-file members, wanted to support Local 574. As a consequence, the demand that we be unseated from the body was brushed aside.

A committee of three was elected to go to the IBT headquarters and present Tobin with a counter-demand that our charter be restored. The committee included Jean Spielman of the bookbinders, Andrew Lief of the carpenters, and Sander Genis of the clothing workers.

The CLU action put the bureaucrats of the Teamsters Joint Council on the spot. They had already aroused rank-and-file criticism within other Teamster locals by moving quickly to unseat our delegates to the Council when our charter was revoked. Now a special committee from the AFL central body was going to Indianapolis to demand that the whole thing be reversed. So they decided to get in on the act, both as a cover against further criticism and to keep abreast of events. This led them to arrange for the inclusion of Patrick J. Corcoran, an official of the Milk Drivers Union, on the CLU committee.

Since it was highly unlikely that the committee would get anywhere with Tobin, we did not sit with bated breath awaiting the outcome of the Indianapolis session. Our attention was concentrated, instead, on strengthening Local 574's position in preparation for a prolonged struggle.

A general unionization drive was launched, which spread rapidly to all unorganized sections of the trucking industry. Steady gains in membership strength resulted and additional companies were brought under contract with the union. Workers' grievances over contract violations by the bosses were given prompt and effective attention. The latter task had become a big one, because the local now dealt with almost 500 employers, most of whom had never before had anything to do with a union.

Then the veterans of 1934 got a small financial boost on June 1. Under the terms of the strike settlement their hourly wages rose 2 1/2 cents an hour on that date. This meant an hourly rate of 55 cents for truck drivers and 45 cents for helpers, platform workers, and inside workers.

At this point the workers' devotion to the union was graphically demonstrated. A general membership meeting voted to pay an extra months' dues to help clear up outstanding strike debts for medical services and food.

In keeping with its continuous growth the local rented a new, more spacious headquarters at 257 Plymouth Avenue North. The main hall would seat 2,000. There were also smaller rooms for meetings and conferences, along with office space, a library, and a club room. Kitchen facilities were available for social affairs and a checkroom accommodated 600.

The power of a union needing such facilities for its normal operations was soon shown to the building-trades workers. They were trying to unionize a big construction job but the employers, as had long been their habit, sought to run it on an open-shop basis. Local 574 refused to allow any trucking of material to scabs on the job and the bosses had to agree to 100 percent unionization of the project. This act of solidarity with the building-trades unions, which strengthened their good will toward us, came at a most opportune time. The special committee sent by the CLU to see Tobin was about to present its report to the central body.

As we expected, the IBT president flatly refused to reinstate Local 574. A new charter for a General Drivers Union would have to be issued, he insisted, subject to a series of harsh restrictions.

First: Various sections of the local would have to be chopped off and organized on their own as distinct crafts. As a starter ice and coal workers were to be put into separate unions, also taxi drivers.

Second: All inside workers were to be denied membership. To be a member, 51 percent of one's time had to be spent either driving or doing other actual work on a truck.

Third: The present officers of Local 574 were to be excluded from the new local and all membership applications were to be subject to approval by the International. The local was to come under the direct supervision of a special representative of Tobin.

Fourth: The new local was to pay the back per capita taxes owed by Local 574.

These demands made Tobin's intentions clear to most everyone. He sought to cut up Local 574 into small, helpless units on a narrow craft basis. The fact that this would strip the local of its fighting ability at terrible cost to the workers did not bother him. His main concern was to keep the union under his bureaucratic control, and to do so he was ready to weaken it. On top of that he intended to force the AFL unions of the city to help him break us.

While they were in Tobin's office, the CLU committee reported, he telephoned William Green, the AFL president, who promised him full cooperation. The committee interpreted this to mean that attempts by the CLU or any of its affiliates to defend Local 574 would result in the loss of their AFL charters.

Although most CLU delegates were outraged by Tobin's arrogant demands, they voted to formally unseat Local 574 from the body rather than risk punitive action at Green's hands. At the same time a majority insisted that we continue to sit in on their sessions as unofficial delegates, which we did. On the surface, it might appear that we had lost a round, but in reality a deep polarization, largely favorable to us, was taking place in the AFL central body.

Shortly after the CLU had complied formally with his demand that we be unseated, Tobin chartered a "Local 500," which he intended to use to destroy Local 574. He then ordered the Teamsters Joint Council to proceed against us, in accordance with the dictates he had laid down to the CLU committee. At the same time he reconstituted Taxi Drivers Local 125, which had earlier been displaced when the workers involved had voted to join Local 574.

Pat Corcoran was assigned to direct Tobin's campaign locally. He, in turn, designated Cliff Hall, whom we had fired from his former post in Local 574 for incompetence and disloyalty, as business agent of "Local 500." Together they went to talk to the bosses with whom the old Local 574 officialdom had maintained class-collaborationist relations prior to 1934. They asked help in forcing the workers at these companies to switch over to the Tobin-sanctioned paper union, but little came of it. "Local 500" began what was to be a short life with only 26 members, as compared to over 3,000 in Local 574.

Corcoran's line with the bosses was to stress the "legitimacy" of the new paper union. He also gave assurance that it would take in only "responsible" members who knew how to get along

with their employers. On that basis he and Hall went to the
local Chamber of Commerce to ask help in organizing a "safe
and sane" drivers local. This led to a meeting on June 24
at the Nicollet Hotel with trucking employers, who were asked
to break their contracts with Local 574 and deal with "Local
500."

The bosses were, of course, sympathetic to the request, seeing
in it an opportunity to smash the union power in the industry.
But they had a problem. Local 574 not only had contracts
with them, it had their workers solidly organized. They knew
that an attempt to go along with the Tobinites would lead to
a battle which they weren't sure they could win. So they decided
to play it cool.

On the same day that Corcoran and Hall met with the trucking bosses, Local 574 held a general membership meeting. It
took place at our new headquarters, which had in itself become
a symbol to the workers of their union's strength. News about
the bosses playing footsie with the Tobin gang was received
with anger and indignation. All phases of the situation were
discussed, as the members expressed their determination to
fight Tobin — and the bosses too, if they decided to stick their
oar in. A motion was then adopted authorizing the leadership
to take the initiative in organizing a united front with AFL
unions sympathetic to our cause.

This decision led to the formation of a Joint Transportation
Council, composed of two AFL unions — the garage workers
and filling station attendants — and Local 574. It was envisaged
primarily as a union-building instrument, devoted to organizing
all transportation workers and engaging in common struggle
against the bosses. At the same time our relationship with
these AFL unions helped to develop a nucleus around which
to build an organized left wing in the Central Labor Union.

The latter effort got a further boost on July 20, the first
anniversary of the "Bloody Friday" police riot in 1934. A
memorial meeting, officially endorsed by the CLU, was scheduled at the Parade Grounds, a large open field on the edge
of the downtown district. Thousands of workers attended, representing almost every union in the city. Prominent AFL officials felt compelled to participate in the speaking program
and to mention the vital role Local 574 had played in making
Minneapolis a union town. Afterward over 2,000 marched from
the meeting through downtown streets to the scene of the
shooting, tying up traffic for almost two hours. The renewed
spirit of solidarity engendered by this event gave fresh encour-

agement to Local 574's friends and made it harder than ever
for the AFL bureaucrats to carry out Tobin's orders to stig-
matize us as "outlaws."

Under the impetus of the July 20 demonstration, new steps
were taken to build an organized left wing within the Central
Labor Union. A special conference of AFL unions was called
on the initiative of the garage workers and filling station attendants. Local 574 was invited to attend with full voice in
the deliberations.

Official delegations came to the conference sessions from
many unions. Included were locals of carpenters, lathers,
painters, garage workers, filling station attendants, upholsterers,
ornamental iron workers, city and sanitation drivers, flour
and cereal workers, building service employees, laundry
workers, stationary engineers, building laborers, restaurant
employees, and bakers. Participation by the city and sanitary
drivers was unusually significant, since it marked a breakthrough for us within the Teamsters Joint Council.

By unanimous vote the conference adopted a resolution demanding the reinstatement of Local 574 into the IBT and AFL.
This action not only helped to stymie Tobin's attempts to have
us read out of the labor movement; it strengthened our hand
in enforcing existing working agreements with the trucking
bosses and in renegotiating contracts that were coming up for
renewal.

When the agreement with the Yellow Cab Company expired
in June, we had little difficulty in negotiating a one-year continuation. The new terms brought further gains in wages and
conditions for the workers involved, thereby binding them
even more closely to Local 574. Since this company employed
the great bulk of the city's cab drivers, Tobin's reconstitution
of Taxi Drivers Local 125 was made relatively meaningless.
It was able to corral nothing more than a handful of individual cab owners and their relief drivers.

Similarly, we had little trouble with the coal bosses, who
had been the first to battle us in 1934. For a brief time a
few of them toyed with the notion of using the Tobin gang
against us. Then the General Labor Committee of the coal
employers sent a letter to the industry advising that it take
" . . . no interest in quarrels between competing labor unions."
In effect the bosses were being reminded that Local 574 had
the power in the industry, and nothing could be done about
it at the time. Without further ado, new and improved terms
of agreement were reached, extending through the fall and
winter of 1935-36.

Matters were somewhat more complex in the ice industry. For years Ice Drivers Local 225 had existed in the city and had more or less confined itself to class-collaborationist relations with the Cedar Lake Ice Company, a big firm operating its own fleet of trucks. In the meantime there had been a steady growth of broker operators in the industry. These outfits confined their capital investment pretty much to the production of ice, hiring independent truck owners to make deliveries. The latter were workers who had bought trucks, usually through long term financing, which they drove themselves on a commission basis for truck and driver.

Many of these workers spent the winter hauling coal, and they had joined Local 574 during the 1934 struggle. Now they wanted to extend the gains the union had won for them in coal into the ice industry, where they worked during the summer. Our efforts to cooperate in this legitimate aim quickly brought us into conflict with the petty bureaucrats of Local 225. Although they had no intention of doing anything for the independent truck owners, they objected to efforts on our part to help these workers on the ground that Local 574 shouldn't "interfere" with their jurisdiction in the ice industry. Since their argument was phoney, we brushed it aside and proceeded to act.

A coverage agreement was negotiated with the major broker operators, providing significant gains for the workers who delivered ice for them. Ray Rainbolt and Harry DeBoer of the Local 574 staff were then assigned to bring holdouts among the small-fry outfits under the contract. As a first step Lucas Ice and Fuel was struck.

At 5:00 A.M. one morning we put a picket line around the place. Several squad cars filled with cops soon showed up, and before long a scab driver went through the motions of preparing to load a truck. The union responded by moving quickly to bring in reinforcements. Then a big-mouthed cop began to bray about being sworn to uphold "law and order." We took this to mean that they were getting themselves psyched up for an attack on the picket line, and we braced ourselves to receive the expected charge.

About that time the lieutenant in command came out of the company office, but he didn't order the cops to get ready to convoy the scab truck. Instead he motioned for a couple of them to follow him, walked out about half way between the opposing lines and indicated that he wanted to parley. DeBoer, Rainbolt, and I stepped forward to meet him.

"Mr. Lucas is ready to sign up with you," he said, "but he

wants you to remove your pickets first."

"Will you pull out your cops, too?" we asked.

"No, I can't do that," he replied. "My orders are to give him full protection."

After further discussion we came to an understanding. Both sides would withdraw their forces a carload at a time, doing so alternately, until only one detachment of pickets and one squad of cops remained. At that point Lucas would be expected to put his name on the dotted line.

The lieutenant then went to consult Lucas about the proposed arrangement and returned in a short time, looking quite relieved.

"Okay," he said. "That's the way we'll do it."

Around 6:45 A. M. Rainbolt walked into the company office and the contract with the union was signed.

In a tension-filled confrontation, lasting a bit less than two hours, we had won a decisive victory. A demonstration had been given that, despite Tobin's attack on us, Local 574 retained the fighting power for which it had become famous.

All that remained now was a mopping up operation. Yet that took a lot of doing because anarchy was rife within the ice industry. Several skirmishes still had to be fought before the job was done. In one case, for example, a cockroach boss tried to get Rainbolt jailed for allegedly breaking his leg in an altercation that grew out of an attempt to deliver ice with scab drivers. Rainbolt beat the rap.

Finally the whole situation was brought under union control and after that the ice drivers' earnings improved steadily.

A different problem arose concerning firms where Local 574 had lost the collective bargaining election after the 1934 strikes. Among these was La Belle Safety Storage Company, one of the largest outfits in the transfer industry. As in most other situations of the kind, the workers at this company had come to regret their vote against the union. One by one, all but a handful of them had since joined Local 574, and we were now in a position to demand that the company sign a working agreement.

In this case "Local 500" sought to intervene against us. Corcoran and Hall tried to get the transfer bosses to help them freeze Local 574 out of the industry. As an inducement they shaped their contract proposals around a pledge that union members would "work for the interests of the Company at all times." This led the Transfermen's Association to call a meeting to consider a "movement started . . . in the last few days . . . which is of the most vital importance."

Local 574 responded to the threat by striking La Belle. This action put "Local 500" in a bind. Hall had signed up four men at the company, whom the other workers considered finks. In doing so he had promised them protection so that they could continue working, no matter what Local 574 did. Now we had put a strong picket line around the place and Hall could do nothing about it. Neither could the bosses. So La Belle signed an agreement with Local 574 after a three-day tie-up.

Soon thereafter the transfer bosses decided as a group to slam the door on "Local 500." They proceeded to negotiate a new agreement with Local 574, even though the 1934 strike settlement did not expire until May 31, 1936. The new contract, which ran for one year, went into effect on November 1, 1935. Under its terms all transfer workers got a further wage increase of five cents an hour, effective June 1, 1936. This time the bosses signed directly with the union, instead of dealing through the Labor Board, as they had done in 1934.

In summing up the meaning of these experiences, the *Northwest Organizer* asserted: "Local 574 is an established, deeply rooted union. It is here to stay and it is here to build."

Clearly we were holding our own against Tobin in Minneapolis, but we didn't stop with that. Steps were also taken to carry the fight to him in the International. An IBT convention—which was held every five years—was about to take place. This gave us a vehicle for an appeal to all Teamster locals in the country. We sent them an open letter, stating our case and asking their support in our fight for reinstatement in the International.

Since Tobin ran everything with an iron hand, we had no illusions about the convention overruling him. Yet our counterattack might possibly have some good effects. Mass moods were changing within the labor movement under the radicalizing conditions of the time, and the IBT could not remain entirely unaffected by the process. There was a good chance that we could evoke sympathetic responses among rank-and-file members, perhaps even among a few secondary officials. This probability was enhanced by the national reputation Local 574 had gained through its militant 1934 struggles.

We realized that significant opposition to Tobin's line could not be developed in time to affect the forthcoming convention, but that was a secondary consideration. As we saw it, the fight over IBT policy would be a long one. What had started in 1934 was bound to run much deeper than many realized. For these reasons the success or failure of our efforts did not hinge upon the outcome of immediate events. It remained entirely possible that in the long run our fight could bring about some basic changes in the International.

Concerning the immediate question, the Tobin machine rammed through a convention decision upholding the revocation of our charter, as had been expected. In addition the IBT constitution was amended to bar communists from membership.

The two actions were interrelated, both being intended to prevent the spread of a rebel movement within the national organization. Establishment of an exclusionary membership policy laid a basis for expulsion of left wingers on trumped-up charges. At the same time it provided a device for indiscriminate red-baiting to fog the issues in dispute. Along with these threats, oppositionists got a reminder that they would also be subject to blanket acts of reprisal. Notice had been served that defiant local unions could expect to lose their charters.

Measures of this kind, Tobin obviously assumed, would enable him to carry out his plan to split up Local 574 and reorganize the remnants under his bureaucratic control. On balance, however, the situation in Minneapolis raised serious doubts as to whether he could succeed in that aim. After months of sustained effort, his flunkies had managed to sign up less than fifty workers in "Local 500." That figure amounted to only a shade more than one percent of Local 574's membership.

"If this represents a split," the *Northwest Organizer* observed, ". . . Webster didn't understand his own dictionary."

8. Federal Workers Section

There was one important sphere in which we had a complete advantage over Tobin.

Like most AFL bureaucrats, he wanted nothing to do with the unemployed. To him these workers were little more than riffraff, potential strikebreakers, with whom "responsible" trade unionists should not become involved. If anything was to be done for them, his school of thought contended, let the welfare agencies take sole responsibility. For a time the AFL hierarchy even opposed unemployment insurance.

We had an opposite view, based on objective reality. Many millions were jobless nationally. All were victims of the capitalist economic system, forced into miserable circumstances under depression conditions. As workers, they deserved trade union support in a fight for social concessions from the capitalists to improve their lot. Such aid would not only be a necessary act of class solidarity, important though that was as a matter of principle. It was the best way to prevent the bosses from duping the unemployed into taking the places of trade unionists who went on strike. Therefore, we insisted, organized labor should do everything possible to help the jobless.

This policy dispute, over what might seem an unrelated issue, had a direct bearing on our clash with Tobin inside the trade union movement. A background sketch of the unemployed struggle should clarify this connection.

After the 1929 stock market crash, layoffs in industry mounted steadily. More and more workers were thrown into personal economic crisis. Yet Herbert Hoover's administration persisted in treating the developing social catastrophe as a temporary interlude of economic readjustment, repeatedly assuring the country that prosperity was "just around the corner." Nothing was done by the federal government to give direct aid to the jobless. They were left to the tender mercies of local systems for doling out public relief. These were generally archaic setups that gave only grudging help to the needy, doing so in ways that caused humiliating experiences for relief clients.

At the outset this situation was tolerated by the victimized workers, who tended to accept Hoover's assurances that their difficulties would only be temporary. Organized activity among the jobless was confined mainly to "self-help" tactics. Committees were formed to chisel food, clothing, and other items from merchants willing to contribute as an investment in good will. Organized searches were instituted for odd jobs through which a few dollars could be picked up. The fruits of such efforts were then shared fairly among those participating in the activities.

Before long the merchants became reluctant to continue their donations, which had become rather costly to them. Efforts were then made among unemployed groups to develop barter systems. These centered on efforts to produce simple consumer items through projects organized along commune-type lines. Scrip was generally used as a means of payment by merchants who agreed to handle such products, and it was then honored for the purchase of certain commodities from stores participating in the overall plan.

After a time the "self-help" type of activity began to fade into the background. To an increasing degree the unemployed were coming to realize that their difficulties were not temporary, that their problems were not about to be resolved through early reemployment. This gave rise to a trend toward new forms of mass action.

Techniques were developed to resist the eviction of tenants by landlords. Demonstrations — marked by an upward acceleration of their scope and militancy — were organized to bring pressure upon city, state, and federal officials for improvements in public relief. At the same time it was made clear that the unemployed were not fighting primarily for a dole. What they wanted, above all, was to have steady work.

With their turn toward mass pressure on the capitalist government, political consciousness began to rise among the jobless. This opened the way for radical parties to gain increasing influence within the unemployed movement. At the same time chances were improving for class-conscious militants to play a leading role among workers who had jobs, many of whom were becoming quite combative. By 1933 the combined development had advanced to a point where it was objectively possible to achieve a qualitative leap in the fighting capacity of the labor movement. If employed and unemployed workers could be drawn into mutual support of their respective struggles, a powerful team could be organized in opposition to the capitalist class.

Achievement of this necessary aim stood as a key challenge to the revolutionaries of that period.

Proceeding accordingly, the Trotskyists within Local 574 had set out in 1934 to draw the unemployed into an alliance with the union. A considerable force was involved. Measured loosely, in terms of families of jobless workers, it came close to representing a third of the city's adult population. On top of that there were periodic downturns in the economic status of other workers. Many went through cycles of being employed, only to be temporarily laid off and forced to exist for a time on public relief.

Hundreds within Local 574 fell into the latter category. These members had a direct stake in the fight being waged by the jobless to improve their situation and they wanted the union to get into the battle. Thousands among the totally unemployed, in turn, felt a growing affinity with Local 574. If they helped the union establish itself as a power in the city, they realized, the way would then be open to gain meaningful support of their own struggles. Taken as a whole, these interrelated factors made possible the forging of a powerful united front within the working class.

To assure a firm alliance with the unemployed, steps were needed to show that it would not be a one-sided affair. Trade union support had to be mobilized in the fight for improved public relief. Collaboration had to be maintained on the federal "made work" projects which Roosevelt had set up. At the same time it was necessary to develop close cooperation with leaders of the unemployed in shaping plans for their help in Local 574's battle against the trucking bosses.

A tactical problem arose in this connection because of Communist Party policy. The Stalinists had gained some influence among the jobless by setting up unemployed councils. Trotskyists had been barred from these formations, which were under rigid CP control and operated in conformity with the ultra-left line it was still following in 1934. Instead of helping to promote working class unity, the Stalinists could be expected to use their councils as a weapon for factional attacks on Trotskyist-led Local 574. A means, therefore, had to be developed to outflank them in the unemployed movement.

This aim was accomplished through the Minneapolis Central Council of Workers (MCCW). It was a delegated body of representatives from unemployed formations, a few trade unions, labor political groups, and other workers' organizations. The MCCW had been created for the express purpose of fighting in behalf of the jobless, and it had the endorse-

ment of the AFL Central Labor Union. Through this body
Local 574 was able to develop highly effective working relations with the unemployed, based on reciprocal collaboration
in all spheres of struggle.

Jobless workers flocked onto the Teamster picket lines in
both the May and July-August strikes in 1934, giving a good
account of themselves in battle. The union, in turn, backed
them in their fights on the federal Emergency Relief Administration (ERA) projects during that period. This dynamic alliance brought victory for Local 574 in its conflict with the
trucking bosses and, in the course of the action, the MCCW
membership rose to an unprecedented 4,000.

A new problem developed, however, when settlement of the
1934 Teamster strike brought a sudden decline in the tempo
of mass action. The changed atmosphere caused many of the
jobless, who had responded to the dramatic trade union struggle, to lapse into inactivity. A lull followed in the unemployed
movement and the MCCW suffered a sharp drop in membership. This experience underlined the need for greater stability
in the unemployed organization. It also verified Local 574's
contention that the organization of jobless workers under trade
union sponsorship had become an absolute necessity.

This could be done, we argued, in a manner that would
enable the unemployed to retain their own distinct formation,
along with their full democratic rights. The main change would
be their affiliation with the trade union movement. Through
this step the necessary inner stability could be imparted to
the unemployed movement. At the same time, new leverage
would be gained through direct union aid in fighting to advance the interests of jobless workers.

These views met with approval among the MCCW leaders,
and they expressed readiness to dissolve their organization
into a new trade union setup of the kind we proposed.

It was also agreed that efforts should be made to have the
AFL Central Labor Union take responsibility for the new
step. There were many jobless members among its various
affiliated unions, all of whom needed the collective labor support that could best be organized through the central body.
A resolution to this effect was introduced in the CLU by Local 574's delegates. It passed by a big vote and a committee was set up to formulate policy for the proposed new form
of union activity. Then Tobin revoked our charter, the CLU
backed off from its commitment, and the task rested entirely
upon our "outlawed" union.

Once again, Local 574 was about to take a pioneer action

designed to increase the combat power of the working class.

Basic guidelines for the project were set down in the local's by-laws. The pertinent section read: "It is the duty of the unions to assist the unemployed workers to organize and improve their living standards. To fulfill this obligation the union shall maintain an auxiliary section of unemployed workers to be known as the Federal Workers Section of Local 574. This section shall function under the direct supervision of the union Executive Board and shall have the full assistance of the union. Members of the Federal Workers Section shall not have voice or vote in the regular meetings of the union."

There were several reasons for the latter provision. Enrollment in the Federal Workers Section (FWS) was not confined to Local 574 members who had been laid off. Its ranks were open to all the city's unemployed, including jobless members of other unions. Thus it was bound to be a heterogeneous formation and, hopefully, one of considerable size. Such a body could not be formally incorporated into the union with voice and vote. That would have distorted the local's basic character as an organization of workers employed in the trucking industry. The resulting problems would have weakened the union base upon which the unemployed movement was to be built. Hence the new body had to be structured as an auxiliary section of the local.

Special union buttons and membership cards were issued to workers who joined the FWS. They paid dues of twenty-five cents a month, which was about all they could afford. Additional funds needed to carry on the necessary activities were provided through subsidies from Local 574 and, after a time, through donations from other unions. Regular meetings of the section were held at which its members hammered out a program and shaped a course of action to deal with their specific problems as unemployed workers.

As they moved into battle with the public authorities, these workers now had some unprecedented advantages. They had gained organizational equilibrium from their close attachment to a stable union. Leadership assistance was available to them from experienced class warriors on Local 574's executive board. In fact, the board assigned one of its members to work regularly with the unemployed, usually Grant Dunne. He not only consulted with the FWS leaders about their problems, but one of his functions was also to help them in their dealings with city, state, and federal officials. Since he spoke for the union as a whole, Grant's role served to emphasize that the jobless were backed by the full power of Local 574.

Across a period of some months an effective staff was built up for the Federal Workers Section. None of those involved were salaried functionaries. All got by on the same basis economically as the unemployed, being on public relief or having a job on a federal "make work" project.

A major component of the staff consisted of former MCCW leaders. Among them were Ed Palmquist, Carl Kuehn, Roy Orgon, George Viens, Louis White. In addition Marvel Scholl became a staff member, functioning like all the others without compensation.

Political leadership within the FWS staff fell mainly upon Max Geldman, who had been a Trotskyist since 1930. From the outset he played a key role in the struggles conducted by the section. In addition he was instrumental in recruiting most of the former MCCW leaders and several rank-and-file members of the FWS into the Workers Party. The latter accomplishment added a new dimension to the building of a broad left wing within the labor movement.

As soon as the FWS had geared itself for action, a fight was launched to improve the public welfare system. There were many ills to be combatted. Relief clients got insolent treatment from investigators and city officials. Discrimination against individual workers living on the dole was commonplace. Destitute families were evicted from their homes because the Relief Department had evaded payment of rent allowances.

Such practices, which added to the miseries of the jobless, were brought to a halt through pressures upon city officials by the FWS. At the same time a battle was opened for major improvements in the budgets allocated to families on relief. Several aspects of this fight were recorded later by Marvel Scholl.

"Dorothy Holmes [who later married Henry Schultz] and I collaborated in revamping the relief budget upward, in terms of specific demands upon the authorities," she wrote. "We did this with the help of faculty members and students at the University of Minnesota Agricultural School. The old budget under which the unemployed lived was totally inadequate. For instance, it was based on minimum (I do mean minimum) calory needs of different age groups within the family. Teen-aged boys got the highest calory allowance. Girls and younger children, even babies, mothers and fathers were allowed far less. But even the higher levels for teen-aged boys were wholly inadequate.

"When we had a food budget worked out the Federal Workers Section presented it to the City Council. Some on the Council tried to brush our demands aside with the argument that they had no funds to meet them. We replied: 'Get the funds for relief from those who have them — the rich.' Our reply brought vigorous applause from unemployed workers who had packed the Council chamber for the hearing. We also got sympathetic help in our struggle from two Farmer-Labor aldermen, I. G. Scott and Ed Hudson.

"It took about three such sessions," Marvel added, "before the Council gave in. The food budget was expanded. In addition we got action on our demands that allowances be increased for rent, clothing, utilities, coal and medicine. Now Minneapolis had the highest relief budget in the country, and the unemployed had an organization capable of enforcing it."

Her concluding point was underlined by an episode that soon followed. The ruling class sought to negate the workers' victory by pressing the City Council to "hold in abeyance" the promised relief increases. A majority of the Council buckled under the pressures from the bosses and the whole issue was thrown up for grabs. The FWS countered by initiating a call for an unemployed demonstration outside City Hall, which took place September 18, 1935. A police assault was made on the demonstrators, but they refused to be cowed, making it plain that acts of intimidation would not settle the matters in dispute. This confrontation was followed by a tug of war in which the FWS succeeded, step by step, in winning improved conditions for workers forced to live on public welfare.

Attention was also given by the FWS to another type of relief, administered through the Hennepin County Welfare Department, known as Aid to Dependent Children (ADC). In the early Thirties it involved cash grants of twenty dollars per month, per child, to mothers whose husbands had either died or had left them. An account of the difficulties for these women was included in Marvel Scholl's recollections mentioned above.

"ADC recipients were subjected to more harassment than regular relief clients," she observed. "While they received no grant for their own livelihood, they were not allowed to work if they were under the program. Any evidence of a man's residence in the home was cause for immediate withdrawal of the grant. ADC investigators were known to arrive in the middle of the night, trying to catch a man in the mother's bed; they searched the homes for male clothing, pipes, etc.

"Another organization in Minneapolis, which worked closely with the ADC, was a private 'charity' known as the Children's Protective Association. Its main aim in life was to break up families, especially of women on ADC. When their agents got their hands on a woman — through the ADC mostly — they prowled the neighborhood, interviewed neighbors and trades-people, built their case and then hauled the mother into court to take her children away from her.

"Our members always brought these cases to us. We had one cardinal rule. We made our own investigation, basing our findings always on what was best for the children. And our members knew and understood this from the first.

"Then we would appear in court with the member. The judge in Children's Court had developed a healthy hatred for the 'Protective Association' investigators, calling them in our presence, 'snooping old maids, male and female.' He took to calling George Viens and myself into his chambers before a case came into court, discussing it with us, asking our opinion.

"In every case in which we appeared for one of our members formal custody was awarded to a representative of the union and we placed the child in the 'foster home' of its mother. Many tragedies were prevented this way. Farrell and I, for example, were at one time jointly and separately guardians for 14 children.

"Sometimes," Marvel added, "when illness of a mother made it necessary to place the children in an actual foster home for a period, we were faced with a dilemma. None of the existing boarding homes met with our approval. So we established our own. An appeal was made to union families, some with children of their own, some whose children had grown up and left home. A half-dozen couples applied and were accepted as boarding homes by the official agency. We put our wards into these union homes."

While fighting out such issues with the local authorities, we were also organizing workers on the federal government's Emergency Relief Administration projects. These "made work" setups represented little more than a token gesture to the idle labor force. Available jobs were limited, as was the length of employment. Wages were set at a bare subsistence level. Open-shop conditions prevailed, with government flunkies lording it over the workers.

Unemployed assigned to these projects—who came to be known as "federal workers"—needed an organization akin to a trade union to defend themselves. One of our key aims was to help fill that need, thereby strengthening the overall ties between employed and unemployed. For that reason Local 574 named its special unemployed unit the Federal Workers Section.

As FWS recruitment proceeded on the ERA projects, steps were taken to prepare for action. Delegates were elected by the workers on each project to handle their grievances. Collective discussions were then held by these delegates to prepare policy recommendations for submission to the section's membership as a whole. This process had scarcely started, however, when Roosevelt scuttled his ERA program in mid-1935 and changed the entire federal relief system.

Roosevelt's action stemmed from the same coldly calculated policy that he had regularly followed. His aim was to provide just enough federal relief to prevent a major upheavel among the unemployed — and no more. To keep the situation under control within this contradictory framework, he developed a cyclical pattern of operations. It had begun with the setting up of a Civil Works Administration a few months after he assumed the presidency in 1933.

The unemployed reacted to this initial measure with a fresh sense of hope, thinking that the federal government was really going to solve their problems. Then it gradually became clear that this was not the case. Not all the jobless got federal aid and those who did received far too little. They began to put pressure on the government for increased relief, and unemployed organizations were formed on the basis of this struggle. For a time Roosevelt made grudging concessions under these pressures, although he resisted doing so every inch of the way and actually conceded very little.

Then, early in 1934, he turned the whole thing around in his favor by scrapping the original relief program. A transition was then made to a new federal relief setup designated as the Emergency Relief Administration. With the government deliberately sowing confusion during the process of the change, several losses resulted for the workers. Some of the financial gains they had previously won disappeared in the shuffle. Existing unemployed organizations were thrown into confusion, many of them tending to disintegrate. In general, the jobless then found it necessary to reorganize themselves, overcome the demoralization caused by Roosevelt's trickery, and start again from scratch in the battle for their rights.

By mid-1935 they had managed to revivify their struggle nationally to the point where they were pressing vigorously for federal concessions. So the great liberal in the White House decided to break it up by repeating the 1934 cycle. A transition was set into motion from the ERA to a new federal setup called the Works Progress Administration (WPA).

It was precisely at this point that the unusual effectiveness of a union-sponsored unemployed organization was demonstrated. Members of the Federal Workers Section were not left adrift without a rudder in the changed situation, as were most of the unemployed. Their association with a strong trade union became a stabilizing factor for them in their moment of crisis. This meant concretely that they got effective aid in moving swiftly to remobilize the unemployed generally for continuation of their struggle.

As soon as the new WPA projects got started the FWS launched an organization drive among the workers involved. Elections of job stewards followed on all projects, leading to a union representation structure of the kind Local 574 had established in the trucking industry. A fight was then opened for the adjustment of grievances submitted by the workers, and there were many.

Unemployed workers were being removed entirely from the city's relief rolls and put to work under the new WPA setup. In many cases there were big time gaps between their last relief check and their first payday on WPA. After a big hassle the city authorities were forced to cease their practice of removing these workers so hastily from the relief rolls, and compensation was secured for individuals who had thus been victimized.

A general grievance affecting all on WPA arose over the rate of pay. The scale was $60.50 a month, truly a starvation level. In fact it was below the budgetary level the city of Minneapolis had been forced to establish for relief clients. As a result workers who were transferred from direct relief, paid by the city, to the federal "work-relief" system got an automatic cut in income.

The FWS set out to block this swindle by mobilizing the workers around a demand aimed at the city fathers: either get the WPA to pay more, or provide supplementary relief for those on WPA. Our campaign was effective. Supplementary relief was granted by the city, raising the total received by WPA workers back to the amount they would have gotten if still on direct relief.

By this time the Federal Workers Section was establishing itself as the major organization of the city's unemployed. New recruits were entering its ranks by the hundreds. Some had never before been associated with a trade union; others among these jobless were, or had been, members of various AFL organizations. All were staunch partisans of Local 574, with nary a friend of Tobin's among them.

We were gaining a whole new category of allies in the local's fight for survival.

9. New Strike Wave

Further support was coming our way from yet another quarter. Employed workers throughout the city were experiencing a rise in militancy that led to a new strike wave. Their combative mood stemmed from frustrations caused by ruling class policy during the previous two years.

Roosevelt had launched his "New Deal" program in 1933 with assurances that something truly meaningful would be done for the "ill-fed, ill-clothed, ill-housed" of the nation. His demagogy raised great hopes among the workers. This led them, at the outset, to depend on the government to solve their problems. Then they began to learn, through a series of experiences, that there could be no substitute for their own action.

One of these experiences had to do with the National Industrial Recovery Act (NRA), which was among the initial measures instituted by Roosevelt. Typifying the norms of capitalism, the Act was intended primarily to do some economic pump priming by increasing private profits. This objective was prettied up by the Washington propagandists as a move that would bring "public" benefit.

NRA codes of "fair competition" were set up to end competitive price cutting among the capitalists, who were trusted to "regulate themselves." An "easy money" policy was instituted to raise profit levels. This, of course, resulted in climbing prices.

Concerning labor, provisions were made for codes to set minimum wages and maximum hours. Actual decisions on these matters, however, were left entirely to the employers in each industry. No voice whatever was accorded to the workers under the law.

Section 7(a) of the NRA did give assurance on paper of the workers' right to organize and bargain collectively with the bosses. In practice, though, the Roosevelt administration sought to impede struggles undertaken by the trade unions.

Its aim was to divert industrial conflicts into the swamp of
government mediation, always at labor's expense. As a result,
evidence began to mount that the "New Deal" was a raw deal
for the workers.

Yet these accomplishments under the NRA did not satisfy
the greedy capitalists. They wanted still greater profits. So
they set out to curb the authority they had allowed Roosevelt
to assume in 1933. At that time there had been great fear
among the bosses that the severe economic depression might
precipitate a labor uprising of such magnitude that it would
imperil their rule over the country. Their disarray and alarm
had caused them to give the incoming president free rein, temporarily, to do whatever he could to ward off the danger.

Now the situation had changed. With help from the AFL
hierarchy, the demagogue in the White House was slowing
down the objective trend toward working class revolution.
Although the trend had not yet been fully reversed, the
capitalists were regaining self-confidence. That emboldened them
to press for a return to unrestricted "free enterprise."

To attain their objective the profit hogs resorted to the U. S.
Supreme Court. The response of that august body to their
demands illustrated its servility to the ruling class. In May
1935 the court declared the NRA unconstitutional.

Roosevelt's next move on the trade union front was to push
through Congress the Wagner Labor Relations Act, which
he signed into law in July 1935. The new measure formally
required employers to bargain with unions representing a majority of their employees. A National Labor Relations Board
was set up for the mediation of industrial disputes. In addition
a category of "unfair labor practices" was established, which
served as a means to put such disputes under the jurisdiction
of federal courts. Supposedly the latter provision was aimed
at the bosses, but in time it came to be used more and more
against the workers.

Class collaborationist union officials hailed the Wagner Act
as "Labor's Magna Charta." This, of course, was utter non-
sense. Their lavish praise of the new law was really an expression of hope that it would enable them to keep the workers
suckered into reliance on the capitalist government as a substitute for use of union power against the bosses.

In Minneapolis, however, right-wing AFL officials were not
to have much luck along those lines. Large numbers of
workers, who had never been organized, got some idea of
their inherent class power from Local 574's victorious struggle
in 1934. Then they had seen the Arrowhead and garage

workers organize and win strikes for union recognition, which
also brought those involved immediate material gains. Now
the unorganized toilers were ready, in increasing numbers,
to move into action on their own behalf.

Many were joining the AFL. Upon doing so they pressed
the union officials to lead them in battle against the bosses.
In fact, this trend was about to result in two hard-fought
strikes. Under the impact of those struggles, compelling desires
to have it out with the bosses spread to other workers and
a new course of procedure developed. In some cases unorganized workers simply went on strike spontaneously. Then
they came to the union movement in a body, asking help to
get themselves properly geared for battle.

On the whole, workers involved in the unfolding struggles
recognized instinctively that they needed guidance from union
leaders with proven fighting ability. They wanted nothing to
do with class collaborationists who toadied to the boss class.
This naturally led them to ask Local 574 for assistance, and
they couldn't have cared less that Tobin had declared us
"outlaws."

These developments were accompanied by a change in the
city administration.

In the June 1935 municipal elections Mayor Bainbridge,
whose strikebreaking role had earned him the hatred of the
working class, put in a bid for reelection. An aroused labor
movement then went all-out in support of Thomas E. Latimer,
the Farmer-Labor candidate for the office. Latimer was elected,
leading most workers to believe that they now had a mayor
who would side with them against the bosses. But things didn't
work out that way. Latimer soon showed himself to be as
slippery and treacherous in public office as Governor Olson
had been during the 1934 strikes.

A preview of what was to come in this respect could be seen
in an item carried by the *Minneapolis Tribune* on June 30,
1935: "The fleet of six armored cars for use by police in
waging war on bank robbers is nearing completion, and will
be ready for use next week. Half the cost of the armored cars
was contributed by bankers and business men of Minneapolis."

Under a headline warning, "Trouble Ahead," the *Northwest
Organizer* responded to the news by putting a rhetorical question to the labor movement: "Do you doubt that these armored
cars will be used primarily, not against bank robbers, but
against workers who are out on strike?"

Latimer didn't take very long in giving the answer.

He had scarcely taken office when about 250 ornamental

iron workers went on strike at eight shops in the city. The walkout was conducted by Local 1313 of the International Association of Machinists (AFL). Demands upon the bosses centered on union recognition, along with improved wages and conditions.

Although a delegation of strikers soon came to Local 574 with a formal request for help, there was resistance within Local 1313 when we attempted to respond. It came from the Stalinists. Since their recent turn in trade union line, they had established a foothold in the machinists' locals. Now they wanted to use the ornamental iron walkout to strengthen their union base, and they looked upon any intervention by us as an obstacle to their political ambitions. But the struggle soon took a turn that made it impossible for them to keep us out of the situation.

One of the larger firms involved was the Flour City Ornamental Iron Works, located where the Milwaukee Railroad tracks crossed Twenty-Seventh Avenue South. The head boss, Walter Tetzlaff, stood high in the councils of the Citizens Alliance. He sought to break the strike, and as a preparatory step he had gotten a court injunction against picketing.

The next move against the union came on the morning of July 26. Mayor Latimer appeared in person at Tetzlaff's plant, accompanied by around seventy cops. They escorted a couple of dozen finks inside, meeting with no difficulty in crossing the small and surprised picket line. This strikebreaking action constituted a challenge to the entire labor movement, and the Stalinists could no longer make it a private fight, even if they had still wanted to.

When word of Latimer's treacherous deed got around, Local 574 sprang into action. As a first step Henry Schultz and I went to consult the Local 1313 leaders at the strike headquarters near the Flour City plant. We found an air of gloom about the place.

The Stalinists understood that reinforcements had to be brought in, if a fight was to be made, but their past policies had so isolated them from the mass movement that they didn't know where to begin such an effort. All they had done was to arrange an afternoon appointment with Latimer to protest his action. We asked about the scabs and were told that the union expected them to be escorted out of the plant at 4:30 that afternoon. This information provided the cue for our intervention. What the situation called for was the presence of a big reception committee to greet them.

Local 574 quickly set its machinery into motion to mobilize

volunteers, including a call by the Federal Workers Section
for help from the unemployed. Other militant unions were
contacted and they, too, responded to the emergency. By 4:30
over 1,000 pickets were on hand at the plant.

At the appointed hour police reinforcements arrived. A few
cops were assigned to the company lot where the scabs' cars
were parked, and the rest were concentrated at the main plant
gate. The intended tactic was easily perceived. Cars would
be brought up to the gate, one at a time. There, under police
protection, finks would pile into the cars, which would then
dash past the picket line.

We devised what proved to be effective countermeasures.
Only a lesser part of the pickets was put at the gate. Our
main force was used to form a gauntlet along Twenty-Seventh
Avenue, down which the scabs' cars would have to travel.
This gave the cops a mistaken idea of the union strength,
and they were further confused by a diversionary tactic we used.

Among the volunteer pickets was Elmer Crowl, an official
of a building trades union. He was a fighter, but like a bull,
he had only one battle technique; that was to lower his head
and charge. On some occasions this tendency had caused problems. In the present case, though, a negative could be turned
into a positive trait.

Crowl was allowed to take command of the pickets at the
plant gate. When the cops started to bring the scabs out, he
immediately led a charge on them. That kept the police
command so busy that scant attention was paid to what the
carloads of finks were being sent into.

The main union force, having found some rocks in the
neighborhood, had prepared the real reception. Pickets lined
a considerable stretch of the planned escape route. When the
cars started to leave the plant, they were given a tattooing
that the scabs inside weren't likely to forget soon.

Such an effective response from others in the labor movement,
at a time when the strikers badly needed help, gave them fresh
inspiration. Instead of weakening Local 1313, Latimer's action
had brought it new strength. To consolidate the gain, the strike
committee asked that other unions send representatives to participate in its sessions, which was done. In the changed situation
Tetzlaff abandoned his attempt to open the plant, and for a
time the strike remained quiet.

Less than a month later a new battle erupted, this time in
the hosiery industry. It involved the Strutwear Knitting Company, situated on Sixth Street South a few blocks from the
downtown area. The firm employed around 1,100 workers.

For some time a campaign had been conducted by Roy Wier, the Central Labor Union organizer, to bring them into the American Federation of Hosiery Workers, AFL. His efforts had centered on organizing skilled men tending the knitting machines; women employees, who constituted a majority of the work force, had been neglected.

In fact, Wier was proceeding generally in a half-thought-out, vacillating manner. This helped to bring about the firing of eight machine tenders for union activity, as a warning to the other workers. With his hand thus forced, Wier led the organization out on strike without adequate preparation. The main demands were union recognition, reinstatement of the eight to their jobs, and a raise in pay.

The strike began on August 16. Of the 200-odd skilled knitters, less than a dozen tried to scab. The latter were herded into the plant under police protection, along with 50 or so women employees, who had been shunted aside by the union and misled by company propaganda. With this skeleton force, the bosses started up the machinery, hoping to weaken the strikers' morale by creating the impression that production was underway. But the workers knew the sounds of the factory too well to be fooled.

Notice was then sent to all employees that full-scale operations would resume under police protection on August 19, and those who failed to report for work would be fired. The labor movement responded to the threat by sending reinforcements to the picket line. They came mainly from Local 574, the Federal Workers Section, Local 1313, and the lathers' union, which was also on strike. By 6:30 A.M. on August 19, a union force of over 500 had gathered to back up the hosiery strikers.

Close to 100 cops soon arrived at the plant. They were accompanied by the armored cars, which were taking a day off from chasing bank robbers. Around 8:00 A.M. the scabs, who had huddled together, began moving toward the entrance. When the pickets intervened, the cops charged our line, swinging their clubs viciously. Quite a battle took place before the finks — among whom there were now professional strikebreakers — managed to get into the building.

During the fight the cops surrounded Ray Dunne and dragged him into the factory. Then they vented their wrath against Local 574 by beating him unmercifully. After that he was smuggled past the picket line in an armored car and hauled off to jail. Only upon Ray's insistence was he finally taken to a hospital, where X rays showed that three of his ribs were broken. He was held under arrest on a charge of "failure to obey an officer." Local 574 promptly bailed him out and arranged proper medical care, but he was laid up for some time.

Around 3:00 P. M. preparations were made to start the strikebreakers on their way home for the night. It wasn't going to be easy. This time they wouldn't be coming from various directions to congregate under police protection, as they had in the morning. Just the opposite. Sooner or later the cops would have to turn them loose to go their separate ways.

The evacuation began by taking the scabs out the rear door of the plant, where the armored cars were lined up to protect them. They were formed into a column of fours, women being placed in the outer files to shield the men in the center. Police on foot were drawn up along both flanks of the formation. The procession then started down Seventh Avenue South toward the loop shopping district. Somewhere along the way, the cops seemed to assume, their charges would be able to scatter out safely on their own. But it didn't work out that way.

News of the morning battle had brought reinforcements to the picket line, which now numbered about 1,000. These forces were quickly formed into two strong lines, paralleling the fink march. As the remarkable parade moved slowly along, an occasional male scab got clobbered; spectators shouted encouragement to the pickets; and a traffic jam developed. Nothing was going right for the cops, who had gotten themselves into a real bind.

We made a guess that the finks would be herded into Dayton's, a big department store between Seventh and Eighth Streets on Nicollet Avenue, where they could lose themselves among the shoppers. So a picket detachment was rushed down Eighth Street to enter the store from that side.

As we had anticipated, when the march got to Seventh and Nicollet it halted. The cops formed protective lines at the entrance to Dayton's and pushed their charges through the revolving doors. Inside the store the pickets went after the male scabs, undertaking to teach them that they should mend their ways.

The women, it was felt, had not been given a fair shake by Wier. They were approached accordingly, and a number of them attended the next union meeting.

Concern about the labor militancy shown at Strutwear and Flour City was not confined to the bosses. The AFL bureaucrats were equally upset over their inability to control the newly organized workers. In an effort to change things around, they demanded that Wier keep Local 574 out of the Strutwear situation. He complied with the demand, informing us in a shamefaced way that our help was no longer needed. Fortunately, this turn of events did not immediately jeopardize the strike, as could easily have been the case. The Strutwear management, stunned by the outcome of the August 19 struggle, had decided to postpone any further attempt to reopen the plant.

Next the AFL officialdom undertook to carry through some unfinished business of the Citizens Alliance. This had to do with the "Committee of 100" strikebreaking scheme, projected by the Alliance in early April, which had failed to get anywhere at the time. The scheme still appealed to the union bureaucrats, who shared the bosses' desire to prevent militant labor struggles. So they now pressed for establishment of a "public" body to pass judgment on worker-employer disputes.

On August 24 a meeting was held between Mayor Latimer and officials of the Minnesota State Federation of Labor, the Minneapolis Central Labor Union and the Teamsters Joint Council. A joint statement was issued by those present deploring the "recent small deluge of industrial controversies in the city." Blame for the situation was placed upon "racketeers." A proposal was made that union officials meet with "employing and business interests" in an attempt to "remove this industrial strife."

It happened that Local 574 had just set a deadline for a strike at Glenwood Inglewood, a firm distributing spring water, which had refused to sign a union contract. When the company president read the joint Latimer-AFL statement in the papers, he made a public appeal to the mayor for protection. A propaganda campaign was immediately launched, aimed at building up this incident into proof that Local 574 was the prime source of all the labor trouble in town. Then the whole thing began to backfire. The Glenwood Inglewood boss suddenly decided that the smartest thing for him to do was to sign the union contract without forcing us into a strike.

We followed this up with a statement by the Local 574 executive board, which took note that all the strikes going on in Minneapolis at the time were being conducted by AFL unions. Concerning these struggles, the statement added: "Local 574 still stands by its policy of giving whatever assistance it can whenever it is officially asked to do so. We do not seek to run the affairs of other unions."

Soon thereafter Latimer appointed an Employer-Employee Board, on which he put three AFL officials: T. E. Cunningham, J. B. Boscoe, and Guy Alexander. He then called upon all striking workers to return to their jobs and let the new Board adjust their differences with the bosses.

A choice between opposing policies had been put to the strikers. They could return to work, entrusting their fate to the AFL business agents and Latimer; or they could accept Local 574's offer to help them fight on until they won union recognition and concessions on their other demands.

Before long the first reply was given. It came in response to a new strikebreaking attack on the ornamental iron workers.

Taking the "labor statesmen's" pitch as a sign that union militancy had been undermined, Tetzlaff set out to resume operations at Flour City. He began with a "work force" of about twenty supervisors and professional strikebreakers. They were housed in the plant, guarded by privately hired armed thugs.

There was a city ordinance against such housing of scabs in an industrial establishment. Pointing to that fact, the strikers demanded that the authorities remove them. Tetzlaff got around the obstacle by turning to the courts. He was granted an injunction against enforcement of the ordinance.

On September 9, a protest demonstration was called by Local 1313, with little advance preparation. The turnout was not as large as it could have been, but word of the action got around. This brought out reinforcements for a second protest rally the next evening, held on a vacant lot across from the plant. Suddenly, without warning, the police assaulted the rally. Tear gas was fired into the gathering from armored cars. Then cops on foot charged in viciously with clubs to break it up.

Reports in the boss press the next morning played up the success of the police attack. This provoked an upsurge of anger among the workers of the city. The stage had been set for another battle royal.

By 9:00 P.M. the following night, September 11, over 5,000 workers had gathered outside the Flour City plant. The police were also on hand in large numbers, as were a half-dozen armored cars. For a time things remained relatively quiet, the main activity being a speaking program conducted by various union leaders.

Then, around 11:00 P.M., the cops moved in to break up the gathering and clear the streets around the plant. In no time at all a full-scale police riot was underway. The armored cars advanced first, their crews firing tear gas from the portholes. Cops on foot were deployed behind them, like infantry behind tanks in military combat. They clubbed the crowd mercilessly, making no distinction as to age or sex. Not even the residents of houses across the street from the plant, most of whom had been seated on their porches, were exempted. If they resisted, the berserk cops in some cases followed them right into their houses to give them a beating.

In the meantime, veteran picket line fighters among the demonstrators had conducted an organized retreat. They filtered back between the houses opposite the plant to alleys in the rear. There they regrouped and launched sorties against the cops. Soon the armored cars came into the alleys, the foot patrols again following them. In this case the demonstrators gained advantage from the absence of street lighting and some of the fiercest combat took place. Before it was over the cops had pulled their guns and fired point blank at the workers.

There was one scene I shall never forget. Emil Hansen of Local 574 — a huge, powerful man — had found half of a concrete building block. Time after time he hurled the missile at the windshield of an armored car, trying to shatter the glass. Although he didn't succeed, his valiant attempt epitomized the anger, determination, and courage of the union fighters.

The battle lasted until about 2:00 A.M. By then the whole area was saturated with tear gas. Two workers had been killed by the cops: Melvin Bjorklund and Eugene Casper. Several others had been wounded by police gunfire. Numbers had been injured on both sides by clubs and rocks. But there had been relatively few arrests. The cops had proven to be more eager to inflict casualties than to take captives.

As the night's confrontation plainly showed, working class resistance to Latimer's strikebreaking actions had become so pronounced that his policy in the Flour City situation had to be changed. Tetzlaff was informed that the expected police support could not be provided. The scabs and thugs were removed from the plant and it was again closed.

On the heels of the September 11 atrocity the grand jury issued a finding absolving the mayor and the cops of any crime. After this whitewash of their criminal actions, the Non-Partisan Labor Defense organized a public trial, with Latimer as the main defendant. It was held on September 16, before an audience of close to 1,000 workers, at the Local 574 hall.

Bill Brown, the Local 574 president, was elected presiding judge. Louis Roseland of the carpenters was designated clerk of the court. Francis Heisler, who had previously helped the Fargo strikers, came from Chicago to serve as prosecutor. The audience selected a jury of twelve workers, none of whom had been present at the scene of the crime.

Latimer had been formally invited to appear in his own defense but he refused to do so. Brown, therefore, appointed Gilbert Carlson, a Minneapolis labor attorney who handled legal matters for Local 574, to defend the mayor, and he was tried in absentia.

Over two dozen witnesses were heard. Among them were pickets, residents of homes opposite the Flour City plant, and people who just happened to be passing by when the police assault occurred. They gave eyewitness accounts of shooting by the cops, of hapless victims dragged from passing cars, and of people hit in their homes by stray police bullets.

The jury found Latimer and the Police Department guilty of murdering Bjorklund and Casper and injuring many other workers.

Newspaper reporters had been invited to attend and considerable publicity was given to the trial in the daily papers. A transcript of the proceedings was printed in an expanded edition of the *Northwest Organizer* on September 18 and copies were distributed throughout the labor movement.

About a week later Local 1313 won its fight. Tetzlaff and the other ornamental iron bosses recognized the union. An agreement was signed providing for the reinstatement of all strikers without discrimination and an increase in wages, along with other gains for the workers. Once again the Citizens Alliance, which had been behind the strikebreaking moves, had taken a beating.

The union victory set off spontaneous walkouts in other industries. A typical example was the action taken by unorganized workers at the Powell Candy Co. One day the management announced a pay cut and what happened next was described later by Marvel Scholl, who was at the Local 574 hall at the time.

"It sounded as though a herd of elephants was tramping up the stairs," she wrote. "Everyone ran out of their offices to find the hallway crowded with workers, candy factory employees, all still dressed in their smocks, aprons and caps. And the sugary kind of soil which they pick up on the job.

"A spokesman said, 'We are on strike. Organize us.'

"The bosses had cut wages. And spontaneously, the whole crew decided they had had it. Without leadership, without any organization, they just walked out of the factory, down Washington Avenue in a body, and presented themselves to the leadership of 574."

We helped them set up a picket line, draft demands, and select a negotiating committee. A Local 574 staff member then went with the committee to meet the boss. At the same time Roy Wier was contacted to find out what AFL union had jurisdiction in that sphere. He came over and enrolled them in the Food Workers Union. At 4:30 that afternoon, Powell signed a contract which recognized the union, rescinded the pay cut, and granted concessions involving wages and conditions.

Bill Brown spoke the simple truth when he remarked one day after this episode: "Nobody likes the 574 leaders, except the workers."

Tobin's prospects of reading us out of the labor movement were degenerating from bad to worse. Not only was he unable to win the rank-and-file workers to his side, but a revolt against him and his local counterparts had developed among the officials of some unions.

An organized left wing had taken form within the Central Labor Union, supported by fifteen AFL locals. On September 30, these locals held a conference at which they reiterated earlier demands that Local 574 be reinstated into the IBT. They also took a stand against the collaboration of right-wing union hacks with Latimer, who had prostituted himself to the Citizens Alliance. The conference called for dissolution of the Employer-Employee Board and reaffirmation of the workers' right to strike.

This action underlined Tobin's failure to mobilize the local AFL movement against us. On top of that, problems were arising for William Green, the AFL president. He, too, was experiencing defiance of his arbitrary directives to the city's labor movement. So the two of them got together to figure out what to do next.

Being typical bureaucrats, they decided to send an overlord into Minneapolis to kick dissident AFL members back into line.

10. We Win Another Round

On October 30, 1935, a press conference was held in Minneapolis by a newcomer, Meyer Lewis (no relation to John L.), who introduced himself as a special representative of William Green. He chose as his central theme what had become a rather tired subject locally. Green had sent him to the city, he said, to rid the labor movement of "reds."

His plan of action, as reported in the *Minneapolis Journal*, was to contact employers who had been "victims of communist aggression in labor disputes"; to urge union members to repudiate radicals; and to "combine the entire citizenry under one common banner to completely purge the city of communism." Toward that end he made a fervent plea for help from civic clubs, the clergy, and the police.

Green's emissary then met with leaders of the Citizens Alliance, who expressed their approval of his objectives. The Alliance arranged for him to get a spread in the daily papers urging the trucking bosses to break their contracts with Local 574 and deal only with "responsible" AFL business agents. The bosses were interested in Lewis' aims, but past experience made them cautious about openly siding with him.

Instead they launched an oblique attack on Local 574 by digging up forgotten court cases from the May 1934 strike. In several instances "disorderly conduct" charges against pickets had been handled at that time by technically defaulting on bail of twenty-five dollars each. Now the bosses had the city prosecutor issue new warrants against those involved. Two arrests were then made. The men picked up were Harry DeBoer of the Local 574 staff and Phillip Scott, who had earlier been acquitted of charges that he killed C. Arthur Lyman, a special deputy in 1934. Both cases were finally dropped for lack of evidence and no more arrests of the kind were made.

Clearly, if Local 574 was to be successfully attacked, Meyer

Lewis would have to make good on his public boasts. But
he quickly found that he was a general without an army.
Within the labor movement he had few to rely upon other
than right-wing bureaucrats in the Central Labor Union. So
he went into conference with the most reactionary of these
craft union hacks to plan a strategy for the "takeover" of
Local 574.

As a starter Lewis called a special meeting of all AFL business agents to demand their support. Among them were friends
of Local 574, who were angry about what they had been
reading in the papers. They tore into Lewis and made a motion
to ask Green to recall him. After heated discussion the meeting
was adjourned to prevent the motion from coming to a vote.
As a parting shot Green's henchman threatened to revoke
the CLU charter if the left wing was not curbed in that body.

Meanwhile we had launched a counteroffensive against the
new red-baiting attack. An editorial in the *Northwest Organizer*
lashed out at Meyer Lewis, who had opened his direct assault
on Local 574 with a brazen lie. He had tried to frame us up as
splitters — by charging that we withdrew from the AFL — in
order to cover up his own splitting role in the service of Tobin.
We had been unjustly expelled from the federation on a sub-
terfuge involving per capita taxes, the union paper reminded
the workers. Since then we had carried on an unceasing
struggle for reinstatement into the AFL, asking only that our
organizaton be accorded its democratic rights. We had consistently supported AFL unions against the bosses, and not
a single strike had been lost in two years.

Tobin's newly arrived henchman, in contrast, had received
public endorsement from the Citizens Alliance, which sought
to restore the open-shop conditions of the pre-1934 period,
a time when not a single strike had been won for many years.

Our counterattack on Meyer Lewis in the union paper was
followed by a protest meeting, open to all trade unionists, held
at the Local 574 hall on November 8. Over 3,000 workers
turned out for the rally. They packed the main auditorium,
the smaller meeting rooms and the street outside the building.
Loudspeakers were used so that everyone could hear the
speakers. Bill Brown gave the main talk in the name of Local
574, and several union officials participated in the program.

Ace Brewer, head of the musicians local, spoke in support
of Local 574 and apologized for the fact that Meyer Lewis
was also a musician. Representatives of the ornamental iron
and the candy workers unions thanked us for the support they
had received and pledged themselves to fight in our defense.

Similar backing was voiced by officers speaking for the firemen and oilers, laundry workers, and structural iron workers. Alderman I. G. Scott, a Farmer-Laborite, called Local 574 "the one really bright spot in Minneapolis," adding that a general dose of "outlawry" would be a good thing for the trade union movement.

Machinists Local 382, which we had helped in the garage strike at the beginning of the year, failed to send a representative to the meeting. Timidity on the part of Herman Hussman, the business agent, was not the sole reason. He was also influenced by William Mauseth, the leading Stalinist in the local, who didn't want any plaudits given to the Trotskyist leaders of Local 574. The *Northwest Organizer* went after Hussman and Mauseth by name, pointing out that they had made a mistake. Their absence from the protest rally would be taken by Lewis as a capitulation to him, even before he had turned his guns on them.

Our warning to Local 382 was not based on pure assumption. Meyer Lewis had already moved against Dry Cleaners Local 18005. First he had demanded that the union choose between Local 574 and the AFL. When the membership refused to repudiate us, he revoked their charter. At the request of Rubin Latz, the business agent, Local 574 sent Carl Skoglund to speak to these workers about the fundamental issues in the struggle going on within the AFL. The local then voted to continue its defiance of Green's dictatorial representative.

Right after that we had our first direct confrontation with him. It came on November 12 at the University of Minnesota Student Forum. Lewis, who had yet to address a meeting of workers in town, seemed to think he could get a friendly reception among students. Under a heading, "Local 574 Goes to College," the *Northwest Organizer* reported what happened.

Lewis was seated on the platform, waiting for the meeting to begin, when Bill Brown and Ray and Grant Dunne walked in. To his consternation they went right up to him, introduced themselves, and said they had come to hear what he had to say. Seeming to panic, Lewis made a rather incoherent speech and, upon request, agreed to answer questions. Bill Brown asked to be recognized by the chair.

"I refuse to answer your question before you ask it," Lewis intervened to decree.

"I don't expect you to answer my question before I ask it," Brown shot back, drawing gales of laughter and heavy applause from the audience.

After that students who had been at Local 574's protest
rally a few days earlier took over the discussion. They ripped
into the demoralized union bureaucrat, cutting his arguments
to shreds. Highlights of the event were later broadcast over
the university's radio station, and we won some new friends.

The next day Lewis appeared for the first time at a meeting
of the Central Labor Union. Up to then our representatives
had been allowed to attend these sessions as observers, but
on this occasion they were barred by the doorkeepers. As
it turned out, however, we had no cause for concern — thanks
to the work that had been done to organize a left wing in the
central body.

Under a special order of business Lewis was given the floor
to demand that the CLU declare Local 574 a "permanent
outlaw" and back him in his fight against us. As he spoke,
he was continuously interrupted by hostile remarks from the
floor. Then delegate after delegate rose to lambast him. A
motion was made to demand that Green recall Lewis, and
the meeting ended in an uproar when the chairman, a right
winger, declared the motion out of order.

About a week later a special committee from the Central
Labor Union contacted us, saying that they had been assigned
to work out an adjustment of relations between AFL unions
and Local 574. In the discussion that followed we said that
a fundamental settlement of the existing difficulties necessitated
the reinstatement of Local 574 into the IBT and the restoration
of Local 18005's charter, which Lewis had revoked. All we
wanted was a return to the relations that had existed before
Tobin tried to read us out of the movement. Pending such
action, we did not intend to infringe upon jurisdictions assigned
either to other drivers' locals, or to AFL unions in other industries. We would continue to aid all locals affiliated with
the CLU in every way possible, asking only that they, in
turn, accord us the same consideration.

The CLU committee agreed that our position was reasonable
and that reciprocity called for recognition of our jurisdiction
by AFL unions. It said a recommendation would be made
to the central body that relations be regularized along the
lines of the discussion.

These talks had taken place while Meyer Lewis was away
on a trip to consult Green and Tobin. Upon his return he
set up a permanent office and announced publicly that he
would continue to supervise the local AFL for an indefinite
period. This led to another battle with him at a CLU meeting.
It began with a storm of protest from left-wing delegates over

his public announcement. A second uproar followed when Lewis
tried to block approval of the truce the special committee had
negotiated with Local 574 during his absence. His objections
were disregarded by a decisive majority of the body and the
report of the special committee was approved. A joint Policy
Committee was set up — consisting of a few AFL officials and
Carl Skoglund for Local 574 — to adjust any disputes that
might arise.

After this setback, Lewis got together with his right-wing
cronies to plan an overturn of the "hands off" policy toward
Local 574 that the CLU had adopted. As a starter he hoped
to pound into submission several business agents who had
begun to wobble in their opposition to him. But the class
struggle intervened to upset his plans. A new situation had
developed in the AFL strike at the Strutwear Knitting Company.

Following the earlier request that Local 574 keep out of that
struggle, Roy Wier had gotten the hosiery strikers into a serious
bind. He began with a "statesmanlike" appeal to the company.
The key issue of union recognition, he proposed, should be
settled by a Labor Board election. If the union won, he
promised the bosses, it would be willing to submit all other
issues to arbitration, including reinstatement of the machine
tenders fired for union activity.

Wier's overtures were flatly rejected by the company, which
had no intention whatever of recognizing the union. Then
Meyer Lewis hit town, expressing sympathy for employers who
had been "victims of communist aggression in labor disputes."
This was taken by the Strutwear management as a signal
that a new attempt to resume operations would get support
from within the labor movement.

A dummy corporation was set up in St. Joseph, Missouri.
The fake outfit instituted a replevin action in U.S. court and
federal marshals were ordered to protect a shipment of finished
goods to it from the struck plant in Minneapolis. A hunt then
began for trucks and drivers, with bonus wages offered.

Since trucking was now involved, the strike had entered Local
574's jurisdiction. So we stepped in and took command of the
fight. All local transfer firms were warned that the union would
close them down if they sought to provide trucks for the strikebreaking move being undertaken by the federal government.
None of them tried to defy us. Finally Strutwear was able to
get trucks and drivers from Winona, a small town about 130
miles away.

On November 29 the scab trucks arrived at the plant, accompanied by a score of federal deputies and about 100 city

police. Being experienced in opposing truck movements, we found a way to quickly reinforce the picket line. A call was sent to Local 574 job stewards to get as many trucks as possible headed for the Strutwear scene.

We were not broadening the strike to include trucking firms. Union members were simply using rigs they were driving about the streets on company time as a means to help a good cause. Before long trucks of all sizes, carrying various kinds of loads, began to arrive in the vicinity of the plant. They were double parked on the streets, and the drivers, taking the truck keys with them, walked over to see what was going on where the cops were congregated. The picket line had thus been strengthened and it was going to be hard to move the fink trucks along the clogged streets.

After quite a fight the marshals and cops managed to convoy the scab goods to a nearby rail yard, but not without casualties. Four scab drivers and a deputy marshal had been injured. On the union side a number of pickets had been clubbed and a few arrested.

Even though the trucks were moved, the strikers had won a victory. The whole thing had been a scheme to break their morale by involving the federal government in a violent attack on the picket line. Just the opposite had happened. The strikers gained new confidence from the support they had received in the clash.

A month later some thirty scabs were whisked into the plant in a surprise move against a light picket line. By closing time that day over 600 pickets were on hand and it took repeated police charges on their line to get the finks out for the night. The next morning a still sharper clash took place and during the following hours the picket force steadily grew in strength. By early afternoon it had become evident that a major battle was about to take place between the workers and the cops.

At Latimer's request Governor Olson rushed a National Guard force to the scene and the scabs were removed under its protection. For a short period troops were kept on guard at the plant, which Olson had ordered the company to shut down. The bosses then filed in Hennepin County District Court for an omnibus injunction against picketing at the plant. The defendants included Latimer, the striking union, Local 574, the CLU, and a long list of individual strikers. Nothing came of the injunction attempt and for a time a stalemate existed.

Finally the Strutwear management decided to settle with the hosiery workers. Their union was recognized; all strikers were returned to their jobs, except the eight who had been fired for union activity (their cases were submitted to a district court judge for decision); and wages were increased. Considering that at one point the strike had been almost a lost cause, due to inept leadership, the settlement was about the best the union could secure under the circumstances.

While the Strutwear fight was going on, a new dispute arose in another industry. It took place at the Northern States Power Company, a monopoly utility serving the area. Local 160 of the International Brotherhood of Electrical Workers, AFL, was organizing the power workers, and the union leadership came to Local 574 for help in dealing with the company. I drew the assignment, subject to approval by the Local 160 members. They voted to select me as their spokesman, and I accompanied the union committee to a meeting with R. F. Pack, the company president.

When we entered Pack's swank office, he gave me a cold look but pretended that his stoolpigeons hadn't told him I was coming.

"Are you an employee of the company?" he asked. George Phillips, the union president, then introduced me.

"You will have to leave," Pack told me, pointing imperiously to the door. "I will deal only with our employees."

The union committee informed him they had chosen me to speak for them and insisted that I participate in the negotiations. Pack remained adamant, so we all walked out together.

It was not my personal involvement that was at issue. Pack was challenging the union's right to choose its representatives. He was trying to freeze Local 574 out of the situation. And in the process he hoped to put the union on the defensive right from the start.

He didn't succeed. His arrogance caused so much resentment among the workers that he had to back down on his refusal to meet with me. In the session that followed, however, he evaded discussion of the union demands. Instead he questioned the local's authority to negotiate without the sanction of the International officers of the union.

At this point Meyer Lewis sought to worm his way into Local 160's confidence by calling publicly for Pack's resignation from Latimer's Employer-Employee Board, on which the power executive had been serving. Pack did resign. Lewis then tried to get the union to put its trust in Latimer's Board, contending that, with Pack off it, the Board would be "neutral" and "fair."

Refusing to be sucked in, Local 160 called a special meeting for January 15, 1936, to take a strike vote.

This brought a special mediator into the situation, Fred A.

Ossana, an attorney who had previously represented Local 574 in various court cases. The day before the strike vote was to be taken he arranged for us to have another meeting with the company president. After much argument, Pack agreed to recognize the union, raise wages, and observe seniority rules. But he would neither put the agreement in writing, nor guarantee how long the wage increases would remain in effect. We, of course, demanded a written commitment for a definite period of time. The meeting ended in a deadlock.

All the next day, January 15, the argument was continued by indirect means, Ossana serving as the intermediary by making telephone calls alternately to the union and the company. Finally at 7:00 P.M., one hour before the strike meeting was to convene, Pack capitulated. He agreed to put the settlement terms in writing over his signature and to make the wage raises effective for all of 1936.

Yet another union had been consolidated. The campaign to "Make Minneapolis a Union Town" was rolling along with increased momentum.

January 1936 also saw the first election of officers in Local 574 since the charter was revoked. The four principal offices were not contested. Brown was unanimously reelected president; Frosig, vice-president; Grant Dunne, recording secretary; and myself, secretary-treasurer. Reelection of incumbents was contested only for the three trustee posts.

The new contenders were Oscar Gardner, Curt Zander, Axel Soderberg, L. Abroe, and R. F. DePew. None of them challenged the leadership's basic policies. It was more a matter of militants trying to advance their position in the union by seeking a trusteeship, which was considered a secondary post.

Little interest was displayed in the elections by the membership and the voting was light. When the returns came in the three incumbent trustees — Ray Dunne, Harry DeBoer, and Moe Hork — had been reelected by more than two to one. Ray Dunne, it should be noted, now served the union mainly in an advisory capacity. Much of his time was spent as the central leader of the Trotskyist movement in the city.

The main significance of the membership vote — which other unions, Tobin, Meyer Lewis, and the bosses had watched closely — was the demonstration it gave of the internal solidarity and strength of Local 574.

Also reflected in the outcome of the elections was the failure of the Stalinists to get anything going inside the local against its Trotskyist leadership. They had been trying hard to do so. We got confirmation of that when we came upon a set of directives issued by the "Central Executive Committee of the Communist Party for the Minnesota District." The essence of the directives was reported in *The Militant* of February 1, 1936. Party members in Minneapolis were ordered to "drive the trade union functionaries and membership further away from 574." The local itself was to be colonized and a demand raised to "negotiate" with Tobin.

These directives were more or less identical with the line Meyer Lewis was pushing, and he wasn't having any more luck with it than the Stalinists.

While we were winning new allies by helping the Strutwear and Northern States Power workers, Lewis had spent considerable time conniving with Latimer. At the beginning of 1936 he got the mayor to call the coal and transfer bosses to his office. New pressures were brought to bear in an effort to induce them to break their contracts with Local 574 and force their employees into "Local 500." If they did so, Latimer promised, the police were prepared to deal roughly with us.

After thinking it over in the light of the performance up to then by Lewis and Latimer, the bosses rejected the proposal. They still had little stomach for the kind of fight they knew would result.

Lewis next turned to Corcoran to try to get a drive going at small coal and transfer companies. They got cooperation from two outfits: River Terminal Coal and Dock Company, and Swanson Fuel and Transfer. In both cases the bosses sought to force the workers into the Tobin setup. Local 574 struck River Terminal and threatened to tie up Swanson as well. Corcoran tried to provide finks, but to no avail. The whole thing was quickly settled in our favor.

Such incidents served to intensify the hatred felt toward the Tobin gang among Local 574 members. Besides that, it didn't help their reputation to be seen traveling around with a police escort, as was their practice, and to have cops present when they held a meeting.

Lewis then tried to build a base for "Local 500" by raiding AFL Petroleum Workers Local 19802. When this union was chartered earlier for filling station attendants, Local 574 had transferred its oil drivers to the new organization in keeping with industrial union concepts. Lewis now demanded that these drivers be turned over to Tobin's paper union. To back up the demand he resorted to acts of intimidation. The leadership of the petroleum union was red-baited and revocation of its charter was threatened. Despite these pressures Local 19802 flatly rejected his demand and the drivers remained in that union, where they properly belonged.

After a month or so of "campaigning" along such lines, "Local 500" called a mass meeting, which was given a buildup through extensive advertising. Exactly twelve workers attended. Of those who turned up, some had come to denounce Tobin's agents and to argue in support of Local 574.

As these episodes revealed for one and all to see, we were fighting off the Lewis-Corcoran raiding attempts on every front. At the same time Local 574 continued to gain in internal stability. Steady recruitment added to its membership strength. A highly effective steward system was in operation. Contracts with the employers were fully enforced. And whenever the union had to call a strike against a trucking firm it won the battle.

Our biggest headache in maintaining union activity at the necessary level was a financial one. Because of the wide scope of operations, running expenses were high. After these were met from income derived through membership dues payments of $1.60 a month, not a whole lot was left for staff wages. How we handled that particular problem was later described by Marvel Scholl, whose account of our personal situation reflected the difficulties confronting the whole union staff.

"Whatever money was available," she recalled, "was divided among the staff members every Saturday morning. Those with children got more than the single men — sometimes as much as $20 a week, more often $10 or $15. The single men, who had their own problems in making ends meet, often came to our house for dinner.

"We lived in a little house on Drew Avenue between Cedar and Brownie Lakes. It had four small rooms, and while it was rented to us as a winter home ($20 a month unheated), it was by no means winterized — no insulation, no basement, just a cellar hole for a coal bin. We heated it with two coal burning stoves, a space heater in the living room and a combination range (coal and gas) in the kitchen.

"Every Saturday, if Farrell could not come home, one of the staff members would drive out with our 'pay' and take me grocery shopping. Luckily groceries were cheap. But — starch formed the main part of our diet. A bushel of potatoes (about 50¢), 10 lbs. of sugar, the cheapest coffee available (3 lbs. for $1), a side of bacon, a few cans of corned beef, lots of canned corn and tomatoes (#2 cans about 5 or 6 for $1), butter at maybe 20¢ a lb., several large loaves of white bread, eggs in small quantities depending on the price, navy beans, salt pork, corn meal, flour and — once in a while — a package of chocolate for the three small children.

"I have five dishes which I could make in quantity—corn chowder, baked beans with corn bread (which I always made in two large crocks in the coal stove oven), boiled beans with salt pork eaten over corn bread, Spanish rice and American spaghetti.

"When it came time for the men to come home, dinner was always ready on the stove. One of the children, or I, would stand at the door to count how many men piled out of the car. I never cooked less than a peck of spuds when occasionally we had them with corned beef, but if it was corn chowder, the potatoes were an integral part of the dish, fried crisp with a bit of bacon before the canned corn was added (along with water). If more than three guests got out of the car with Farrell, I would rush to the stove, open more cans of corn for the chowder, a bit more water, etc. If it was baked beans, there was always enough. If boiled beans, some more water went in. If Spanish rice or spaghetti, more tomatoes.

"None of these meals, with the possible exception of the oven baked beans, could be considered quality food, but it was filling.

"After we ate, all the men went back to the hall for their various evening meetings. I did the dishes.

"I had no kicks about the arrangement. During this period our children all had measles, one at a time, colds, etc., so I was literally a captive in the house. While they ate, the men talked about their union problems, their victories and disappointments, what new groups of workers had come to them for help. This was the only way for me to keep abreast of what was my real life.

"We had one luxury during this period. We saved 50 cents a week and with it hired a baby sitter every Thursday night so both of us could go to the Workers Party branch meeting."

Among those coming to us for help that Marvel mentioned were the leaders of Furniture Workers Local 1859 of the International Brotherhood of Carpenters, AFL. They had organized the J. R. Clark Company, which produced woodenware specialties. The firm had recently agreed to a contract recognizing the union and providing wage hikes, along with other improvements. Then the boss sought to trick the workers into signing individual (Yellow Dog) contracts. These ostensibly affirmed the agreement with the union, but they contained a trick clause which read: "This agreement subject to change without notice."

The union had blocked the attempt, moving swiftly to alert the workers against falling for the trick. Soon thereafter the company renewed its attack by firing a union member out of seniority for alleged "insubordination."

On March 23 the 300 workers involved came to the factory at the usual time and took their appointed places. But when the starting whistle blew, they simply sat down, emulating a strike technique that had recently been introduced by the Akron rubber workers. Guards were then posted at all doors by the union leaders, a meeting was held, and a strike committee elected.

A delegation was soon sent to request aid from Local 574. We helped to organize the preparation and transport of meals to the sit-down strikers inside the plant, who stayed there for three days and two nights.

It was a new experience for the bosses of the city, and they didn't know how to go about helping the Clark management try to break the strike. Apparently they feared that an attempt to send the police in would result in damage to the factory, so only a small detail of cops came to maintain a presence on the street outside. Since the forces of "law and order" did not attack the workers, the entire dispute remained peaceful.

On the morning of the third day the Local 1859 president, John Janasco, telephoned me at the Local 574 hall and asked that I come to Clark's and help them negotiate with the boss. He had just been told that the company wanted to come to terms with the union.

When I got there I found a handful of cops outside and a strong union guard at the main entrance. A sign on the door read, "No Help Wanted," having been put up for the attention of would-be scabs. On the inside, doors leading into the factory from the executive offices had been barred. In the biggest office I found the boss, his lawyers, and the union negotiating committee assembled, waiting to begin deliberations.

After some argument the company agreed to a settlement which led to the reinstatement of the fired union member, Walter Lehman, and to the clearing up of other grievances that had arisen out of attempts to violate the union contract. The overall terms were accepted by the strikers and they returned to work the next day, now well protected by a strong union.

By this time the list of unions helped by Local 574 was becoming impressive, as was the quality of the assistance we gave them. We had played a valuable part not only in the winning of a number of strikes by other unions, but also in bringing several thousand new members into the AFL since the fall of 1934. And the AFL had issued charters for many newly formed unions organized largely with our aid. There was scarcely a trade union in Minneapolis that had not grown in power in the aftermath of our victory in the tremendous 1934 struggle against the trucking bosses. The labor movement was gaining the upper hand over the union-hating Citizens Alliance, and everyone understood that Local 574 had provided the key to this reversal in the relationship of class forces. In its great majority the trade union rank and file sided with us accordingly.

For Meyer Lewis, on the other hand, the balance sheet was just the opposite. He had come to town a few months before with the object of isolating us from the AFL unions. At the outset his proclaimed aim in the attack on us had been to "combine the entire citizenry under one common banner to completely purge the city of communism." By now he had been reduced in his perspectives to small-time tactics like those with which Corcoran had begun a year earlier. He could do nothing but attempt petty membership raids on other AFL unions in an effort to build up "Local 500," and he had failed every time.

This ignominious outcome for Meyer Lewis had caused Tobin to switch his strategy. He decided to send Corcoran reinforcements from elsewhere in the IBT. Actually he had little other choice in the matter, unless he was ready to back off from the attack on us.

Meanwhile the AFL hierarchy had become too involved in an internal struggle of its own to pay much attention to Tobin's needs.

11. The Infighting Gets Rough

By the spring of 1936 it had become clear that a split was in the making within the American Federation of Labor.

Workers in basic industry were pressing hard for a turn to the industrial form of organization. Under this form all employees in a given plant or industry would be united into a single union, instead of being divided into separate craft formations, as in the past. To the workers the change was imperative. It was the only way they could struggle effectively against the monopoly corporations that employed them.

Their demand for a shift in organizational policy was being resisted by most of the top union bureaucrats. The clashes that resulted were moving in the direction of a major rank-and-file revolt against hard-core craft unionists who dominated the AFL. This trend had caused serious concern among the more astute federation officials. If the ruling bureaucracy didn't bend some to the mounting pressures from below, they feared, large numbers of workers would come under the influence of radical leaders.

Officials of a bloc of national unions, led by John L. Lewis of the United Mine Workers, had sought action at the October 1935 AFL convention to ease the situation. They presented a resolution calling for a turn to industrial unionism, especially in basic industry. However, the resolution was defeated by a vote of about three to two.

Soon after that John L. Lewis had thrown a bombshell into the AFL Executive Council. He resigned as a vice-president of the federation, an act signifying a declaration of war against the die-hard craft unionists who were setting its policy. Then the Lewis-led bloc formed the Committee for Industrial Organization (CIO). A committee headquarters was established in Washington, D. C., and John Brophy of the mine union was designated organizational director of the new body.

None of the CIO's founding leaders had a clear record of progressivism. Hence their changed stance in support of the industrial union cause had thrust them into a new and rather unfamiliar role. This caused them to proceed in a cautious, hesitant manner, but that was only one aspect of the changed situation. New forces were being set into motion that would sweep them along on a rising tide of class struggle.

In Minneapolis, for example, formation of the CIO gave rise to an immediate upsurge of feeling that a new day was dawning for trade unionists. A conference of industrial union supporters had soon taken place, consisting of delegates from twenty-one AFL unions and Local 574. The gathering had set up a Continuation Committee to take the lead in building a pro-CIO caucus within the city's labor movement.

The changing national situation, and the local repercussions already to be seen, brightened the future outlook for Local 574. If the developing AFL split went deep enough, we now envisaged prospects of finding new allies nationally. So we geared ourselves to a flexible tactical attitude toward the CIO.

While closely watching the changing trade union trends, we were also participating in a new step toward revolutionary regroupment on the national scene.

Young workers and intellectuals were joining the Socialist Party in increasing numbers. A left wing was forming among them and beginning to grope its way toward a revolutionary program. These potential revolutionary socialists faced two major obstacles. Within the SP they were up against a hard-bitten right wing that sought to block their efforts to turn the party in a revolutionary direction. At the same time the Communist Party, in keeping with its "Popular Front" line, sought by various means to steer these young militants back to reformism.

This situation required that the Trotskyists develop close contact with the left wing in the SP and help it evolve toward a full revolutionary-socialist program. To chart the necessary course of action, the Workers Party held a national convention early in 1936. The gathering authorized the party leadership to negotiate an entry of the WP cadres into the Socialist Party as a body, and a few weeks later the desired step was consummated.

The delegation to the Workers Party convention from the Minneapolis branch consisted of Ray Dunne, Carl Skoglund, Henry Schultz, Carlos Hudson, and myself. Since the gathering took place in New York, we decided to drive to Washington, D. C., for a visit to the CIO headquarters. There we had a long talk with John Brophy, the organizational director of the industrial-union formation.

To our surprise we found him quite fully informed about Local 574's fight with Tobin. This encouraged us to sound him out about the prospects of getting a CIO charter for the local. He said it was definitely excluded at that time, since it was quite unlikely that the CIO would involve itself in the trucking industry, even if a split from the AFL should come about.

The discussion concluded with Brophy advising us to continue our fight for reinstatement into the International Brotherhood of Teamsters.

Before long that battle took a new and vicious turn. After failing in his efforts to mobilize the local AFL against us, Meyer Lewis had gone to consult Green and Tobin. He returned to the city the latter part of April, bringing with him the vanguard of a strongarm gang Tobin was sending to launch a campaign of intimidation and terror against Local 574.

The invading force was led by L. A. Murphy, head of a Teamster local in Rockford, Illinois, which was affiliated to the Chicago Teamsters Joint Council. Upon his arrival Murphy set himself up in an office at 306 Pence Building. Operating from there, he proceeded to take charge of the Minneapolis Teamsters Joint Council in the name of Tobin. The gang he used consisted of bureaucrats schooled in IBT practices Chicago-style, along with out-and-out thugs hired for the project. From among this crew a new set of officers was selected for "Local 500," through which they intended to function. A local man was added to the squad, Bruce Vincent, who had been hired earlier as a bodyguard for Cliff Hall. In addition Pat Corcoran gave Murphy full cooperation, as did Meyer Lewis.

Tobin's muscle men, armed with blackjacks and revolvers, began to prowl the streets and loading docks. Attempts were made to compel truck drivers to accept "Local 500" buttons, offered free of charge. Behind this opening gambit lay an implication that it would now be dangerous to venture out wearing a Local 574 button; that only workers displaying the insignia of Tobin's paper union would be safe.

The goons met everywhere with refusals to accept their "protection." They then made direct threats of violence in an effort to sow fear in Local 574's ranks.

Murphy soon moved from threats to actual physical attacks. He did so with confidence that he would be helped in this, not hindered, by the ruling powers. The bosses favored his objectives. Mayor Latimer was prepared to give him police assistance, having the cops look the other way when we were assaulted; at the same time he kept a close watch for chances to frame us on one or another charge. In addition the capitalist press could be counted upon to provide a propaganda cover for the underhanded connivery. Events would be reported so as to make us look bad and to depict Tobin's agents as the injured parties.

Many years later Malcolm X, addressing himself to the subject in a different connection, was to make an eloquent characterization of this age-old newspaper trick. As he put it: "You know, brothers, the press has a grave responsibility, and it also has the responsibility sometimes as an accessory. Because if it allows itself to be used to make criminals look like victims and victims look like criminals, then the press is an accessory to the same crime. They are allowing themselves to be used as a weapon in the hands of those that are actually guilty."

Being aware of such frame-up techniques, we gave careful thought to Local 574's defense against Murphy's attack. Our first move was to alert the whole labor movement to the new danger through the *Northwest Organizer*. As the battle unfolded, each step taken by the Tobin gang was reported and analyzed in the union paper. At the same time all workers were reminded of the stake they had in our fight.

It was not simply a matter of preserving intact the strongest, most progressive union in the city. If we could defeat Tobin, other local unions would be helped in curbing the dictators at the head of their national organizations. Conversely, a victory for the IBT president would constitute a general blow to union democracy. Realizing this, AFL members throughout town continued to support Local 547's defense of its democratic rights.

In the battle itself, Murphy seemed to anticipate that it would be fought along the lines to which he had become accustomed in the Chicago area. He expected us to face him, staff against staff, sap against sap, gun against gun. He also assumed that the union ranks would be little more than spectators, waiting to see who would emerge the winner and proceed to lord it over them. Since the ruling class and its lackeys in public office were on his side, we would be up against loaded dice. For this reason he and his goons were quite cocky at the outset of the conflict.

It didn't take long for Murphy to become disabused of these notions. We had no intention whatever of letting matters proceed along such lines. Our policy was to involve all Local 574 members in the fight, which they knew was vital to their interests. A general meeting was promptly called at which the entire organization was geared for battle. As a result Tobin's invaders were soon exposed for what they actually were, a gang of thugs attacking a mass movement.

Although it would have been a tactical mistake for us to arm ourselves, we did make a propaganda move in that connection. The officers of Local 574 formally requested police permits to carry guns for self-protection. As we expected, the cops denied the request, but a point had been made. Our action helped draw

to the labor movement's attention the fact that we were up
against an armed gang and needed mass support.

Later on, when the going got rather rough, a couple of Local
574's staff members did quietly arm themselves. One of them,
George Frosig, was then picked up by the cops on charges of
carrying a gun, and it took quite a legal battle to save him
from a serious frame-up. After that we had little difficulty in
enforcing the union's no-gun policy.

Just as the fight began to get serious an event occurred that
helped us mobilize broad support. Minneapolis labor celebrated
May Day, an international working class holiday steeped in
revolutionary tradition. The observance took the form of a
parade. It was endorsed by the Central Labor Union, many
local unions participated and over 7,000 workers marched.
They carried banners reading: "For United Labor Action"—
"Make Minneapolis a Union Town."

The event had dual effects. Local 574 members who participated in the march received encouragement from the labor
solidarity thus manifested. Tobin's gang, on the other hand,
began to realize that they faced a far more complex problem
than they had anticipated.

Yet another complication began to worry Murphy. At the
end of May, the 1934 strike settlement would expire, and Local 574's contracts with the bosses involved would be up for
renewal. Since it was already early May, he would have to
move fast on that front. Two things were needed to achieve
his aims: he had to make deals with the bosses through secret negotiations (a step to which they would be amenable);
before that could be accomplished, however, he had to show
that he could take over significant portions of Local 574's
membership (this feat would take some doing).

Murphy decided to make his opening move at the Chippewa
Spring Water Company. We had only part of the workers
organized there, and the bosses seemed to think that with help
from a strong-arm squad he could freeze us out entirely. Consequently, he was ready to make a deal with "Local 500."
This brought an ultimatum to the Local 574 drivers at the
company. They were told that, as of May 16, only members
of Tobin's paper union would be allowed to work there.
Word of this action quickly reached us and we prepared to
intervene.

About sunrise that May morning the entire Local 574 staff
showed up at the Chippewa loading dock. We had not come
alone, though, as Murphy had assumed would be pretty much
the case. Also present was a sizeable body of union members
from other companies, who had taken off from work to help

out. It was not to be a gang fight. The goon squad would be up against a substantial picket line.

When the boss looked out his office window and saw what was going on, he grabbed the telephone. Within about ten minutes some thirty cops arrived. Then Murphy drove up with seven of his henchmen packed into his car.

The police commander asked if we had called a strike. We replied that we hadn't. Our only intention was to talk with the Local 574 members at the company and see that no one interfered with their right to work. This unexpected answer seemed to disorient the head cop. Looking puzzled, he went over to talk with Murphy, who had gathered his crew around him at one side of the dock. About that time the workers, including those wearing Local 574 buttons, got ready to go to work. As the tension rose, we simply waited to see whether our members were going to be interfered with.

Then the boss sent word by way of the cops that he wanted to parley. We agreed, since there was nothing to lose by it. Bill Brown and I went into the company office to speak for our side. Murphy and Jack Smith did the same for "Local 500." The session that followed was distinctly lacking in cordiality.

Pretending injured innocence, the boss proceeded to chicken out of his deal with the Tobin gang. He asked that the two sides find a way to work out the union dispute without interfering with his operations. We replied that so long as our members were allowed to go about their work in peace he would have no trouble from Local 574. Murphy found himself with no alternative but to back off from his attack on us at Chippewa and that particular episode came to an end.

On the heels of this confrontation the package-delivery firms signed a one-year contract recognizing Local 574 as the sole bargaining agent for their employees. This was the first direct agreement we had been able to obtain in this sphere, and we now had the employees so well organized that the companies gave in without forcing us into a strike. The workers won substantial wage increases and various improvements in job conditions.

Shortly thereafter we made a breakthrough in relations with the furniture stores, whose drivers and helpers we had successfully organized, along with shipping-room employees. Union demands were presented to the bosses, who informed us they were ready to negotiate. In the end a contract was signed providing important gains for the workers. As in the package-delivery situation, this was accomplished without our having to take strike action.

In both instances Murphy had been trying to negotiate with the bosses involved. Although talking with him readily enough, even wishing him well, they had in the end capitulated to Local 574. In fact, they were so dubious of "Local 500's" capacity to intervene that they had seen no point in testing our capacity to win a strike against them. Obviously they didn't think Tobin's gang could break it, even with help from the cops and the newspapers.

The way things were going Murphy would soon find himself boxed into a corner, unless he did something in a hurry. Realizing the situation, he made a desperate attempt to goad us into a slugging match, staff against staff. His action no longer represented any illusion that we could be intimidated. By now Murphy knew better than that. The key aim was to give city officials a chance to jail the Local 574 leaders on trumped-up charges. If they could behead the union in this manner, there would be a far better chance to take it over.

On the morning of May 21 the new offensive began. Ray Dunne and George Frosig were distributing leaflets and talking to drivers in the freight yards of the Omaha railway. Suddenly a Buick sedan drove up and a gang of Tobin's thugs jumped out of it and assaulted Ray and George with blackjacks. They were severely beaten.

Ownership of the Buick was traced to L. A. Murphy through a check with the automobile license bureau. This fact, along with an account of the atrocity, was published in the *Northwest Organizer* to inform the labor movement of the new danger. For the record, a protest was also made to the public authorities. But they did nothing about it, as was to be expected.

Local 574 immediately called a mass protest meeting. Word of the outrage had spread rapidly and the hall was jammed with union members, many of them accompanied by their wives. As the latter development indicated, not since the 1934 strikes had the workers been so aroused. They were more than ready to fight back, and combat veterans that they were by now, they knew it had to be done intelligently.

Accepting the executive board's advice, the membership adopted a three-point plan of action: efforts were redoubled to obtain speedy renewal of contracts that were about to expire; an assessment was voted to provide a special defense fund; and a resolution was adopted setting forth the basic line for a campaign to mobilize the city's working class against the new goon attack.

The resolution condemned the gangsterism introduced by Tobin, calling it an open invitation to the enemies of the labor movement. If it could be made to work against Local 574, the other unions were warned, the same methods would be used against them as well. Thus an open challenge had been hurled at the leaders and members of all AFL organizations. It was their duty, acting in their own self-interest, to join in the struggle to free the movement from the menace of thuggery.

Our appeal fell upon responsive ears. Officers, and especially rank-and-file members of AFL locals, poured heat on the right-wing officials of the Central Labor Union and the Teamsters Joint Council. They also brought heavy pressure to bear on Mayor Latimer, as did Farmer-Labor Party ward clubs. Finding himself under heavy fire, the mayor felt he had to do something — so he set out to smear us.

Late in May a small army of police made a surprise raid on Local 574, charging into our headquarters with drawn guns. They were accompanied by news reporters and photographers. Bearing John Doe warrants for illegal sale of liquor, they searched the premises for evidence. Nothing was to be found, except part of a keg of beer which had been stored away after being left over from a social. Twice more in the next few days the cops descended upon us, but they were unable to spot anything that could be used against the union.

It was in connection with these smear attempts that Frosig was arrested on the gun charge mentioned previously.

Taking advantage of the propaganda cover Latimer sought to provide for him, Murphy resumed the physical assaults. In broad daylight on the afternoon of June 3, four rank-and-file members of Local 574 driving along Washington Avenue in a passenger car were forced to the curb and ordered out of their vehicle by two carloads of Tobin's musclemen. Some held guns on the union members, while others pulled out blackjacks and beat them. When the victims ran to escape, a volley of shots followed them.

Bystanders had gotten the license numbers of the thugs' cars, and this information was reported to Latimer with a demand that he take action. As usual though, no arrests were made.

Instead the mayor held a conference with Murphy and Meyer Lewis. Reporters were then summoned and Murphy issued a statement to them. According to the *Minneapolis Tribune* account, he brazenly accused the victims of "firing the shots themselves," falsely asserting that they had done so "after losing a fight with the employes of Stanchfield Transfer Company," a firm located near the scene of the crime.

A week later a Local 574 job steward Harold Haynes was attacked while at work. He had just got back into the cab of his truck after making a delivery. Then the Buick sedan, registered in Murphy's name, pulled up and blocked his way. Five goons leaped out of it. One pointed a gun at Haynes. The other four dragged him out of the cab and beat him with blackjacks and gun butts.

We made a strong protest to Governor Olson. In a letter signed by Bill Brown he was informed that we were holding a special meeting of Local 574 on June 15. We demanded an official answer by then as to what Olson proposed to do about Tobin's criminal attempt, with Latimer's collusion, to destroy a section of the labor movement.

Coming immediately to our support, the fifth ward Farmer-Labor club insisted that Olson take prompt action. Demands were made that he invoke the executive power of the state to put a stop to acts of vandalism in Minneapolis, and that he uncover the instigators of the plot against organized labor.

Similar demands upon the governor came from elsewhere in the unions and the Farmer-Labor Party. Since he was coming up for reelection in the fall, it was politically dangerous for him to ignore these pressures, and he knew it. So he passed word along that he would look into the situation right away, pretending that he hadn't known what was going on. Apparently Olson convinced Latimer that it was politically expedient to quiet things down inside the labor movement, because the physical attacks on us now abated.

Despite these assaults, we had been making headway against the bosses. Early in June the building-material suppliers and the market firms — with one exception — signed direct agreements with the union. In both industries, Local 574 was recognized as the sole bargaining agent for the workers. The new pacts, which ran for one year to May 31, 1937, brought wage increases and improved job conditions. For market workers especially, the advance had become quite dramatic. Since 1933 their wages had almost doubled and the work week had been cut from eighty or ninety hours to forty-eight.

The holdout in the market was Gamble-Robinson, one of the larger firms, which had been exceptionally belligerent in its anti-union stance. We struck the outfit, an action that put the Tobin gang right up against the gun. This was a straight union-employer conflict. If they sought to intervene against us, it would have to be as strikebreakers. Hoping to encourage such an attempt, Latimer immediately offered police protection to the company; but there proved to be little that he, Murphy, or the bosses could do against us.

Local 574 had the workers at Gamble-Robinson completely

organized and the strike was 100 percent solid. The independent grocers announced through their association that any deliveries attempted by the struck firm would not be accepted by them. Then the walkout spread to branches of the company in other Minnesota towns.

After having been shut down tight for about two weeks, Gamble-Robinson signed the same contract with Local 574 that had been agreed to earlier by the other market houses. This was followed by settlements with the strikers outside Minneapolis. In overall terms, unionism had been strengthened in the general area; Local 574 had demonstrated its power; and the Tobinites had exhibited their incapacity to block our offensive on the contract front.

Apparently getting the message, bosses who had been playing it cool now entered into serious negotiations with Local 574. Before long a new contract was signed with sand-and-gravel companies, providing gains for the employees. The coverage agreement with the ice distributing firms was renewed on improved terms. Other settlements followed.

As we registered these victories, a broader wave of trade union struggles was also developing. About 700 sash, door, and mill workers were striking for recognition of their union, Cabinet Makers Local 1865, AFL. Local 574 had turned its main hall over to them for use as a strike headquarters, and they were using our kitchen facilities as a commissary. In addition we helped them with tactical advice, which the inexperienced leadership welcomed.

Seeking propaganda advantage from the Tobin-Latimer smear campaign against us, the struck companies ran paid ads in the newspapers, trying to fog the issue. Their employees wanted to work, they charged, but acts of intimidation, instigated by Local 574, were keeping them off the job. It didn't have the desired effect. The strikers held firm and the industry was kept closed down. A settlement was finally reached on June 24. Local 1865 won recognition, and the workers involved achieved substantial material gains.

Less than a week after Local 1865 left, our facilities were newly occupied as a strike headquarters for the Northern States Power workers. Pack, the company head, was reneging on the agreement he had signed the previous January. This caused some 200 skilled workers in the overhead and underground departments to walk out in protest. The action was led by Henry Schultz, who had been retained by the executive board of the power workers' union, Local 160, to serve as its organizer and spokesman.

The strike, which was conducted with great militancy, lasted only a few days. Pack was compelled to act on the workers' grievances. The previous written stipulation was reaffirmed, and this time Local 160 got full recognition as the sole bargaining agency for the company's employees.

One other dispute is worth noting, just to indicate the breadth of the working class upsurge. At the Minneapolis Golf Club, a course in suburban St. Louis Park frequented by the well-to-do, caddies went on strike. It was a spontaneous action by unorganized teen-agers, who were doing what seemed to them the natural thing those days for young workers who were angered by their employers. Once they had struck, their first step was to contact the "outlaws" of Local 574 for backing and advice. Their fight resulted in some improvements for caddies generally.

On balance, the odds in the fight with Tobin were now heavily in Local 574's favor. As a result of steady recruitment, the union had a stable membership of over 4,000. Contracts with the employers were being renewed and agreements signed in new parts of the trucking industry, all with important gains for the workers. The spirit this had engendered was articulated in a letter written to the union by Oscar Halverson, a rank-and-file member.

"My kids have been eating meat, along with good food, ever since the 1934 strike," he said in one passage, "so with them the sun rises and sets on 574."

Most workers in other industries had sentiments about Local 574 similar to those expressed by Halverson. They knew that in every battle with the bosses we would be there to help them. And all who associated with us found that the experience brought them a better understanding of the class struggle, helping them to become more capable fighters in labor's cause.

As against our growing strength and prestige, "Local 500" remained weak in numbers, and it was getting an increasingly bad reputation. It had been unable to make a meaningful breakthrough anywhere in the trucking industry. Other unions were coming more and more to look upon it as a liability to the AFL. Instead of outlawing us from the labor movement, as they had set out to do, the Tobinites found that they, themselves, were looked upon as pariahs by the great majority of the city's working class.

All this had finally become too much for Pat Corcoran to stomach. Late in June he telephoned Ray Dunne to ask that peace negotiations be arranged between Local 574 and the Teamsters Joint Council.

12. Tobin Backs Down

Formal negotiations began soon after the Tobinite overture. Carl Skoglund, Ray Dunne, and I represented Local 574. Pat Corcoran spoke for the Teamsters Joint Council. L. A. Murphy and Jack Smith presented themselves as officers of "Local 500."

The first talk was held in a charged atmosphere, reflecting the hostility that had developed between the two sides. We took advantage of the fact that our adversaries had sued for peace. When the formalities were over, we simply remained silent, waiting expectantly for them to make the opening move.

Corcoran took the lead. The Joint Council wanted to work out an arrangement whereby Local 574 could be brought back into the Teamsters as a body, he said, but it would have to be done in a special way. He proposed that we merge with "Local 500" under a new charter; that three officers from each side be named to the executive board of the new local; and that a seventh, "neutral" board member be designated by the Joint Council. Murphy and Smith indicated their concurrence in this proposal.

We replied that most of the workers in the general trucking industry were in our ranks, while they had virtually no members in that sphere. This meant that the reality would be a merger with the IBT, not "Local 500." Their paper union should be liquidated, we contended. If they wanted to end the fight, all they had to do was to reinstate Local 574 into the International, with all its members in good standing and with its present officers, who had been democratically elected by the ranks.

Corcoran again stressed that some arrangement would have to be worked out along the lines of his proposal, otherwise they would be unable to get Tobin's agreement to reinstate

us. He suggested that we think the matter over among ourselves and notify him when we were ready to resume the discussion. With that the first talk ended.

We now had a vital decision to make. If the fight with Tobin
was to be settled, it was clear that Local 574 would have
to be reconstituted under a new charter, with changes in the
formal leadership. This raised two key questions for us. Could
a compromise be worked out that would assure the preserva-
tion of Local 574's basic character and principles? If we rejected the peace overture, would we risk isolation from the rest
of the labor movement and ultimate destruction of the union?

The latter danger could quickly become a real one, unless
we showed that we really wanted to help find a solution to
the internal union struggle. We couldn't expect to gain new
strength through formal alignment with the CIO. Brophy had
already told us that the new industrial union formation didn't
expect to enter the trucking industry. Our main support, therefore, still had to come from the local AFL movement. Up to
now we had received backing from that quarter on the basis
of our fight for reinstatement into the IBT. But if we now
let it appear that we intended to pursue an independent course
indefinitely, that support would begin to drop away. The IBT
machine could then get the upper hand and gradually cut
us to pieces.

It followed from these considerations that our best course
was to drive the hardest possible bargain with Tobin. As we
saw it, there were several factors that would enable us to obtain a workable compromise. Nationally a massive strike wave
in basic industry was clearly in the making. Locally the
workers were on the move, dragging the AFL officials more
deeply into conflicts with the bosses. These trends generally
imparted a tone of militancy to the movement that would help
us from within the IBT.

While it was true that Corcoran's plan would reduce us to a
formal minority on the executive board of the proposed new
local, that didn't tell the whole story. The membership would
continue to support the Local 574 officers, as in the past.
We would be backed up by a strong secondary leadership
among the union staff members and the job stewards, all
of whom were battle tested. It would be a situation roughly
analogous to relations between the organizing committee and
the official executive board during the 1934 strikes.

In terms of leadership-membership relations, concerning the
cadres of Local 574, there would be no change. This, we felt,
would make it possible to assure continued rank-and-file con-

trol over all the affairs of the new local. A means would thereby exist to block any Tobinite attempt to alter fundamental policies. From this it followed, in our view, that the local could preserve its basic character and principles under the proposed new arrangement.

For these general reasons we decided within the union leadership that the device of a merger with "Local 500" should be accepted as the basis for reinstatement into the IBT. Corcoran was then notified that we were ready to resume negotiations. Several discussions followed, during which the terms of the merger were hammered out in the necessary detail. The key points involved can be summarized as follows:

1. Local 574 and "Local 500" to be liquidated and a new charter to be issued, constituting one General Drivers Union. (The number later issued to us was 544. Corcoran had induced Tobin to come as close as possible to 574 without allowing our reinstatement under the local's original designation.)

2. The present membership of Local 574 to be reinstated in good standing in the IBT, without any fines or assessments. (Specifically, the latter clause meant that the matter of back per capita taxes we owed the International—the pretext Tobin had used to revoke our charter—would be dropped.)

3. Officers of the new local to consist of two representatives of 574, two representatives of "500," one trustee of 574, one trustee of "500"; the executive board to consist of the above officers and trustees, with the addition of the secretary of the Teamsters Joint Council, acting as the seventh member and chairman. (It was understood in the negotiations that representatives of 574 would have the offices of president and recording secretary of the new local; representatives of "500" would have the posts of vice president and secretary-treasurer.)

4. The organization staff to be set up and chosen by the exexutive board. (On this point it was understood that each side would have half the staff members; that in general the organizers would work in pairs, one from each side; and that the overall size of the staff would be determined by the union's finances. It was also agreed that I would continue as staff director.)

5. All divisions, i.e., the existing sections of Local 574, to stay under the reorganized local for a period of at least one year. (We were not overly concerned about the implication that an attempt to split up the local into separate crafts, each with its own charter, might be made a year later. By then we expected to have sufficient control of the new situation to

readily ward off such a danger. Should that fail to be the
case, it would mean that even bigger problems confronted
us. So we saw no point in making an issue of this seeming
qualification on the future of the local.)

6. The Federal Workers Section to be continued as an auxiliary unit of the new local. (Unemployed members of other
Teamster locals had already been joining the FWS while Local 574 was an "outlaw." This provision meant that such action
was now to become official Joint Council policy.)

7. The *Northwest Organizer* to become the official organ of
the Teamsters Joint Council, under the supervision of its executive board. (It was understood in the negotiations that
Miles Dunne would be designated as editor of the paper. The
first issue under the changed auspices appeared on August 12,
1936.)

8. The above plan to be subject to the approval of the International Brotherhood of Teamsters. (Corcoran assured us
that this was a mere formality, having to do with approval
of the settlement by the International Executive Board. Tobin,
he said, had been kept informed of the progress of negotiations and had already indicated informally that he would
approve the terms set down for our reinstatement.)

Rarely had a top union bureaucrat made concessions of
such magnitude to "subordinates" whom he had initially set
out to discipline.

After revoking our charter in April 1935, Tobin had demanded that Local 574 be completely reorganized as a condition for reinstatement into the IBT. Inside workers were
to be denied membership, which he defined on the narrow
basis of workers actually employed on trucks, as related to
driving, loading, and unloading. Sections of the union were
to be chopped off into separate craft units. The elected officers
and outstanding militants in the ranks of the local were to
be expelled.

All of this had now changed. The entire membership of Local 574, including its officers and organizers, were to be reinstated without a single exception. There was no longer a
demand for immediate dismemberment of the local into separate craft parts. Recognition had been given to our right to
organize inside workers, which meant that the local would
retain its essential character as a semi-industrial union.

As will be seen later, this concession by Tobin on membership jurisdiction marked the first step in a chain of developments that would ultimately change the organizational character
of the IBT itself.

Before we submitted the proposed settlement to the membership for a final decision, two other steps were needed. One
involved formal approval by the International Union of the
terms upon which we were to be reinstated. The other had
to do with broader consultation at the leadership level on
our side.

As soon as it had become clear that there were good prospects of winning reinstatement into the IBT on an acceptable
basis, the development was reported to Jim Cannon, the central leader of the Trotskyist movement nationally. We asked
him to come to Minneapolis for consultation and he soon
arrived in town. Before that he had talked with other leading
Trotskyist comrades within the Socialist Party, to which we
then belonged.

The leading party comrades, including Jim, were hesitant
about our proposed settlement with Tobin. There was concern
among them as to whether we could survive under the terms
involved. It might be better, they felt, to go down fighting
than to risk being compromised as revolutionists, if the
arrangement went wrong on us. However, it was generally
agreed that the views of the Teamster comrades should be
accorded special weight in determining what to do. The policy
decision, it was understood, would have to be made through
direct leadership consultation at the scene of the action.

Jim Cannon met with the party's Teamster fraction at his
room in the West Hotel. Bill Brown was also present. It was
a long session in which every facet of the new situation was
carefully examined.

We explained why we thought the proposed settlement with
Tobin should be accepted. Jim, in turn, informed us of the
hesitations among the national Trotskyist leaders about taking such a course. As the discussion then unfolded the Teamster comrades were unanimous in expressing confidence that
we could retain decisive leadership control in the proposed
new local. We also argued strongly for party approval of
our recommendation.

Being a seasoned party leader, Jim understood the need to
be flexible in this situation. He could advance no important
strategic reason for Local 574 to continue as an independent
union. It boiled down to a question of whether we could avoid
becoming compromised in a joint leadership formation with
the Tobinites. We were confident that we could.

If the party insisted that the offer of reinstatement into the
IBT should be rejected, we were the ones who would have

to carry out that policy. We would be doing so with a feeling of resentment against the imposition of such a line, because we felt that it was neither necessary nor advisable. Therefore, an impairment of party morale was bound to result, with adverse consequences.

Jim was fully aware of these factors. He knew that serious problems were bound to arise from any attempt to force upon us a policy to which we were opposed. There were no questions of principle involved. It was simply a matter of a choice in tactics. So he agreed that the party should give us the benefit of the doubt on the tactical decision. In doing so he showed the mark of a real leader.

"I don't fully agree with your decision," Jim told us, in effect, "but I will take full responsibility with you, even if it goes bad."

By this time the dispute within the AFL over industrial unionism had reached a new stage. The Executive Council had given John L. Lewis and the other CIO leaders an ultimatum to disband their new organization or face expulsion from the federation. Lewis was reported to be defying the order, and an early split had become a distinct probability. (It was actually to occur during August 1936, when the CIO was suspended from membership in the AFL.)

Although it was a long shot, the party fraction meeting decided that a final attempt should be made to get Local 574 into the CIO. Bill Brown and Ray Dunne were sent by plane to consult John Brophy about our prospects. He again told them that the CIO had no plans for the trucking industry and repeated his advice that we accept reinstatement into the Teamsters.

We were now ready to propose the latter course to the union membership, provided that the IBT approved the terms negotiated with the local Tobinites. The required confirmation came on July 9 in a wire from Meyer Lewis, who had gone to the Indianapolis headquarters with a committee from the Teamsters Joint Council. His message read:

"The proposal signed by representatives of Local 500 International Brotherhood of Teamsters and representatives of General Drivers Local 574 as a basis for settlement of Teamster dispute in Minneapolis has been approved by the International Brotherhood of Teamsters through John Gillespie acting president. Both organizations may now proceed to make formal application for new charter to be issued on basis of conditions contained therein. I trust this may open a campaign to completely organize Teamster industry in Minneapolis and that it will be incentive to the organization of the Teamster industry of the entire state. To that end I wish the new organization the greatest success and offer you the fullest cooperation. Copy sent you at request of Smith and Corcoran."

At a regular meeting of the job stewards on July 10 the question of our reinstatement into the IBT was made a special order of business. Reporting for the negotiating committee, I submitted the proposed settlement terms and presented the executive board's recommendation that they be accepted. The telegram from Meyer Lewis was read; also a wire from Bill Brown and Ray Dunne reporting the negative results of their talk with John Brophy.

In the discussion that followed some spoke for the proposal, some against it. To give an idea of the views of those who were opposed, the following are typical comments, as recorded in the minutes of the meeting:

"Gagnon: If the name 574 is taken away we will be looked upon as going back in shame . . .

"Gordon: Under no circumstances will allow Pat Corcoran to act as a dictator.

"Rogers: Not satisfied to allow anyone but our own officers.

"Zander: Would be ashamed to wear an AFL button . . .

"Novey: They will tear us to pieces and knock off our officers.

"Rommerdal: Members will be slugged if they open their mouths in a meeting."

After extensive discussion the executive board's recommendation to accept the reinstatement terms was approved by a vote of about two to one. There was no feeling of having surrendered to Tobin among those who voted in favor; nor would there be any hesitation about accepting the final membership decision on the part of those who voted against. Basically, the job stewards constituted a relatively homogeneous trade union body, ready to act in keeping with the democratic principle of majority rule.

Prior to the general membership meeting, scheduled for July 13, the stewards could be counted upon to faithfully inform the other workers on the job of the discussion they had held with the union officers. This meant that the union members would not be taken by surprise when the matter was put to them for a decision at the meeting.

When the general membership convened, the hall was packed. It was the largest closed meeting of the union in over a year. As at the stewards' gathering, I reported the leadership's recommendation, speaking in the name of the executive board.

The presentation can be summarized with reasonable accuracy from the notes I used, which are still in my files.

It began with a brief review of the negotiations with the Tobinites. The vote at the steward meeting was reported. Then the proposed reinstatement terms were read and the necessary clarifications given. After that I spoke along the following general lines:

"All of us regret that we will lose the designation 574, but it should be noted that 'Local 500' is also out. There is really no alternative on this point. We couldn't convince the rest of the movement that the retention of 574 as our charter number is a fighting issue.

"Although 574 will be in a minority on the new executive board, it will be a powerful one. Our representatives can use the instrument of minority reports to the ranks, if needed. They can count on solid backing from the job stewards and from our fighting membership. On this point we have won a significant victory over the International. No officer is to be expelled, as Tobin has originally demanded, and anyone in good standing is entitled to hold office.

"The executive board has spent long hours over this problem, trying to think out all aspects of it. Here is how we see the situation.

"Our strength in the past has been the slogan: 'We want to be a part of the movement.' Support has thus been gained among the ranks of other unions.

"The International now offers to make a settlement with us. There is no solid point in the offer on which we can seize to defend ourselves, if we turn it down. The rest of the movement does and will call the settlement fair.

"We have not yet been subject to the charge of dual unionism. But if we reject the proposed terms for reinstatement into the IBT, we will become so in the eyes of other unions.

"Can we afford to do this?

"What unions might join in with us? Only those we have built. We all know the weaknesses of other leaders in the movement, who have wobbled throughout the long fight with Tobin. They couldn't be counted upon.

"The *Labor Review* [official organ of the Central Labor Union] has not yet attacked us, but it would. It would become a rival to the *Northwest Organizer*, instead of the two union papers supplementing each other.

"We would lose the weak members of our union almost at once. Our ranks would slowly dwindle to a comparatively small group of bitter end fighters.

"If we accept the International's offer, we will go back in with a strong, fighting membership. We will have three members on the executive board, half of the organization staff and all the job stewards. That constitutes a real power.

"Our officers will become delegates to the Teamsters Joint Council and the Central Labor Union. We can look toward the building of a state organization of Teamsters. And we can get down to business on our plans to organize the long distance drivers.

"There is a new spirit in the city's labor movement. That would make it very dangerous for the International officials to doublecross us. If they do, out we march again.

"We have talked to the CIO about this matter, also with other friends and advisers. After these discussions, and on the basis of the reasoning I have outlined, the executive board has come to a firm decision.

"We recommend that the proposed terms for reinstatement into the International be accepted."

After the report Bill Brown, the union president, called for discussion from the floor. Speaker after speaker was recognized to argue the matter, pro and con. When the question was finally called, the membership voted about six to one to rejoin the International Brotherhood of Teamsters.

A fifteen-month battle had ended with Local 574 the victor.

Officers of the reorganized local had been specifically designated as follows: From former Local 574, William S. Brown, president; Carl Skoglund, trustee; Farrell Dobbs, recording secretary. From former "Local 500," L. A. Murphy, secretary-treasurer; Jack Smith, vice president; Nick Wagner, trustee. Pat Corcoran, secretary of the Teamsters Joint Council, was named chairman of the executive board.

It should be noted that in this changed situation we now considered it possible and advisable for Skoglund to hold union office, despite his citizenship problem.

On July 14 the new officers issued a joint public statement declaring:

"All contracts with the employers formerly held by the dissolved locals will be taken over and enforced by the new local.

"With the splendid harmony made possible through the newly established basis of cooperation between all the leaders and members of the local labor movement, it is assured that the members of the Minneapolis unions and all unions in the state will draw increased benefits from their organizations. The parties to the new agreement pledge themselves to work faithfully and consistently to promote the best interests of the workers as made possible through a united American Federation of Labor movement."

The new charter, as General Drivers Local 544, was formally presented to the union at a large open meeting, well attended by AFL members generally. John Geary, representing Tobin, made the presentation, which was received by Bill Brown. T. E. Cunningham, president of the State Federation of Labor, welcomed Local 544 into the AFL. Miles Dunne spoke as editor of the *Northwest Organizer*. Ray Dunne reviewed the history of the General Drivers since 1933. Jack Smith expressed appreciation of the spirit of harmony and good will he had found in the reorganized local.

Soon thereafter Local 544's delegates were officially seated in the Teamsters Joint Council and the Central Labor Union. In both instances their arrival was greeted with bursts of applause.

After a delay of almost two years, it had now become possible to launch the general organization drive that should have followed on the heels of our strike victory in 1934. This perspective had been set forth in a statement by the executive board of Local 574, issued in connection with the union's return to the IBT. As reported in the *Northwest Organizer* of July 22, 1936, it said in part:

"The drivers must lead the way to the organization and unionization of the unorganized workers of the state and the northwest. Powerful in their own right, the drivers can augment this power in only one way. That is, by following the examples of Local 574, giving aid to other groups of workers in making their way into the ranks of the American Federation of Labor. . . .

"The officers and membership of Local 574, together with the new capable men and augmented forces from the International Union, turn now to the serious job of organizing the drivers, helpers and warehousemen of Minneapolis, of Minnesota and the northwest."

13. New Horizons

Our call for a Teamster expansion drive was not a simple reflex action stimulated by the victory over Tobin. As a matter of deliberate policy we hoped to get such a campaign started at once, both to serve immediate needs and with the longer range aim of widening our influence within the IBT. There were several considerations involved.

National and local trends continued to develop in our favor. The CIO leaders had shown sufficient courage to face a split with the craft union die-hards in the AFL over the industrial union issue. Workers in basic industry were quick to see in this development new chances for a meaningful confrontation with the big corporations. Their combative mood served, in turn, to generate new self-confidence and increased militancy throughout the rest of the working class.

In Minneapolis these impulses were further intensified by Local 574's reinstatement into the IBT. Our return to the AFL not only ended the internal union conflict; it raised to a higher plane the potential for united labor action. Sensing the opportunities presented by the changed situation, the workers of the city were generally eager to launch a new offensive against the bosses.

By helping to get the desired offensive under way quickly, we could strengthen our position within the reconstituted General Drivers Local 544. An aggressive unionization drive would put the Tobinites at a disadvantage. New clashes with the bosses would soon develop. Corcoran, Murphy, and their followers would have to support the fight, or they would lose any capacity to influence the union ranks. At the same time any attempt on their part to introduce class collaborationist policies could be resisted under battle conditions favorable to us. As a minimum this implied the possibility of being able to neutralize them. But we also had a larger aim in mind. It was our intention to draw them into support of a constructive trade union course, if at all possible.

Should we succeed in the latter aim, help would be gained in extending the influence of a militant Local 544 into wider Teamster circles. IBT locals elsewhere in the country, we felt, were taking note of our success in standing up to Tobin. It now seemed reasonable to assume that they would begin to assert themselves more strongly on questions of union policy. If so, we would win allies in seeking to convert the whole International into more of a fighting organization.

As a first step toward this larger end we sought to strengthen the Minneapolis Teamsters Joint Council. The effort began with support to Milk Drivers Local 471 in a campaign to organize several open-shop creameries. For years these outfits had held out against the union. If we could now help kick them into line, it would get us off to a good start in our relations with Pat Corcoran. His first real involvement with us would come through a clash with the bosses in which his union would be the beneficiary.

Corcoran was anxious to conduct such a campaign. Having been a milk driver himself, he was sincerely devoted to the labor movement, especially to the interests of Local 471. He was handicapped as a union leader, however, by strong ambitions concerning his personal career. This weakness had brought him under the tutelage of right-wing AFL officials, who set out to school him in the arts of "labor statesmanship." Such miseducation, along with his careerist outlook, lay at the root of his shabby conduct in supporting Tobin against former Local 574.

With that unsavory episode now behind him, Corcoran was showing signs of a change in perspectives. His interest in battling the creamery bosses, for example, appeared to go beyond a mere desire to strengthen Local 471. He seemed eager to make amends for past misconduct and to improve his image as a union leader. So we took his friendly gestures toward us as sincere, subject only to the test of actual performance.

Corcoran didn't measure up to Bill Brown, either in leadership stature or in political insight. Yet we felt that he could play a useful role, at least partly comparable to Brown's, if properly stimulated and helped. In any case, there was nothing to lose by trying. We, therefore, set out to help bring out the best there was in him.

Toward the end of July the mopping-up operation began in the milk industry. It was a whirlwind action in which the bosses felt the impressive power of a united Teamsters' movement. The staffs of all locals in the Joint Council came to the support of Local 471. Within Local 544's staff a healthy competition quickly developed between those from former 574 and those from former "500," each group trying to make the best showing.

A one-day strike at Engell Dairy Company brought a signed contract with Local 471. This firm, one of the larger holdouts, had long been one of the worst thorns in the union's side. When its resistance collapsed, the other open-shop outfits quickly began to fall into line. In short order the industry was 100 percent organized.

A particular episode enabled Pat Corcoran to make real headway toward gaining respect among the veterans of Local 574. It took place at a creamery located in a small community just outside Minneapolis.

Early one morning a picket line was set up at the place. Before long the village cop showed up carrying a shotgun. He pointed the weapon at the picket line and ordered us to break it up, allowing that he wouldn't tolerate such big-city goings on in his town. Corcoran whirled about and advanced angrily upon the law man, pressing so close that the gun muzzle almost touched his chest.

"If you think you can fire on peaceful pickets and get away with it," he challenged, "try shooting me, you boss-loving sonofabitch."

By then the rest of us were closing in to support Pat. Appearing to have suddenly developed an acute case of bowel trouble, the cop lowered his gun and backed off. Less than an hour later the boss signed the union contract.

At about this time Jack Smith also gave a good account of himself, doing so in negotiations with the Chippewa Spring Water Co. This was one of the places where former "Local 500" had tried to give us trouble earlier. Smith, like Corcoran, now sought to make amends. He asked for the assignment, and the contract he negotiated for the workers at this company met the standards that had been set previously by former Local 574. It was a sign that the Tobinites, who now participated in the leadership of the reorganized local, could be brought around to our way of dealing with the bosses.

Following the mop-up campaign in the milk industry, a general "fink drive" was launched by the Teamsters Joint Council. Job stewards and active members of Teamster locals reinforced the union staffs in carrying out the operation. Squads of four to a car were alloted to the various sections of the city. Streets were combed, docks and warehouses checked, as the Council pressed for 100 percent unionization of the trucking industry. The success of the drive was reflected in the fact that Local 544 alone recruited close to 1,000 new members in one month.

Among these recruits were many workers from the wholesale grocery industry. Their response to the unionization drive indicated that we were in a position to make a major breakthrough in this sphere. Harry DeBoer and Ray Rainbolt were put in charge of a continuing effort to bring Local 544's wholesale grocery section up to full strength. As the campaign progressed, meetings of the workers were held at which demands for a union contract were drawn up. These were then served upon the bosses, who flatly refused to talk with the union representatives.

Behind the employers' adamant stand lay a new Citizens Alliance plot. The Alliance leaders were alarmed by the success of the Teamsters Joint Council organization drive, which had electrified the whole Minneapolis labor movement. In a desperate attempt to stem the mounting tide, they had induced the wholesale grocery firms to spearhead a counterattack on the union movement. Among these companies were units of national chains and big independent houses owned by blue bloods within the city's wealthy class. With these forces in the vanguard, the Alliance planned to use every available trick against us: red-baiting, cops, thugs, government trickery — the works. In the process they hoped to bring enough pressure to bear on the Tobinites now in Local 544 to split the union leadership.

As it turned out though, Corcoran, Murphy, Smith, and Wagner tended from the outset to defer to the Trotskyist leaders in the local. They accepted the fact of our superior experience in fights of this kind, and on that basis cast themselves in a supporting role. Their attitude proved quite helpful in the struggle that followed.

With the employers refusing to negotiate, the union called a strike against them on August 20. Over 400 workers were involved at twelve firms. A strike committee was elected by the ranks of the wholesale grocery section and one of the strikers, Pete Harris, was chosen as its chairman. Picketing began at the struck firms, and a number of cruising squads were organized to provide the necessary mobility of the union forces. Although the industry was effectively tied up very quickly, we expected it to be a long fight and made preparations accordingly. These ranged from the elementary task of setting up a commissary to feed the strikers, to the more complex problem of publishing daily supplements of the *Northwest Organizer* to refute the bosses' lies and tell the workers' side of the story.

The latter step was most vital because the ruling class quickly launched a vicious propaganda barrage against the union. Full-page ads in the daily papers, along with extensive employer statements, sought to raise panic cries about the strikers causing a "food shortage." This was accompanied, of course, by Trotsky-baiting of the union leadership, repeating the canards of 1934. As the *Northwest Organizer* noted, the boss press gave the company statements full coverage, usually on the front page. Of twelve statements issued by the union, on the other hand, only one appeared in the papers and then only in part. It got about two inches of space in an obscure inside section.

At the same time the Citizens Alliance was issuing bulletins to employers throughout the city calling upon them to unite for a "showdown" with the labor movement. With this buildup a boss rally was held at the Radisson Hotel. L.A. Murphy attended the gathering for Local 544, disguising himself as a business man. There he heard the assembled bosses whip themselves into a lather as they started kicking in for a financial jackpot to be used in their strikebreaking campaign.

In this setting Latimer's Employer-Employee Board came forward with a public statement. It called upon the striking grocery workers to return to their jobs, saying that it couldn't mediate the dispute with the employers until they did. Although there were three labor members on the board — T. E. Cunningham, J. Boscoe, and G. Alexander — Local 544 was not consulted before the board issued its unanimous declaration. This disloyal action by the three "labor statesmen" brought a harsh rebuke from the strike leadership. The key issue was union recognition, they were told, and it was not debatable.

Rejection of the Latimer Board's line was followed by a mass rally in support of the strikers. Local 544's general membership turned out in force to show solidarity with the union's embattled section. Members of other locals in the Teamsters Joint Council attended in a body. Inspired by this backing, the grocery workers became more determined than ever to win the fight. Their picket lines remained solid and the struck companies were unable to make any deliveries.

In preparing its next move, the Citizens Alliance used a "civic" organization to hold a "law and order" rally. A demand was raised for more effective police action against strikers. This, in turn, was used as a propaganda cover for a plan to bring in hired thugs. The first move was made against what the Alliance seemed to consider a weak spot in the trade union front.

At the time the Flour and Cereal Mill Workers Union was on strike at the Archer-Daniels-Midland mill. On the evening of September 17 all but a skeleton force of pickets were at a union meeting. Taking advantage of this situation, the company had a railway coach run in on the mill siding. It contained about ten armed men and a quantity of supplies.

Word of the move was flashed to the mill strikers' meeting and to Local 544. Hundreds of mill pickets and sympathizers, including grocery strikers, rushed to the scene. There they gathered around the coach and the thugs soon came out carrying rifles. The cops on duty at the mill ordered them to put away the weapons. They returned inside the coach to do so. Then they came out again, armed this time with revolvers, and fired several shots in the direction of the pickets.

The angry workers responded by charging the thugs, who beat a hasty retreat back inside the railway car. But it had somehow caught fire, during the melee. So the cops had to rescue the company's hoodlums and escort them inside the mill for safety. At the very first attempt, the use of thuggery had backfired on the Citizens Alliance.

Turning to a new tactic, the Alliance set into motion a demand that the governor send troops against the strikers. The appeal for military intervention was made by Sheriff John Wall, who used the Archer-Daniels-Midland episode to make claims of "rioting and violence." Rumors began to appear in the boss press that the National Guard was being "mobilized for emergency action in Minneapolis labor disputes." Scare propaganda about a "food shortage" was intensified, implying that troops were coming to break the grocery strike. Attempting at the same time to give themselves an odor of sweet reasonableness, the grocery bosses were now meeting with the union — but negotiations stood at dead center. It had become quite a strikebreaking ploy.

With the class lines sharply drawn in the conflict, the Central Labor Union and the Building Trades Council made formal pledges of support to the grocery strikers. The Teamsters Joint Council voted to stop all deliveries to chain stores in the neighborhoods. They could no longer get milk, ice, or meat, to say nothing of groceries. Before long the outlet stores of two chains had to close down entirely.

Small wholesale grocery firms were also feeling the pressure. Some of these had already let the union know that they would like to settle the strike, but they were afraid to act because of threats of financial reprisals engineered by the Citizens Alliance. Now they found themselves being forced to the wall

as the big outfits tried to starve out the strikers. As a result
they began to break ranks and sign the union contract, taking their chances on what the future might bring.

Instead of being starved out, as the Alliance hoped, the grocery strikers were getting regular donations of money and
food from other trade unions and from farm organizations.
Generous contributions were made by independent neighborhood grocers, who realized that they had a stake in the union's
struggle against the chains. The Federal Workers Section took
the lead in forcing the city to put the strikers on the relief rolls.

With the tide of battle thus turning against the companies,
the minority of grocery workers who had resisted unionization began to join Local 544. If anything, the strike was gathering new momentum.

Then on October 7, after a war of almost two months, the
big wholesale grocery firms capitulated. A direct contract was
signed with Local 544 giving full union recognition. Wages
and conditions were brought up to the standards we had established elsewhere in the trucking industry. It was a sweeping victory for the workers.

In a number of other instances groups of employers had
been stalling off settlements with the union, waiting to see how
the grocery fight came out. These groups now began serious
negotiations with Local 544. Within a short time contract re-
newals were signed by the coal and transfer employers. An
agreement was obtained for the first time with the big department stores, covering drivers, helpers, and shipping-room and
warehouse employees. In every case important gains were
registered for the workers without having to resort to strike
action.

The mill owners also found themselves compelled to deal
with the Flour and Cereal Mill Workers Union.

A death blow had been struck to the Citizens Alliance as
such. In January 1937 the Alliance was formally dissolved
and the bosses reorganized themselves into a new setup called
Associated Industries. In an editorial headed, "The Leopard
Changes Its Spots," the *Northwest Organizer* characterized the
action:

"The recent announcement in the newspapers that the Citizens Alliance has disbanded, discharged its functionaries and
vacated its offices is to be taken with a grain of salt. . . .

"The same employers, the same labor haters and the same
people whose only outlook is to wreck, destroy and defeat
the trade union movement go to make up the membership
in the new employers' setup.

"But it would be also wrong to think that Minneapolis employers have not changed their tactics, method and strategy in dealing with their employees. The leadership who made up the policy of the 'defunct' Citizens Alliance were believers in head-on collisions with labor organizations and believed in beating the unions down with brute force. . . .

"A powerful trade union movement has grown here in the past three years which absolutely precludes the thought of anyone beating it by strong-armed tactics. A newer, more subtle and more sinister method of dealing with labor unions had to be devised by the employers. . . .

"In place of imported gunmen, thugs and strikebreakers will be substituted a small army of trained employer representatives, labor conciliators and employee relations directors. Their policy will be to outfumble the unions in negotiations, write union agreements with double meanings and buy off union representatives with money and favors.

"The new Minneapolis labor movement has reached a most dangerous stage in its history," the editorial warned. "Trade union leaders whose courage is unquestioned and who have the ability to fight to the death on the picket line are apt to fall a prey to the new spokesmen of employers' groups. Labor must be doubly on its guard."

As the very appearance of the editorial in the union paper testified, things were going quite well on this count within the leadership of Local 544. Experiences in the grocery strike had brought Corcoran, Murphy, Smith, and Wagner closer to our views on union-employer relations. This trend was reflected in a unanimous executive board recommendation that the membership approve a "model contract" intended as a guide for the union staff in negotiations with the bosses. As officially adopted, it contained the following key points:

1.   Contracts with employers to be limited to a term of one year.

2.   Demands concerning wages and working conditions to be decided in consultation with the union members involved in each particular case.

3.   Premium pay to be received for overtime, with the added provision that there be no overtime until all employees on the job worked their full quota of regular hours.

4.   If the work week should be reduced by legislative act, rates of pay to be increased in the proportion necessary to guarantee that there would be no reduction in total weekly pay. (This demand was connected with the general union struggle for a shorter work week to reduce unemployment.)

5.   Disputes over seniority standing to be settled by the union.

The employer to have no voice in the matter.

6. Back pay owed to workers because of contract violations by the employer to be computed at two times the regular wage rate.

7. Formal recognition to be required from the employer of the union's right to operate its job steward system.

8. The union to retain the right to strike over employer violations of the working agreement.

9. No boss to order his employees to go through a picket line of a striking union.

None of these provisions represented mere bargaining points to be used for horse-trading in negotiations with employers. Each and every one constituted a matter of basic policy. All were enforced accordingly in actual practice. As staff director, it was my job to see that this was the case.

So far as possible the members of the union staff worked in pairs: one from former Local 574, the other from former "Local 500." This helped us not only to exert progressive influence on the newcomers to the staff, but also to instill in them the team concept of leadership. The latter objective was also helped along by our success in retaining the policy of equal staff pay at a level no higher than that received by skilled workers in the industry.

Organization of staff work had to be carried out under complex conditions. The fusion in practice of two previously hostile forces was only part of the problem. There was a very substantial and rapidly growing union membership. Contracts had to be negotiated with a large number of employers, and they had to be enforced. New patterns of expanded organizational activity also had to be developed if the full potential of favorable objective conditions was to be realized.

To attain these various ends, staff operations were divided into three broad categories. Some teams were assigned to field work, looking toward expansion of the union power. Others were given the task of handling negotiations with the bosses. Still others got the job of settling grievances arising from employer violations of existing contracts.

Standard procedures were codified for the handling of grievances, as had been done in the case of contract negotiations. A suitable form was devised for the recording of all grievances in writing, both to assure that the necessary information was provided by the workers involved and to make certain that their complaints did not get lost in the shuffle. It was union policy to assume that the worker was always right. If a boss claimed that a grievance had been filed unjustly, the burden of proof was upon him. In every instance the grievance report had to be returned to me, as staff director, with a written account of the disposition of the case.

Verification of contract enforcement along these lines gave rise to a problem involving two organizers who had come onto the staff from former "Local 500," Eddie and Al Firotto. Neither of them seemed to have had much trade union experience, yet they insisted on working together. This made it hard to use their services. So I did the best I could by assigning them to handle grievances at small companies where the problems were relatively uncomplicated and the union could easily bring the necessary pressure to bear upon the bosses.

After a time they were found to be accepting favors from employers. In reporting the matter to the executive board I also mentioned that they showed little interest in trade union work and might not be adverse to looking elsewhere for employment. It was agreed that I should talk with them along these lines. I did so, and seeing the logic of the situation, the Firotto brothers voluntarily withdrew from the union staff.

Before long another situation arose, this time concerning Joe Bellini, who had also come onto the staff from former "Local 500." He was found to have assaulted a rank-and-file member of the union. Brown, Skoglund, and I made a motion in the executive board that he be fired forthwith. Murphy, Smith, and Wagner voted against our motion.

Up to this point we had been able to reach the necessary decisions by concensus in the executive board. In the given situation it had been the best procedure, both sides seemed to feel, since we were in the process of shaping principled leadership cooperation with good will on both sides. Now, however, we were deadlocked, and for the first time Corcoran would have to cast the deciding vote in his capacity as "neutral" chairman of the board.

Corcoran—like Murphy, Smith, and Wagner—seemed to feel a sense of obligation toward Bellini, who had served with them in the earlier fight against us. At the same time he knew that we were deadly in earnest about our motion. If he voted against us, we would immediately take the issue to the union membership. A matter of principle was involved. Under no circumstances could physical abuse of rank and filers by union officials be tolerated.

Corcoran decided to resolve the bind by voting with us, and Bellini was summarily fired from the union staff.

Murphy, Smith, and Wagner accepted the decision with good grace. Our collective leadership relations continued as before, even when one or two others from former "Local 500" dropped off the union staff voluntarily, not seeming to like the discipline that had now been firmly established.

A point had been reached where the former Local 574 members on the union staff were ready to initiate the surviving newcomers into the "Order of the Fourth Degree." The ritual was simple, though somewhat violent. A candidate for the degree was taken to a bar by four members of the order. There he was seated with them in a booth, the seating being arranged so that he could not escape. Drinks were then ordered, naturally at the candidate's expense. Glasses were raised for a toast, and when the novice attempted to take a sip, the others set to pounding him lustily on the arms, causing him to spill the drink. The process was repeated until the victim managed to sip his potion. Then, battered and bruised, he was proclaimed a member of the order.

Since initiation was offered only to individuals for whom those holding the "Fourth Degree" had respect, it was actually meant as an honor, even though the procedure was rough. In this case, therefore, it was a sign of the growing affinity of the two components in the union leadership, an affinity that was now based largely on common adherence to principled union policies of a class-struggle character.

Advances were also being registered in yet another way. Pat Corcoran had become impressed with the potential for union growth that was apparent in the new situation. He began to respond to the opportunity in a way that reflected a capacity to envisage union-building on a larger scale. As a starter he initiated several steps to strengthen the Teamsters Joint Council, using his post as its organizer for the purpose.

A new charter, as Local 289, was obtained for bakery drivers, among whom an organization campaign was just beginning to take hold. Harry DeBoer, who had been an officer of former Local 574, was elected organizer of the new local. Later he became its president.

Ice Drivers Local 221 — which had long existed as little more than a caricature of a union — was completely reorganized. Two members of former Local 574's organization staff, Ray Rainbolt and Kelly Postal, were elected as the principal officers of the reorganized local. Rainbolt became president; Postal was designated secretary-treasurer.

As part of this project Local 544 turned its ice drivers over to Local 221, doing so with the agreement of the workers involved. The opposite course of liquidating 221 into 544 could not have been taken without risking friction with Tobin. Since that would have been unwise — and since the reorganized

local would now be under capable leadership — we thought
it best to transfer the ice drivers. It seemed to be the only
way in which the necessary working class unity could be at-
tained within the industry.

Except for our voluntary transfer of the ice drivers, no
other section of Local 544 was touched in any way during
the following period.

Another forward step was taken when the offices of the Teamsters Joint Council and all its affiliates were moved to the
Local 544 headquarters. The entire building was taken over
for the purpose, almost doubling the available space. Considerable remodeling was done to streamline the office and
meeting facilities to suit expanded needs.

Space in the remodeled headquarters was also made available to Power Workers Local 160 and Furniture Workers
Local 1859. Both these organizations had become staunch
allies of the Teamsters, because of the help we had given them,
and they wanted to come as close as they could to having
an integral part in our operating structure.

Another occupant was Warehouse and Inside Workers Local 20316, which had recently been chartered by the AFL.
This local, led by James Bartlett and Robert F. Tibbetts, was
organizing among some of the most exploited sections of the
working class; young, unskilled, and women workers. One
of its first campaigns, for example, was conducted at Sears-
Roebuck, an open-shop, low-wage outfit of national notoriety.

All in all, quite a powerhouse was becoming concentrated
at 257 Plymouth Avenue North. New leverage was thus gained
in the drive to widen our influence within the IBT, an effort
that had already gotten under way.

14. We Reach Outward

A draft program for a Teamster expansion drive had been published in the *Northwest Organizer* of July 15, 1936. It said in the key passages:

"The first move that must be made is the erection of a Northwest Teamsters Joint Council. This organization must act as a clearing house and should coordinate the organizational activities of a staff of trained, efficient organizers. . . .

"The hardest part of such a program would be the bringing under Union conditions of drivers in small centers of population and those who are employed in more or less isolated communities. The only logical way that truck drivers and transportation workers employed in small towns and villages can be unionized is by setting up local unions in various strategic centers throughout the state which would draw their membership . . . [from] various small communities located within the radius of, let us say, 50 miles from the place where the drivers' local is situated. . . .

"No better proving ground for the attempted solution of this problem can be imagined than Minnesota where there already exists a progressive, intelligently directed labor movement."

In the same issue the union paper discussed the organization of over-the-road drivers, who hauled freight, household goods, etc., between cities, sometimes across very long distances. The central problem was stated as follows:

"Attempting to organize long distance truck transportation drivers in various local communities, without a national program to coordinate the efforts of various local agencies, can never accomplish the desired results.

"Overland truck drivers occupy a position in industry very similar to that of the railroad worker. He cannot be a non-union man at one end of his run and a union man at the other. . . .

"It becomes obvious that what is needed, before the long distance driver can be unionized, is a well planned, well financed and well directed national campaign. The old haphazard manner of attempting to organize the overland drivers in one community at a time will achieve just about the results that have been accomplished up to now. That is, practically nothing. . . .

"Hundreds of thousands of long distance truck drivers are awaiting some agency that can improve their conditions of employment and bring their wages to a living level. The time is right for such a campaign to be started."

Unionization of over-the-road drivers and organization in depth of Teamster formations in new localities were interrelated tasks, as the *Northwest Organizer* pointed out.

Take the case of line drivers from open-shop towns coming into a union stronghold like Minneapolis, for example. They had to join the IBT and their employers were compelled to pay the wage scale we had established for such work. The bosses involved could scarcely refuse to meet these conditions, because the alternative was to cease operating in the city.

An organizational nucleus came into being at the open-shop end of such over-the-road runs. The impetus this gave to unionization in those localities was further reinforced by the wage hikes the line drivers received, which were often quite dramatic.

Leverage thus gained could be used, in turn, for a breakthrough in the local cartage setup, which serviced the now-unionized line operations. From that foothold, organization could then be extended to other branches of local trucking and the associated occupations.

This process, of course, presupposed support of budding organizations by other, stronger IBT units in the area. The direct help of experienced organizers was needed. Backing had to be forthcoming when a new union was forced to take strike action — in order to win recognition and make gains for the membership.

To the extent that organization in depth could be accomplished along these lines in outlying towns, the way would be opened to use the new strong points for the unionization of line drivers coming from even more remote open shop terminals. At the same time, chain grocery firms, wholesale distributing networks, etc., could be brought under union control on a district basis. Before these objectives could be realized, however, a Teamster conference of broad geographic scope had to be constructed.

As a first step toward that end we arranged early in Au-

gust 1936 for joint consultation with two other Minnesota
unions holding General Drivers jurisdiction: Local 120 of St.
Paul and Local 346 of Duluth. An understanding was reached
with them, in principle, on the need to develop more extensive Teamster cooperation, beginning on a statewide basis.

In addition Local 120 agreed to join with Local 544 in a
combined drive for the complete unionization of freight trucking
in Minneapolis and St. Paul. An initial move of this kind was
especially important, because the two cities actually constituted
one metropolitan area with an artificial dividing line between
them. Divergences in the progress of Locals 120 and 544,
therefore, were bound to be harmful. Mutual gains achieved
through close working relationships, on the other hand, could
forge a formidable Teamster base in the Twin Cities from
which to reach outward.

Further progress was registered a few weeks later at the
Cloquet convention of the Minnesota State Federation of Labor.
A caucus of Teamster delegates to the convention was held
to discuss the need for organized collaboration. The discussion brought to light numerous problems confronting IBT
locals in various parts of the state. A decision was reached
then and there to form a provisional state council and create
a central agency to unify and coordinate Teamster activities.

About this time we were able to help the Fargo truck drivers
begin a union comeback in that North Dakota city. Early
in 1935 Tobin had revoked their charter, thereby contributing
heavily to the defeat of a bitterly fought strike. Since then
they had held together a nucleus of militants, waiting for an
opportunity to resume their fight against the bosses. Pat Corcoran, now able and willing to give them a boost, backed
them in obtaining a new IBT charter, this time as Local 116.
Already a relationship was being reconstituted that would take
us across state lines.

As had been agreed in the Cloquet talks, a conference of
Teamster locals was held in Minneapolis on January 10, 1937.
Pat Corcoran gave the main report. The old ideas did not
suit the needs of the day, he said. New methods and forms
were required to organize workers engaged in trucking. As
that step was accomplished, our purpose should be to establish uniform wages, hours, and working conditions throughout the entire district. There were no ulterior plans for cap-
turing any local unions to build a power bloc, he assured
the delegates. Nothing more was intended than an honest,
sincere program of cooperation.

The conference decided to launch a North Central District

Drivers Council (NCDDC). Corcoran was elected president and I was designated secretary of the new body. The scope of the district was tentatively defined to include the Dakotas, Iowa, Minnesota, Wisconsin, and upper Michigan.

St. Paul Local 120 did not participate in the conference. Tobin's agent, John Geary, seemed largely responsible for the local thus reneging on its earlier commitment. Apparently he didn't want the Minneapolis rebels messing around in the nice, tidy, old-line Teamster setup over which he presided in that city.

We bypassed the St. Paul problem for the moment and gave immediate attention to Wisconsin. Another of Tobin's general organizers, Henry Berger, who based himself in Chicago, was riding herd over Teamster locals in this bordering state. Rumors persisted that Berger was bad mouthing us wherever he went. So Corcoran and I decided to attend an IBT conference held in Green Bay toward the end of January.

There we found the delegates badly misinformed about the aims and objects of the NCDDC. They seemed eager to get the facts, though, which gave us an opportunity to get in some licks about the need for a change in Teamster organization methods. Although our efforts didn't bring the eastern Wisconsin locals directly into the council, as we had projected, at least we had made some friends among them.

Following this episode, Corcoran, L. A. Murphy, and I went to a meeting of the International Executive Board held in Washington, D.C. It was the first time Tobin and I had met personally. Both of us observed the amenities of the occasion, but with a stiffness that reflected our hostile relations of the past.

Corcoran spoke for us before the board. The tenor of his remarks was to give assurance that matters were going well in Local 544 and that harmony prevailed in the Minneapolis Teamsters Joint Council. Afterward Tobin asked for a private talk with Corcoran and Murphy. They later informed me that he had questioned them concerning the district council we were building. Their replies, they felt, had eased his suspicions about the project.

During the trip we also stopped in Chicago. Primarily through Murphy's contacts in the city, we were able to explain our expansion plans in Teamster circles and even stimulate some interest in the project. Berger's voice was no longer the only one heard there on this count.

Beginning in March, Corcoran and I made an extensive tour of Minnesota and the Dakotas, speaking as officers of the NCDDC. The itinerary included the towns where Teamsters locals already existed and others where we sought to get new formations started. Pat's former conservative role in the AFL was useful in advancing our aims. His reputation among right wingers enabled him to solicit active cooperation from officers of the AFL State Federations in North and South Dakota, which proved to be most helpful.

Our tour served primarily as a groundbreaking operation. Wherever we struck pay dirt, follow-up action was taken by other organizers from the stronger unions, especially Minneapolis Locals 544 and 471, also Duluth Local 346. After a time Walter Hagstrom, a Local 544 job steward at the Yellow Cab Company and a Trotskyist, was put on full time as an NCDDC Organizer. He worked mainly in North Dakota, where the organizational tempo was rapidly accelerating.

Elsewhere in the district a dispute soon developed with the Gamble-Robinson wholesale produce chain (also known as Nash-Finch). It started in northern Minnesota. The company was prepared to negotiate with Local 346 in Duluth but it refused to deal with the union in Hibbing. In keeping with NCDDC norms, Local 346, the stronger union, refused to settle until Hibbing was included. This forced the company to grant concessions to its employees in both towns.

About a week later IBT Local 662 in Eau Claire, Wisconsin, struck the Gamble-Robinson branch in that city. The NCDDC gave maximum support to the embattled workers and they soon won. In a settlement reaching far beyond Eau Claire, the company signed a blanket agreement covering all its branches in the district where a union contract had not previously been obtained. In some of these branches, especially in the smallest towns, wages were almost doubled. Termination dates were made identical, putting the workers in a strong position to renegotiate improved terms a year later.

The NCDDC had thus been directly instrumental in switching cash from the bosses' pockets into those of the workers. Moreover, it had been done against one of the biggest, most notoriously antilabor outfits in the region. News of the victory swept across the prairies like a grass fire. Workers in town after town were inspired to pitch into the Teamster campaign with renewed vigor.

Their response was a mark of the way in which the radicalization of those days was spreading among the masses, extending from the major cities to the most isolated pockets in the country's population.

Reacting logically from their class viewpoint, the capitalists undertook to weaken the growing Teamster power at its source, Local 544. In Minneapolis they were now better organized than ever through their new setup, the Associated Industries. Its counterpart had also been developed in St. Paul, with a setup in trucking known as the Employers Compliance Committee. Acting together, the Twin Cities bosses sought to use against us the shortcomings of Local 120, which was poorly led.

Their plan was to stand firm against renewal of contracts with Local 544 until the harshest possible terms had been imposed upon the weaker union in St. Paul. A propaganda basis would thereby be laid to refuse new concessions in Minneapolis and to demand instead that we give up previously won gains. By launching a flank attack of this nature upon Local 544, rather than trying head-on to deal it a crushing blow as in the past, they hoped to undermine the local's power.

Our first response was to let the bosses know that we understood what they were up to, hoping thereby to throw a scare into some of the more jittery ones. Through an editorial in the *Northwest Organizer,* we declared: "If Minneapolis employers want war they shall have it, but the blood will be on their hands, not ours."

Meantime we set to work on the problem of developing joint action with Local 120. In this connection Corcoran, Murphy, Smith, and Wagner gave a big assist in their capacity as members of Local 544's executive board. They used their influence in the IBT to arrange a meeting with International officials on the subject. A session was held in Indianapolis, with committees from both locals and with John Geary present. There an understanding was reached that the two unions should cooperate in an effort to equalize wages in the Twin Cities trucking industry.

Common demands for a higher wage scale were then agreed upon. This meant that St. Paul workers, whose pay rates had lagged, would get a bigger raise than workers in Minneapolis. No problem resulted for us, however, because our membership understood the need for this seeming inequality in the process of establishing wage parity. It was recognized that attainment of the goal would in the long run lead to far greater gains.

When the demands were served upon the transfer firms, Local 120 indicated that it would go on strike if they were refused. In Local 544's case, the membership voted blanket strike authority to the executive board. This was done since contracts up for renewal involved other sections of the industry besides the transfer companies and delicate matters of timing in developing our tactics were to be considered.

To show that we meant business, Local 544 first struck the big furniture stores on June 16. A week later the Minneapolis transfer bosses capitulated, as a strike was about to be called against them. They signed a contract conceding the demand for a minimum wage of seventy cents an hour, which set a new high in the industry. Our victory broke the united front of the Associated Industries. It also reversed the strategic situation the bosses had tried to create on a Twin City scale.

In St. Paul the transfer companies refused to accept the Minneapolis settlement terms, and Local 120 called a strike against them on June 23. Local 544 immediately went all out to support the picketing and to contribute know-how from its own considerable strike experience. Specialists were assigned to help in every department of activity.

With the aid of these experienced hands, cruising squad techniques were introduced into the picketing. Commissary facilities were set up. A womens' auxiliary was formed to take part in the struggle. The *Northwest Organizer* staff got out a daily strike bulletin. At the strikers' request, a representative of Local 544 also assisted in negotiations with the bosses.

Unions outside the Twin Cities, belonging to the NCDDC, supported the fight by refusing to truck anything normally handled by Local 120.

The strike had scarcely begun when the Regulated Motor Transportation Association broke the bosses' ranks and signed up with the union (a subject to which we shall return later). Since the Association represented big firms engaged in long distance hauling, their action represented a major breakthrough for Local 120. Despite this change in the situation, however, the companies engaged in local hauling persisted desperately in their efforts to defeat the union.

Paid ads were run in the daily papers attacking Arthur F. Hudson, Local 120's president, in an effort to sow dissension among the strikers. After twisting the issues involved, one ad brazenly asserted: "The only conclusion to be drawn is that the president of your union, dominated by the leaders of Local No. 544, has considered his personal power and program of more importance than the welfare of both St. Paul truck drivers, and the public."

An episode in the strike was then seized upon to press even more viciously the fake issue of Local 544's "domination." One day a scab truck went off the highway into a ditch. Bill Brown, who happened to be in the vicinity, was arrested. He was charged with "highway robbery," which carried a prison sentence of five to forty years. A smear campaign was launched in the press on the basis of the charge, and the bosses showed every sign of seeking to convict him.

The threat brought a declaration from the NCDDC that it would call a forty-eight hour protest strike of its 20,000 members in four states if Brown was prosecuted. An attempt to weaken the Teamsters' council at its center was turning into a new danger for the bosses on the periphery of the district. This caused cooler heads within the ruling class to intervene and the charges against Brown were finally dismissed.

While all this was going on, the picket lines had remained solid. Close feelings of comradeship had arisen between Locals 120 and 544 as we stood shoulder to shoulder in struggle. If there was to be any surrender, it would have to come from the bosses, and that is exactly what happened.

After an eight-day walkout, the transfer companies came to terms with the union. Wage rates comparable to those paid in Minneapolis were established. In fact, the gains in the contract generally were so impressive that the strikers could hardly believe what they were hearing when the settlement terms were read at the ratification meeting.

Considering the victory they had won — and the help they had received — there was no longer any question whether the officers and members of Local 120 would thereafter be active supporters of the NCDDC.

Now that the key fight had been won, Local 544 turned its attention to its own contract problems. The furniture store strike had already been settled to the workers' advantage. Before long, renewal of agreements with other sections of the trucking employers were negotiated without a fight. In every case the bosses gave in on the main points. The Associated Industries scheme to undermine the union's power had burst like a bubble in the wind.

As though to add a touch of irony, Local 544 organized the private chauffeurs of the wealthy class. The move was started by former cab drivers now holding such jobs. There were no negotiations. The union simply sent the individual employers a letter setting the minimum wage that they had to pay, as it had been decided by the workers involved. Few of them offered any objections. They apparently feared that union cruising squads would force their limousines to the curb if they resisted.

Summing up the general wage gains of Local 544 members in his own inimitable style, Bill Brown wrote in the *Northwest*

Organizer: "Remember, about three years ago we were just winning our 42 1/2¢ an hour, which the bosses insisted was nothing more nor less than Communism. The 70-75¢ hourly that we are now getting must put us in some advanced stage of Utopia that hasn't been named yet."

Our leap forward in the Twin Cities gave fresh impetus to the Teamster campaign throughout the district. New locals were chartered in three towns, making a total of eleven such units formed since the drive began. Two of them were in Marshalltown and Mason City, which signified the start of a penetration into Iowa.

The third was in Winona, located in southeastern Minnesota. This region of the state had always been a stronghold of anti-unionism. In fact, it was from Winona that scab trucks had been sent to Minneapolis during the 1935 Strutwear strike. Now, two years later, the AFL was making its first breakthrough in that vicinity.

During August newly formed IBT Local 799 struck Winona's ice, coal, lumber, and transfer industries, where about 250 workers had been organized. The union won substantial wage gains and other advances, firmly establishing itself in the town.

In this period strikes against various types of trucking firms were also conducted in Brainerd, Eau Claire, Mankato, and Minot. The bosses tried in some cases to form company unions in an effort to beat the IBT; in others, railroad police, along with the town cops, were used against strikers; and in Mankato attempts were made to organize vigilantes, factory whistles being used as a signal for mobilization. However, none of these anti-union ploys worked.

All the strikes were won by the Teamsters. Pay increases of as much as 64 percent (Minot) were registered. Hours, which had mostly been insufferably long, were cut to forty-eight a week. Union recognition was reinforced by setting up steward systems to assure employer compliance with the contracts. In some cases the union victories were followed by "fink drives," emulating Local 544's technique.

With its campaign thus rolling along, the NCDDC held a conference in September 18-19, 1937, at Hibbing, Minnesota. There were eighty-three delegates present, representing twenty-nine IBT locals in the district. Deliberations centered around a report by the Field Committee, the council's leading body, which was included in the minutes of the gathering. The key passages stated:

"It is important to recognize that the general work of the

Council is now rapidly passing into a second decisive phase. During the first stage the work centered mainly around the establishment of Local Unions and the creation of machinery for the organization of these unions and the drafting of demands to be presented to the employers. This phase of the work still remains to be done in several localities.

"However, a large section of the Council has now passed into that stage of development where negotiations are underway with the employers and strike action may become necessary. This creates a great demand for experienced men to meet with the employers and generally to direct the strategy of the Union in taking the necessary action to secure signed contracts. It further requires that the closest possible cooperation be established between the various Local Unions and the Field Committee of the Council.

"Many mistakes will be made, but it is vital to remember that a serious blunder by a Local Union, which results in defeat at the hands of the employers, would have a detrimental effect on all Local Unions in the Council.

"It is also important to keep uppermost in our minds the fact that we have in the first stages caught the bosses off their guard but they will resist vigorously our efforts at unionization and will use every instrument at their command to this end. . . .

"It must be remembered that in the final analysis the Council represents only a voluntary organization of Local Unions acting in concert so that the strength of one may be the strength of all. It therefore follows that the weakness of one Local becomes the weakness of all Locals and when a Local Union does not carry its share of the load, the work of the Council is seriously hampered. . . .

"We clearly understand that we are dealing with human beings and not with blue prints and that under the happiest of circumstances we all have many shortcomings; but it is just because of these facts that we earnestly appeal to all of the delegates and to all of the Local Unions to recognize the nature of our Council and the handicaps under which it functions and do all in their power to exert a full degree of initiative and cooperation in making successful the organization of all the drivers in the district."

The conference approved the perspectives set forth by the Field Committee. In addition, a resolution was passed advocating that the AFL adopt the industrial type of organization, a form which the newly created IBT locals were tending to emulate. Feeling themselves better geared for the struggle, the delegates returned to their various localities, and a new wave of battles against the bosses soon developed.

During October a three-week strike was conducted in Fargo at over-the-road and local cartage firms. The union won a solid victory, gaining full recognition by the employers. Marked advances were scored on wages, hours, and working conditions. After a delay of two years and yet another stiff fight, Local 116 had overcome the defeat which Tobin had imposed upon its predecessor in 1935.

While this action was taking place, a walkout also developed some miles to the north at Grand Forks, North Dakota. It involved workers in the transfer, bakery, market, and wholesale grocery industries and the conflicts lasted from a few days to three weeks at the various companies. Despite ruling class use of violence against the workers, IBT Local 581 broke through on every front. Significant concessions were won from the employers. A new and higher level of trade unionism had been reached in that previously benighted town.

In the neighboring state of South Dakota a bitter conflict developed within a few weeks at Sioux Falls. Jack Maloney and Happy Holstein, of the old Local 574 staff, had been sent there at the request of Teamster Local 749. This union, which had only recently been chartered, was concentrating at the time on the organization of long distance and local cartage drivers. The bosses refused to deal with it, and a strike was called during November.

Scabs were brought in and the police were issued riot gear in an attempt to crush the walkout. Two pitched battles resulted, one at Munce Bros. Transfer, the other at Wilson Transportation. Although several workers received injuries when the cops attacked with gas and clubs, their picket lines were firmly held. In the end the companies capitulated to the union and yet another advance was registered by the NCDDC.

In the meantime, though, a grievous blow to the Teamster campaign had been struck in Minneapolis.

SPECIAL BULLETIN

THE NORTHWEST ORGANIZER

Official Organ of the Minneapolis Teamsters Joint Council

MINNEAPOLIS, MINNESOTA, FRIDAY, NOV. 19, 1937

P. J. Corcoran Slain; Rites Saturday—
TJC Calls Holiday For Morning, 9-12

Governor Benson Offers $500 for Pat's Murderers

On Thursday Governor Elmer A. Benson offered a reward of $500 for information leading to the arrest and conviction of the slayer or slayers of Patrick Corcoran. In a statement accompanying the offer, Governor Benson said: "The murder of Patrick J. Corcoran of Minneapolis is a challenge to the forces of law and order in this state and no effort must be spared to solve this brutal crime . . . This case cannot be allowed to rest until the killer or killers have been brought to justice."

STATEMENT OF MINNEAPOLIS TEAMSTERS JOINT COUNCIL

Minneapolis Teamsters Joint Council No. 32, is horrified at the apparent cold-blooded slaying of Patrick J. Corcoran, Secretary-Treasurer of the Teamsters' Joint Council.

Pat Corcoran has led an uncompromising fight against Minneapolis employers and has unquestionably been in the interest of the interest of the workers encurred the enemity of a large section of Minneapolis employers and their agents. There can be little doubt but that many of the employers who have dealt with Corcoran during the past two years have reason to wish for his elimination. It is obvious that one who fights consistently in the interest of the workers makes enemies. Those enemies are known and threats received over a period of time, indicate how seriously Corcoran's death was desired.

The Teamsters' Joint Council and all of its affiliated locals hold nothing but the highest respect and admiration for the work that Corcoran has carried out. He knew of the danger that confronted him but in spite of this insisted on carrying on his struggle to improve the conditions of those who toil. We are convinced that the dastardly murder of Pat Corcoran will only serve to spur the Drivers' Unions to even greater organizational efforts. His murder will not go unavenged. Teamsters' Council No. 32 pledge themselves to carry forward to a successful conclusion the campaign which was inaugurated by Corcoran. If the employers and their agents think that by murdering individuals they will be able to wreak their will upon the working class, they have murdered in vain.

We will carry on.

STATEMENT OF GENERAL DRIVERS LOCAL 544

Local 544, Minneapolis General Drivers Union, is moved to sorrow as Patrick J. Corcoran, official of the Local Union, falls to his death under assassins' bullets. Pat Corcoran and the Drivers Union at one time were on opposite sides. Since that time, however, and since the time the Local Drivers Union returned to the Drivers' International, there has been no more staunch supporter, or truer friend, than Corcoran. Since the rapprochement between the one-time outlaw union (574) and the A. F. of L. there has been no one who has accorded greater support to the Drivers than Pat Corcoran. He has been our friend and has indicated by his every act that he has been actively interested in furthering the interest of the Minneapolis Teaming crafts. Not only has he actively participated in the organization of the General Drivers Union, but he has in that same period assisted in the unionization of the Bakery Drivers, Laundry Drivers, Tea and Coffee Drivers and several other hitherto unorganized sections of the Drivers movement.

Corcoran was one of the foremost movers in the formation of the North Central District Drivers Council, a union Council which brought into its fold all of the northwest teaming craft locals. During his fight for unionization of Northwest Trucking Workers, Corcoran had made enemies, who, no doubt, desired his death. If assassination of teaming craft leaders is the answer of the employees, then Local 544 says, you may kill who you may think are the leaders. But we have trained people who will go forward with the fight. When all of the Driving Craft Work-

Teamsters Offer $10,000 For Corcoran's Assassins

Labor Movement Joins Drivers in Observance of Holiday Saturday; Funeral at St. Mary's Basilica

On Wednesday night around ten o'clock Patrick J. Corcoran, Secretary-Treasurer of the Minneapolis Teamsters Joint Council and Chairman of the North Central District Drivers Council, was foully and brutally assassinated near his home.

Earlier in the evening, he had attended a meeting of the Laundry Drivers Local, held at the headquarters of the Council, 257 Plymouth Avenue North. He left the meeting for his home, put his automobile in his garage, and started for the door. It was then that his assailant or assailants attacked him, beat him, crushed his skull, and sent a bullet crashing into his brain. His snow-covered body was discovered by a neighbor at 11:30 p. m.

A Cowardly Act

It was some time before the horrible news of his assassination leaked out. With sorrow, with anger, his trade union brothers, his friends, members of the trade union movement, heard of the cowardly, dastardly act.

The body of the martyred trade union leader was taken to the county morgue. Later, officials of the Teamsters Joint Council and a representative of the Northwest Organizer went to the morgue, identified themselves and asked to see the body. They were refused admission. Representatives of the daily press had no difficulty in viewing the body of the murdered man.

Surviving are his wife, two sons, Edmund and Patrick, Jr., two daughters, Betty and Janet, three brothers, John, James and Alphonse. He lived at 28 Penn Avenue South.

Council Meets Immediately

On Thursday morning at 10 o'clock a special executive meeting of the Minneapolis Teamsters Joint Council was held in the Council headquarters.

The executive meeting decreed that the Council offers a reward of Ten Thousand Dollars for the apprehension and conviction of those responsible for the murder of Corcoran. It further decreed that a Holiday of all members of the Teaming Crafts in Minneapolis be held Saturday, November 20, to permit members to attend the last services for the martyred trade unionist, to be held at 11 a. m. Saturday at the Basilica of St. Mary. Members observing this Holiday need not fear that either their jobs or their standing in their Union will be jeopardized. Miles Dunne was elected to fill temporarily the post of Secretary-Treasurer of the Council.

Saturday Union Holiday

The rest of the Minneapolis trade union movement is called upon by the Council to join with it in observing the Holiday on Saturday. All unions affiliated to the North Central District Drivers Council, of which Patrick Corcoran was chairman, have been notified of the actions of the Minneapolis Joint Council, and invited to send delegations to observe the funeral. Thursday afternoon, officials of the Warehouse and Inside Workers Union, Local 20316, called upon all of its members to join with members of the Teamsters Joint Council in observing the Holiday. Officials of the Federal Workers Section of Local 544 had already taken similar action. It was believed that many other unions would rapidly follow suit.

After 12 o'clock noon on Saturday, any driver if he so wishes, may take his truck on the street, with the full sanction of the Teamsters Joint Council. Milk and bakery drivers will begin deliveries at midnight Friday, and are to be off the street by 9 o'clock Saturday morning.

PAT CORCORAN'S UNION RECORD

Prior to 1922—Active in the railroad unions.

June, 1922—Initiated into Milk Drivers Union Local No. 471.

April, 1932—Elected Business Agent of Local 471.

April, 1935—Elected Secretary-Treasurer of Local 471, which office he held until January, 1937. He then became Business Representative and Financial Secretary-Treasurer of the Teamsters Joint Council No. 32. He was also Chairman of the North Central District Drivers Council; Chairman of the Board of Union Business Agents; Vice-president for the Fifth District of the Minnesota State Federation of Labor.

ers in the Northwest are organized and operating under union conditions, we will be satisfied.

Pat Corcoran is a martyr and has suffered a martyr's fate, but his martyrdom will only spur us on to greater efforts.

STATEMENT OF YELLOW CAB SECTION, LOCAL 544

The membership of this section wishes to express its deepest concern and sympathy in the loss of a leader who has so ably demonstrated in the past his ability fearlessly and courageously to lead his followers in organization drives . . . In our estimation . . . Continued on other side

Patrick J. Corcoran

"Mourn not the dead who in the still earth lie,
Dust unto dust,
That calm sweet earth that mothers all who die,
As all men must.

But rather mourn the apathetic throng,
The cowed and meek,
Who see the world's great anguish and its wrong
And dare not speak."

$10,000 Reward is Offered for Slayers

Front page of the November 19, 1937, Northwest Organizer following the murder of Patrick J. Corcoran (shown in photo).

15. Murder in Cold Blood

"On Wednesday night around ten o'clock Patrick J. Corcoran, Secretary-Treasurer of the Minneapolis Teamsters Joint Council and Chairman of the North Central District Drivers Council, was foully and brutally assassinated near his home.

"Earlier in the evening, he had attended a meeting of the Laundry Drivers Local, held at the headquarters of the Council, 257 Plymouth Avenue North. He left the meeting for his home, put his automobile in his garage, and started for the door. It was then that his assailant or assailants attacked him, beat him, crushed his skull, and sent a bullet crashing into his brain. His snow-covered body was discovered by a neighbor at 11:30 P.M."

In these terse paragraphs the murder of the Teamster leader on November 17, 1937, was described in a special edition of the *Northwest Organizer.* The union paper also reported:

"On Thursday morning at ten o'clock a special executive meeting of the Teamsters Joint Council was held in the Council headquarters. The executive meeting decreed that the Council offers a reward of Ten Thousand Dollars for the apprehension and conviction of those responsible for the murder of Corcoran. It further decreed that a Holiday of all members of the Teaming Crafts in Minneapolis be held Saturday, November 20, to permit members to attend the last services for the martyred trade unionist, to be held at the Basilica of St. Mary. . . .

"Miles Dunne was elected to fill temporarily the post of Secretary-Treasurer of the Council." (Later Miles was formally elected by the Joint Council delegates to a full term in the post.)

The executive meeting of the Council also issued a public statement, which declared: "Pat Corcoran has led an uncompromising fight against Minneapolis employers and has unquestionably by his unswerving loyalty to the interests of the workers incurred the enmity of a large section of Minneapolis

employers and their agents. There can be little doubt but that
many of the employers who have dealt with Corcoran during
the past two years have reason to wish for his elimination."

In a statement issued simultaneously, Local 544 asserted:
"Pat Corcoran and the Drivers Union at one time were on
opposite sides. Since that time, however, and since the time the
Local Drivers Union returned to the Drivers' International,
there has been no more staunch supporter, or truer friend,
than Corcoran. Since the rapprochement between the one-time
outlaw union (574) and the AFL, there has been no one who
has accorded greater support to the Drivers than Pat Corcoran.
He has been our friend and has indicated by his every act
that he has been actively interested in furthering the interests
of the Minneapolis Teaming crafts. . . .

"During his fight for unionization of Northwest trucking
workers, Corcoran had made enemies, who, no doubt, desired
his death. If assassination of teaming craft leaders is the answer of the employers, then Local 544 says, you may kill
who you may think are the leaders. But we have trained people
who will go forward with the fight."

The next day Miles Dunne and Ray Sawyer, president of
the Milk Drivers Union, went on the radio. They broadcast
to the whole city the Joint Council's offer of a $10,000 reward
for the apprehension and conviction of Pat's killers. In addition
they notified all workers of the plans for a truck stoppage
during the funeral.

Throughout Friday night and early Saturday morning an
unending stream of trade unionists filed silently through the
flower-packed home of the Corcoran family to pay their last
respects to Pat. From nine that morning until noon, while
the funeral services were being conducted, not a truck moved
in the city. Over 10,000 workers came to the Basilica for the
last rites, packing the big church and overflowing into the street
outside. Delegations were present from towns throughout the
region, representing Teamster locals affiliated to the NCDDC.
With sorrow and with anger, all had come to give Pat the
send-off he deserved. And they were more determined than
ever to go forward in the trade union struggle that had cost
him his life.

After the funeral Local 544 held a general membership
meeting to assess the changed situation. All present were agreed
on the key problems now confronting us. If there was to be
any chance of finding Pat's assailants, organized labor would
have to put heavy pressure on the government for action. This
would no doubt have to be done in the face of a new capitalist

attack, since the bosses could be expected to use his tragic death against the union.

Recognizing that other killings might be attempted by labor's enemies, the meeting voted to take protective measures. Arming of the Local 544 staff was authorized. A decision was also made to provide bodyguards from the union's ranks for its officers.

In the present case arming of the staff took place under circumstances different from those that had prevailed in 1936. This time there was no internal union struggle involved. One of our people had been murdered by agents of the ruling class, we had to assume, and there was an implied threat to others. So the union purchased .38 caliber revolvers for defensive use. As a safeguard against being framed by the cops for carrying these weapons, official permits were requested. When the request was refused by the authorities, we acted to cover ourselves by registering the serial numbers of the guns with the chief of police.

L. A. Murphy handled these arrangements. Then, when the assignment had been fully carried out, he resigned as secretary-treasurer of Local 544. In doing so he explained that compelling personal reasons required his return to Rockford, Illinois. There he resumed, after a time, his previous activities as a Teamster official in that city.

(The person who returned to Rockford was different from the one who had left town in the spring of 1936 to serve Tobin in Minneapolis. While fighting Local 574, Murphy had come to respect its Trotskyist leaders. Then his association with us on the executive board of Local 544 had attracted him, at least in part, to the class struggle principles by which we lived. In his own way he had become a Trotskyist sympathizer. Until his death years later, Murphy made occasional financial contributions to the party, doing so through Ray Dunne.)

Meantime, Jim Cannon had rushed to Minneapolis as soon as he received word of Corcoran's assassination. As in earlier times of crisis, he worked closely with the party's Teamster fraction, helping us in every possible way. In addition Jim brought with him Felix Morrow, an able party journalist, to assist the *Northwest Organizer* staff. On both counts the aid was indeed welcome. We were faced with complex problems in shaping the union's strategy and in counteracting propaganda attacks from its enemies.

For one thing, a smear campaign was already developing in the daily papers. The capitalists had been quick to seize upon this new opportunity to hit the Trotskyists, against whom they had deep grievances. Since 1934 we had been instrumental in forcing the bosses to part with millions of dollars for increased wages. And by 1937 we had become a key factor in a unionization drive throughout the region that would add huge new sums to company payrolls. Thus there were material incentives for a ruling class attempt to use Pat's murder as a means to turn the tide against us. Demands for an investigation of the unions could be expected. The minimum aim would be to sow division in the labor movement and demoralize the workers. A danger also existed that an attempt would be made to cook up a legal frame-up against the leaders of Local 544.

At the same time the Stalinists would undoubtedly make use of this opportunity to launch an unprincipled factional attack upon us. Moreover, they were sure to do so with utter disregard for the consequences to the workers' movement. Of that we could be certain, because time after time they had done the same thing at previous critical points in the unfolding class struggle.

There was also the possibility of new difficulties with Tobin, since our peaceful relations with him at the time were of a rather tenuous nature.

In these general circumstances, a quick counteroffensive against the ruling class was needed. As the first step in that direction, we shaped concrete demands for vigorous governmental action in the search for Corcoran's killers. Efforts were then initiated to develop the broadest possible united front within the labor movement, centered around these demands.

The counteroffensive began with the drafting of two resolutions. One demanded that County Coroner Gilbert Seashore summon a coroner's jury to proceed with an inquest into the murder. The other called upon Minnesota Attorney-General Ervin to appoint a special investigator to ferret out the killers. Specifically it was asked that Ervin appoint Sam Bellman, a Farmer-Labor state representative who was well known and widely trusted in labor circles, to the investigative post.

Both resolutions were first adopted in the Teamsters Joint Council. Then representatives from the IBT body got them passed at a meeting of the Minneapolis Board of Union Business Agents. The latter formation, which consisted of officials from all AFL unions, was broadly representative of the city's labor movement. Thus a significant united front had rapidly been formed around the two specific demands, which were seconded shortly thereafter by the Central Labor Union.

Next a big trade union delegation met with both Ervin and

Seashore to request immediate action on labor's demands. Ervin refused to appoint a special investigator, pleading lack of funds. But the state administration, being Farmer-Laborite, had to make some gesture of cooperation with organized labor. So Governor Elmer Benson (who had assumed the office after Floyd Olson died in 1936) passed the buck to Roosevelt by requesting FBI help in finding the murderers. U.S. Attorney-General Cummings replied that Washington would not enter the case "unless evidence is produced that a federal crime was committed." As the *Northwest Organizer* observed, the assassination of labor leaders did not appear to merit federal attention.

However, Coroner Seashore did respond to the trade union demands. He convened a jury that was surprisingly favorable in its composition from labor's viewpoint. It consisted of T. E. Cunningham, president of the State Federation of Labor; Allen Sollie of the AFL City and County Employees Union; I. G. Scott, Farmer-Labor county commissioner (formerly a city alderman); Sam Bellman, whom labor had wanted as a special investigator; Charles Horn, an employer with liberal leanings; and former Minneapolis Mayor Kunze, a bank official.

The jury met on November 30 and conducted an inquest that lasted five days. About 140 persons were subpoenaed to appear for questioning. Highlights of the proceedings were summarized in the *Northwest Organizer.*

Alice Corcoran, Pat's widow, and Frank Dorrance of Local 471 told of various threats that had been made against the murder victim. In one case gangsters had threatened Pat's life, it was reported, in an effort to prevent him from organizing ice cream drivers.

Dr. Russell Noice stated that he had heard threats made against the Dunnes and Bill Brown by four men in a beer parlor.

Ray Dunne testified that threats against labor leaders are regular occurrences, particularly when labor is making great strides. "A short time before Corcoran was killed," he told the jury, "we turned some of them over to the police."

While I was on the witness stand, juror Horn queried me about possible resentment against the union among low-wage trucking outfits coming into Minneapolis from other cities. His questions enabled me to stress the possibility that Pat had been killed by agents of the bosses.

Throughout the inquest sessions, continuous complaints were made by the capitalist press that Grant Dunne was running the investigation. Actually Grant had been assigned by the union to assist Coroner Seashore in all possible ways. This attitude on our part stood in marked contrast to the failure of the official forces of "law and order" to render any meaningful aid to the coroner's jury. Due in no small part to the noncooperative attitude of the police, the inquest failed to turn up any clues to Corcoran's killers.

Taking note of the lack of concentration on efforts to find the criminals, the *Northwest Organizer* asserted: "Our enemies prefer to have the identity of the murderers remain a mystery. First, because those murderers certainly came from the enemies of labor. Second, because only so long as Pat's murderers are not found, only that long can our enemies go on trying to pin it on the trade unions for which Pat lived and died."

Police lethargy in the Corcoran case was symptomatic, as was smearing of the labor movement in the capitalist press and continued threats against other workers' leaders. These had become the norms of the day. Life for trade unionists under these conditions was reflected in experiences recounted later on by Marvel Scholl.

"It would not be entirely true to say that the terror began for me with the murder of Pat Corcoran," she wrote. "Actually the whole period of our ouster from the Teamsters, with the presence of Tobin's goons in the city, was one of uncertainty for the lives of our comrades.

"But the real terror began early that November morning, when suddenly someone pounded on our door and we wakened to hear Harry DeBoer call, 'Wake up, Farrell. They murdered Pat last night.'

"We did not have a phone then. But after that Farrell gave in to my pleas to have one installed, even though it meant he would no longer get the small amount of peace and privacy which not having one had given him.

"When Tommy Williams [a cab driver belonging to Local 544] became Farrell's bodyguard, he practically lived with us — even to the point of going along to the movies on Saturday night, although we both insisted that on those occasions he bring Violet [his wife] with him.

"Farrell hated having a bodyguard and carrying a gun and every time he could he sneaked away and drove home by himself. Finally he quit carrying the gun and put it, unloaded, on a high shelf in the kitchen.

"One night when I was writing my Picket Line [column for the *Northwest Organizer*] our little dog, Lady, kept barking at the kitchen door and I scolded her. Then suddenly there was a crash of glass in the basement, from the front part where there was a storage room.

"Then I knew somebody was in the basement. Apparently they had studied Farrell's habits. He used to drive the car into the garage, come into the house through the grade door on the side and go down into the basement to stoke the furnace for the night.

"I called the headquarters of the oil station attendants, where I knew Farrell and Tommy would most likely be, since they were on strike. I got Tommy on the phone but he couldn't find Farrell, which meant he was probably on the way home alone. My concern for him led me impulsively into a foolhardy act.

"I got the gun off the shelf, didn't even attempt to load it, and with Lady beside me, we went down into the basement to stoke the furnace. That someone was in that small storage area was evident. Lady stood in the door to that front part of the basement barking her little head off, while I loaded the furnace, and then both of us ran upstairs.

"A few moments later I heard the basement stairs creak and the grade door to the outside close. So I stationed myself in our front door, watching for Farrell to come home. As his car turned into the driveway I ran out, yelling for him to get out and into the house. I was certain that the assassin would still be waiting for him in the garage.

"Another incident, which took place while Farrell was out of town, happened like this:

"Around midnight I went out onto the closed-in sun porch to check the front door lock before going to bed. Right across the street, but opposite the vacant lot between our house and the Zimmerman's, stood a car. Since that entire block across the street was all weed-grown vacant lots, and since I could see no lights in any of the houses on our side, I knew the car didn't belong to some neighbor's visitors. While standing there watching in the dark, I saw someone light a cigarette, and then two more cigarettes were lit in the back seat of the car.

"I turned out the living room and dining room lights, left the light shining for a few moments in the bathroom and then turned it off. Thus I was entirely closed in with no lights showing anywhere. Then I called 544's office but no one was there. Remembering that the power workers would be meeting at the union headquarters, I called them. Luckily I got George Phillips [the Local 160 president].

"As he instructed, I sneaked back to the sun porch and waited. While I stood there someone got out of the car and went into the weeds across the street. Probably to relieve himself, because he came back in a few minutes.

"In about 15 minutes cars began streaming down Fortieth and Forty-first Streets to converge from both ends onto the 19th Avenue South block where our house was located. The people in the car saw what was happening and took off like a bolt of lightning. The union fellows said there were four or five men in the car.

"They all came in, searched the house, including the basement, and checked the garage in the back. After they had satisfied themselves and me that there were no lurkers, and had got me calmed down, they prepared to leave.

"As they were going out one worker — probably rather new to the class struggle — asked me, 'Why didn't you call the police?' And a roar of laughter went up from everybody else."

Small wonder that seasoned trade unionists laughed cynically at any notion of getting police protection against assassins. Since Pat's death it had become increasingly clear that the authorities were making, at best, only a perfunctory search for the killers. From time to time the cops would announce an anticipated "break" in the case, only to admit later that they were right back where they started. Their performance was, in fact, becoming an obvious charade.

Meanwhile the smear campaign in the capitalist press continued. Efforts were made to link Corcoran's death to "gangsterism" in the labor movement. A typical characterization appeared in the *St. Paul Daily News*, which referred to "labor czars, levying tribute through violence." In its issue of November 29, 1937, this same paper asserted: "If the terrorism continues, a vigilante movement will develop."

It was in this setting that the Stalinists made their contribution. They needed neither an investigation nor evidence to fix the blame for the assassination. The *Daily Worker* of November 23, 1937, merely announced that in Minneapolis there was "a rising popular indignation against disclosures that racketeering and gangsterism imported into the labor movement here and linked with the Trotskyites in the leadership of the Drivers Union has been at the root of the killing."

The charge was repeated by a so-called "Hennepin County Industrial Council of the CIO," which at that time was largely a paper formation used as a mask by the local Communist Party hacks. Through this setup they alleged that the "assassination was the logical outcome of the gangsterism and racketeering fostered in the Minneapolis labor movement by the Dunne-Brown-Dobbs leadership of 544 and their allies."

This action was quickly repudiated, however, by George Cole, the Regional Director of the CIO. Use of the CIO label to make such accusations, he stated publicly, had not been authorized. His repudiation was soon followed by another from the Minnesota Council of CIO Packinghouse Workers. This real flesh-and-blood organization called the Stalinist-engineered charges against the Teamsters "most harmful to the welfare and future of the CIO and a united labor movement."

Finding itself stymied on the CIO front, the CP turned its attention to the AFL. Harold Bean, a Stalinist union official, took the lead in forming a "Volunteer committee for driving gangsterism out of the labor movement." It was then announced that on December 1 the committee would hold a "mass public hearing on gangsterism in the Minneapolis labor movement which resulted in the murder of Patrick J. Corcoran."

Those individuals listed as sponsors of the "public hearing" were immediately summoned to appear before the coroner's jury. There they were put on the witness stand and asked to report the evidence on which their allegations were based. Having none to offer, they were exposed as liars.

Under this pressure eleven AFL officials, who had been listed as joining in the call for the December 1 affair, repudiated the whole scheme. They claimed that their names had been fraudulently used without their knowledge or consent. This stripped the "volunteer committee" down to none but known Stalinists and rendered it impotent.

Following the coroner's jury episode, over 150 officials of the Minneapolis labor movement assembled at the call of the Board of Union Business Agents. The gathering adopted a resolution which declared:

"Every attempt to attribute the murder of Corcoran to forces inside the labor movement, and to besmirch the trade unions with the accusation that 'gangsterism and racketeering' inside labor's ranks is responsible for the murder, constitutes a foul slander on the bona-fide labor movement and its martyred officer, and shields the real murderers and the dark forces behind them. . . .

"We condemn the mass meeting announced for Wednesday, December 1, at Eagles Hall, as in no way representative of the attitude of organized labor, as being an aid to the mortal enemies of organized labor, and further evidence of an unscrupulous campaign by irresponsible elements to discredit and split the labor movement of Minneapolis."

This condemnation of the Stalinists effectively blocked their vicious attempt to turn the murder investigation into a lynch attack on the leaders of Local 544. But these unprincipled factionalists had already done grave injury to the labor move-

ment. They had helped the bosses divert suspicion from themselves and use the killings as a weapon against the unions.
In fact their atrocious conduct had given artificial respiration
to the smear campaign in the capitalist press. The *Minneapolis
Star*, for example, pointed gleefully to "charges made by union
leaders" as the issue of most importance concerning the assassination.

Under cover of the running attack on Local 544 in the daily
papers, the bosses next undertook a probe to see if the union
had been weakened internally. Once again the lead was taken
by the wholesale grocery firms, whose contract with the local
had recently expired. In the negotiations the companies issued
an ultimatum: If the union did not accept at once their terms
for renewal of the contract, they declared, all offers would be
withdrawn. Clearly they wanted to force a strike, and the
workers accomodated them by voting to walk off the job on
December 9.

On the second day of the shut down the bosses got an assist
from Mayor Leach (an outright reactionary who had won the
1937 mayoralty election, displacing Latimer in that office).
Leach went on the radio to deplore the interruption of work
by "a faction of certain self-appointed leaders of labor," and
to call upon the union movement to "purge itself."

Then the mayor tried to help swing a company union move
by asking the grocery workers to bypass Local 544 and sign
individual pacts with the bosses. He did this by mailing copies
of the employers' proposals to the strikers at their homes,
asking them to write down their vote on the question and send
it back to him. This caper was played up in the daily papers
as a "secret ballot" through which the workers could speak
for themselves.

Leach's union-busting attempt failed completely. The strike
remained solid, giving proof that Local 544's fighting power
was as great as ever. Having become fully aware that this
was the real situation, the bosses did not even wait for the
results of the mayor's "secret ballot." On the fourth day of the
dispute they signed a contract renewal. It brought wages and
conditions at the grocery firms abreast of advances that had
recently been made elsewhere in the trucking industry.

Soon after the victory over the grocery bosses, Local 544
gave another demonstration that its internal stability had not
been shaken by the smear attack following Corcoran's murder.
The vehicle was the election of union officers. Of the seven
posts to be filled only five were held by incumbents from the
previous selection of a full executive board. Two vacancies

had been created by Pat's death and Murphy's resignation.

The elections were held in strict conformity with the procedures established earlier by former Local 574. Nominations
took place at a general membership meeting, which also selected election judges from the ranks. A month of campaigning
was provided. Then the membership voted by secret ballot,
the polls being open for two days at the union headquarters.

In the nominations a slate composed of current leaders of
the union was presented. It included: Bill Brown for president;
Jack Smith for vice president; Grant Dunne for recording secretary (to replace me in that post); Farrell Dobbs for secretary-
treasurer (to replace Murphy). Three trustees were also nominated: Carl Skoglund and Nick Wagner (both incumbents);
and Miles Dunne (to replace Corcoran).

Only one post was contested. Oscar Gardner, a job steward,
ran against Brown for union president. In his campaign
Gardner raised no important programmatic differences with
the incumbent leadership. So far as I can recall, his main contention was that he could do a better job than Bill in carrying
out union policy. The membership disagreed with that argument.
Brown was reelected by a vote of about three to one.

A heavy vote was cast, even for those candidates who were
running without opposition. The turnout at the polls was
almost twice what it had been in previous elections. This was
plainly the workers' way of telling Local 544's enemies that
they retained full confidence in their leaders.

It was especially significant that Smith and Wagner, who
had come from former "Local 500," were not opposed for
reelection. Through their conduct as officers of Local 544,
they had won approval in the union ranks. This, in itself,
reflected the extent to which they had come to accept the trusted
policies of the former Local 574 leaders, who now constituted
a solid majority on the executive board of the reorganized
local. The union's leadership was again becoming relatively
homogeneous.

Confronted with a manifest failure to chip the most solid
rock in the city's labor movement, the capitalists tapered off
their propaganda offensive against us. At the same time the
daily papers reduced their coverage of the search for Corcoran's
murderers. Before long the authorities were able to shunt the
case aside, and it has never been solved.

Even though labor was frustrated in its efforts to find the
killers, a victory had been won in a certain sense. The union
movement fought off a ruling class attack that was in many
respects the most vicious since the cops used riot guns on

us in 1934. This meant that the Teamster campaign throughout the region could again get rolling with the throttle wide open.

At least that would have been the case if we had not run into new difficulties with Tobin. As secretary of the NCDDC I wrote to the IBT head shortly after Pat was killed. My letter gave him an account of the tragedy and our efforts to find the assailants. Whatever Tobin's thoughts were on the subject, he did not trouble to communicate them to us. It was not a good sign.

16. A Major Breakthrough

We proceeded with the expansion drive by holding a session of the North Central District Drivers Council in Minneapolis on December 5, 1937. Art Hudson, the head of St. Paul Local 120, was elected president of the body to fill the vacancy caused by Pat Corcoran's assassination. Plans were then discussed to move toward enlargement of the area embraced by the NCDDC.

As experience had already confirmed, the key to this objective was the over-the-road drivers. Therefore a series of contrete steps was projected to mobilize these workers and bring their power to bear against the long distance trucking bosses.

These steps included: launching the broadest possible organizational campaign throughout the North Central states; establishment of an area-wide contract providing uniform wages, hours, and working conditions for intercity hauling; development of coordinated action between Teamster locals involved in the fight for these goals; and creation of a representative leadership formation, commensurate with the expansion of the area, to direct the battle.

The workers aimed at in this drive toiled under inhuman conditions. Hours of labor varied widely. Trips of from 80 to 120 continuous hours — with catnaps snatched here and there — were quite common. Even longer stretches of continuous driving were obtained through the use of sleeper-cabs.

Usually the "sleeping" device consisted of a flat slab behind the drivers' seat with a thin, hard, often lumpy mattress. Two drivers were assigned to these operations, alternating between a turn at the wheel and "resting" on the slab. Genuine relief from exhaustion was impossible under these rude, unsanitary conditions in a moving truck. Yet the bosses often sought to deduct bunk time from the drivers' pay, claiming that they were "not working."

Such long hours of continuous travel dulled the drivers'

reflexes. To make matters worse, they often had to operate
defective equipment. In addition, the dangers implicit in this
situation were sometimes compounded in winter by the numb-
ing effects of steering a big rig along slippery roads without
a heater in the cab. Because of these combined factors, acci-
dents occurred frequently.

Rates of pay for this hazardous work were a confused jum-
ble. Earnings were variously computed on the basis of flat
rates per hour, per mile, or per trip. Mileage was not figured
according to the actual distance traveled; it was usually fixed
arbitrarily through what the employers called "short line distance" tables, a chiseling device that had little to do with the
realities of highway driving. Through similar deviousness,
trip rates were calculated without any provision for time lost
because of operational difficulties, a factor that was more likely to be encountered than not.

Whatever the form of flat payment—by the hour, mile, or
trip—allowance was rarely made for anything other than driving. The workers were expected to donate their time and labor
for loading, making pickups and deliveries en route, and unloading at the end of the run. They also had to take the rap on
time lost due to tie-ups waiting for freight, breakdowns, and
layovers.

With all these factors taken into account, over-the-road drivers
often received as little as thirty cents an hour, in some cases
even less. And out of that princely wage they usually had to
pay for their meals and lodging while on the road.

As though being underpaid wasn't bad enough, many of
these workers had only uncertain employment. The bosses took
full advantage of the surplus labor pool created by economic
depression. To get work the drivers had to hang around the
company premises without any compensation, waiting to be
called on a run. In handing out job assignments the bosses
ignored length of service. Toadies received favored treatment
and rebels were given a hard way to go.

The stiff competition for jobs enabled the companies to gouge
their employees in yet another manner. Some workers were
induced to buy a piece of trucking equipment under a long
term finance plan. Firms holding official carrier's rights issued by the government then employed rig and driver by the
mile, ton, or trip. From the fee paid him the owner-operator
had to cover the cost of equipment, including operating expenses, and the problem of its replacement when it wore out.
After meeting these costs it wasn't easy for an owner-operator
to scratch out a living as a working driver.

To make matters even worse, ambitions developed among individual owner-operators to expand their holdings and go into business for themselves. This sowed division in the workers' ranks, giving tactical advantage to the bosses.

All in all, there was burning need for improvements in wages, hours, and conditions for over-the-road drivers. It followed that a meaningful trade union campaign would get a big response among these workers. As matters stood, however, little had been done by the IBT to organize them, and even less had been accomplished in bringing their employers under union contract.

Behind this default lay the outlived policies of the Tobin regime. The IBT's focus had been determined by earlier conditions, when cartage by dray or truck was confined to local operations, and railroads handled long distance hauling generally. Under these circumstances union activities in a given city remained sealed off from those in other localities. Structurally, therefore, the organization as a whole was little more than a loose federation of city formations over which Tobin presided much like a feudal monarch.

To finance his regime, the IBT head levied per capita taxes on the dues collections of local unions. A staff of well-paid general organizers, permeated with his old-line ideology, was maintained to supervise all union activities. In this and other ways favors were dispensed to loyal servitors. They, in turn, were expected to ferret out violations of IBT "law" and help punish the offenders as decreed by the general president.

Within this framework relatively strong Teamsters Joint Councils had arisen in a number of cities, especially the larger ones. Such formations developed as more or less insular baronies, presided over by dictatorial local bureaucrats. Inside their particular domains these worthies were allowed considerable latitude, so long as they did nothing that directly crossed Tobin.

The Joint Councils were founded on the organization of drivers in the local trucking industry. None of these setups had paid serious attention to the rise of highway trucking operations and the needs of the workers involved. More often than not, drivers entering a unionized terminal from an open shop town were merely required to join the IBT local at that terminal. All they got in return for paying union dues was a membership book; most often they still had to work under nonunion conditions. In this connection, locals affiliated with the Chicago Teamsters Joint Council were among the worst offenders.

If a Teamster local in a big town did make an occasional gesture toward doing something for highway drivers, nothing much came of it. The bosses usually got around the problem by basing their drivers at the opposite end of the run. There the wage scales would be lower, because either the town was unorganized or the IBT local at that end was relatively weak.

Plainly enough, effective action required cooperation between IBT locals on an area basis. Only then could open-shop terminals be brought under firm union control. In addition, it was the way to overcome the diversities between the few over-the-road contracts that then existed and to establish uniform terms for all line operations.

Yet the Joint Councils, rooted as they were in the concepts of yesteryear, failed to respond to the new needs. Instead, the bureaucrats ruling over these formations tended to be suspicious of any moves toward intercity cooperation. They looked upon such ideas as a threat to their control over the baronies alloted to them under IBT "law." They wanted no part of an organized area program.

Tobin shared this tendency to put concern for personal power above the needs of the workers. He wanted no formations within the IBT broader than the Joint Councils, each restricted to a specific city. In his view, a broader area body meant the threat of a rival power arising to challenge him. In fact he had questioned Corcoran and Murphy rather closely about the NCDDC, quite obviously with that concern in mind. Since then Corcoran had been killed and Murphy had gone back to Rockford, leaving the Trotskyists in unquestioned leadership authority within Local 544. It followed, we had to assume, that our efforts to expand the NCDDC would now be viewed by the IBT head with greater suspicion than ever.

The solution of the problem lay in a basic contradiction operating against Tobin and in our favor. His policies and organizational forms had not changed with the changing times. Thus his position was weakened by stubborn refusal to make the necessary readjustments. In contrast, we sought to modify the union's strategy, tactics, and functional norms so as to meet the needs of the day.

Our line, if properly applied, could fulfill the desires of the workers to fight in defense of their class interests. For that reason the objective potential for an effective campaign was immense. In fact spontaneous efforts to get some action going in the sphere of over-the-road operations were developing in town after town across regions beyond the existing NCDDC territory. All the situation needed for the creation of a real powerhouse was further extension of organizational cooperation and leadership guidance.

Concerning the latter need, there were several factors that would aid us in extending leadership influence across a broader area. Many of the locals trying to organize over-the-road drivers were relatively weak. More often than not the leaders of these units were rather inexperienced. Consequently they tended to welcome support and guidance, looking especially to Local 544 for aid.

They turned to us in part because of the power we had demonstrated in 1934 and also because of our successful battle to win reinstatement into the IBT. We could show them how to fight, they seemed to feel, and we appeared to know how to keep Tobin from fouling up the struggle.

If we were to take full advantage of this favorable situation, there were delicate problems of timing to be considered in developing our tactics. As had been the case in preparing the 1934 struggle, it was necessary to avoid a premature showdown with the IBT head over the present campaign. Such a confrontation would inevitably occur, we had to assume. When it came, however, it would be vital to have built up an organizational force and a struggle momentum going beyond his power to control. For this reason we had moved deliberately, from one planned step to the next, even since our expansion drive was first launched in the summer of 1936.

At the outset we had concentrated on organizing some 2,000 highway drivers moving trucks into and out of Minneapolis. Part of them worked for employers based in the city; others were employed by truck lines operating from elsewhere in the area. Whichever the case, the employers were required to pay no less than the wage scale established by Local 544, which generally meant an automatic raise in pay for over-the-road drivers from other towns, whether organized or not. Recognition was accorded by us to membership in local unions located elsewhere. We merely insisted that no worker hauling to and from Minneapolis should receive cut-rate pay.

As previously described in some detail, this policy served as an important means to promote the rise and growth of the NCDDC through the following period. In the course of applying it, however, some misunderstandings arose with IBT locals situated beyond NCDDC territory. A typical example involved Local 90 of Des Moines, Iowa.

Carl Keul, the head of that local, turned up in Minneapolis one day with a Des Moines trucking boss in tow. He complained that we were interfering with members of his union coming into the city. After getting rid of the employer, we had a fruitful discussion with Keul.

He had thought we were following the Chicago practice of making all drivers who came into town join our local, even if they already belonged to another IBT unit. We refuted this report, which had come to him from the boss. Then we explained why Local 90, which had a contract providing wage scales lower than ours, should cooperate in making the bosses pay the higher scale on runs into Minneapolis. Once he saw the light, Keul became a supporter of our program for the creation of an effective IBT force throughout the entire bank of North Central states.

Similar problems had arisen with Teamster locals in eastern Wisconsin, which had not joined the NCDDC. Some of these units had contracts with long distance trucking companies, but their wage scales were generally below the rate that by mid-1937 prevailed in both Minneapolis and St. Paul. In their case, as in Keul's, misunderstandings had arisen from our policy of enforcing the higher scale for their members entering the Twin Cities.

This led Hudson and me, as officers of the NCDDC, to attend a meeting of Wisconsin locals held in December 1937 in Milwaukee. There the immediate problem was settled through acceptance of our policy of enforcing the higher scale wherever a contradictory wage situation existed. Agreement was also reached that a standard over-the-road contract was needed, which could be applied throughout the entire area. Once again, new momentum had been added to the movement for a change in IBT policy.

Overall developments in our campaign reached a qualitatively new stage at an NCDDC conference held in St. Paul on January 8-9, 1938. Delegates were present from forty-six local unions already affiliated with the body. These included the most recent affiliate, Local 383 of Sioux City, Iowa, where Jack Maloney had just been assigned by the NCDDC to give the local direct help as an experienced organizer.

In addition observers came from IBT locals in Des Moines, Iowa; Omaha and Lincoln, Nebraska; Kansas City, Missouri; and to our pleasant surprise, from as far south as Tulsa, Oklahoma. The grapevine was really carrying word of the campaign along the highways.

As the first order of business I presented the report of the Field Committee. It opened with a summary of the gains registered since the NCDDC was formed a year earlier. The rolls of local unions in larger cities had been substantially swelled. Old locals were being revived and new ones created in smaller towns. Pressure by the Council had helped the locals negotiate working agreements with employers that brought significant improvements in wages and conditions for the membership. Where strikes had been needed to accomplish this, the IBT had won in every instance. There had been a narrowing of wage differentials between larger and smaller towns. And in the course of these struggles the way had been opened to organize big chain outfits on a district basis, as had been accomplished in the case of Gamble-Robinson.

Turning then to the over-the-road question, the report dealt with problems arising from the lack of a uniform wage scale in existing contracts with long distance trucking firms. It was also stressed that in many cases the situation was further confused by the absence of any contract whatever. This resulted in pressures from the bosses to hold all wage scales down to the lowest rate. In these circumstances locals often became involved in misunderstandings and quarrels, which helped nobody but the labor haters. To get the IBT on the right track in this connection, the report set forth two prime essentials: cooperation between local unions; a uniform wage scale for the area.

After a preliminary discussion of these perspectives the gathering recessed for the day. It was intended that the resumption of deliberations the following morning would focus on the shaping of a broad plan of organizational expansion and the selection of a joint wage-scale committee. As it turned out, though, the agenda had to be changed.

Between the sessions John S. Picago, a general organizer stationed in Milwaukee, arrived in town. He brought with him a directive from Tobin issued in the name of the International Executive Board. The board, it was asserted, did not approve of general meetings between local unions to discuss general matters. Any conference of the kind had to be confined to specific issues involving specific locals. In effect, we were being ordered to disband the NCDDC.

When the conference reconvened the next day, it opened with a reading of the directive we had received. An explosion followed. Delegate after delegate took the floor to denounce Tobin's dictatorial action, which cut squarely across the needs of the times. The defiant attitude was further reflected in unanimous approval of a recommendation by the Field Committee that a delegation be sent to Indianapolis to lodge a direct protest with the general president.

Those who made the trip as representatives of the NCDDC included: Art Hudson, St. Paul Local 120; Carl Keul, Des Moines Local 90; Jack Maloney, Sioux City Local 383; Fred Smith, Duluth Local 346; Thomas V. Smith, Omaha Local

554; Jack Wirth, Fargo Local 116; and Farrell Dobbs, Minneapolis Local 544.

We also took along John Geary, the general organizer stationed in St. Paul, who was a staunch Tobinite. We wanted to nail him down as a direct party to any understanding that could be reached in a showdown with his boss.

Our session with the IBT head opened with a pompous lecture from him on the "laws" of the organization, to which we listened courteously. Then he got a shock. With the sole exception of Geary, every member of the delegation talked back to him, pointedly and emphatically.

After an hour or so of increasingly heated argument, during which we counterposed urgent necessity to his points of "law," a couple of basic facts seemed to percolate through to Tobin. Things were changing within the industry and inside the union faster than he had realized. Unless some readjustments in policy were made, he could have a major revolt on his hands. So he decided to be a bit more flexible.

In the end he offered an acceptable compromise. Intercity cooperation between locals to deal with critical problems would be allowed, provided there was no violation of the rights of Teamsters Joint Councils. Such collective action was to be restricted to the handling of special problems in specific spheres. Among these were to be creameries and produce chains, the delivery of goods for bakery combines, and highway construction work. Also, and most importantly, we were authorized to proceed with the necessary measures to establish uniform wage scales for long distance hauling throughout the North Central states. In all these activities, it was understood, Tobin would be kept informed of what we were doing.

Although the NCDDC could no longer function in its previous form, with unrestricted scope and a wide range of activities, a major breakthrough had been accomplished. We now had Tobin's approval of the key project, a sweeping organizational campaign among over-the-road drivers on an area scale. Once these key workers became unionized, the IBT would be able to grow apace in all quarters of the trucking industry. This growth would require the ultimate development of a broad and sophisticated form of area organization along the lines initially conceived by the NCDDC (as proved to be the case when the Central Conference of Teamsters was formed later on).

Before the ground could be prepared for the achievement of these broader aims, however, we had a battle to win against the companies engaged in long distance hauling.

17. Eleven-State Campaign

Now that we had extracted Tobin's approval of collective action in the over-the-road sphere, a planning session was quickly held in Minneapolis. It was attended by local union representatives from Iowa, Minnesota, and Wisconsin. Our discussion centered on steps to form an area contract committee and to find a way to open area-wide negotiations with firms engaged in highway transportation. A division of labor was agreed upon to begin these efforts.

Chicago was the hub of such trucking operations in the upper reaches of the Mississippi river valley. Thus it was the key terminal for our campaign and the movement there had to be drawn into collaboration with us. So the Wisconsin locals, which had the best relations with the Chicago unions, took the initiative in setting up a meeting with the appropriate Teamster officials in that city.

It was also understood that the rest of us would meanwhile concentrate on mobilizing additional forces in the southwestern quarter of the area. In fact a first step in that direction had already been taken. Right after the session with Tobin a request had been received from Omaha Local 554 that some of us come there to give them a boost. So Jack Maloney, Carl Keul, Art Hudson, Carl Skoglund, and I had gone to Omaha for a weekend of talks with these workers.

Our discussions led to a decision by Local 554 to expand its staff of organizers and to extend its unionization drive deeper into the state of Nebraska. A membership rally was also held, at which over 400 drivers packed the local's newly opened hall at 1222 Harvey Street. Those in attendance manifested great enthusiasm for the area campaign to bring the over-the-road bosses to book.

Inspired by the mood we found in Omaha, we proceeded on February 19-20, 1938, to hold a working conference at Sioux City. Delegates came from local unions in Minnesota, Iowa, the Dakotas and Nebraska. The gathering made two key decisions. A recruitment drive was organized to extend along the Missouri river valley from South Dakota to Kansas and Missouri. In addition, a general understanding was reached on contract demands to be presented to the employers.

Concerning the latter decision, the necessary groundwork had already been under way for over a year. It was started in Minneapolis during the fall of 1936 as one of the measures in our general expansion drive. In keeping with our established practice, we had begun by seeking broad consultation with the workers involved in long distance hauling. In this case, however, the aim could not be fully accomplished through collective discussions. So many of the drivers were always away on runs that few could be assembled at any one time.

To solve the problem we prepared a questionnaire designed to obtain their views. One set of questions sought information about the exact conditions under which each driver worked. A second category asked for recommendations on demands to be served upon the over-the-road bosses. Space was also provided for general comment. Since the desired information could best be obtained by soliciting anonymous contributions, no signatures were requested.

Packets of the questionnaire were given to union militants working in the industry. These were taken along on road trips and passed out to other drivers. Copies were accepted by many who never got near Minneapolis, and in these cases, requests were often made for some extras, which they could hand out themselves. Later on these workers would give filled-out questionnaires to a driver heading for Minneapolis, asking that they be returned to Local 544. As a result we had quite a clear picture of the workers' views on an area scale.

Information thus gathered was then classified and generalized. Out of the process emerged a concrete set of union demands which we could be certain would be strongly supported by over-the-road drivers generally.

In May 1937 the demands were served upon the Regulated Motor Transportation Association. As previously mentioned, this formation consisted of Twin City-based firms engaged in long distance hauling. The Association set up a committee to meet with representatives of Locals 120 and 544. Then, soon after negotiations opened, the St. Paul transfer strike had erupted. Finding themselves caught in a bind, these firms deserted the united front which the Twin City bosses had formed and made a speedy settlement with the IBT.

Early in June of that year they signed a contract which

did more than meet the union demands related to local cart-age. It also covered their over-the-road operations. Among the main provisions of the latter agreement were the following:

The union to be the sole representative of road employees.

A fifty-four hour week for line drivers, with premium pay for overtime. If called to work, a minimum guarantee of forty hours. Drivers not required to load or unload at terminals before or after an eight-hour driving period.

Drivers to receive a minimum of seventy cents an hour. Time to begin upon reporting to work and to continue until released from duty. This to include time spent on delays, pick-ups and deliveries, loading and unloading, breakdowns and tie-ups.

Drivers not to be required to take rest in sleeper-cabs. The employer to furnish proper sleeping facilities away from home. While on the road, drivers to get lodging and meal allowances.

Seniority rights to prevail in all respects.

Drivers not to be required to take out unsound equipment or violate speed laws. Heaters to be installed in all over-the-road trucks.

The employer to recognize the union's job steward system.

The union to retain the right to strike over contract viola-tions by the employer.

At the Sioux City conference these provisions were used as the basis for the preparation of demands to be made upon the bosses for a uniform, area-wide contract. With only a few exceptions, the terms of the Twin City agreement were incor-porated verbatim into the area demands. The exceptions were as follows:

It was decided that we were now in a strong enough posi-tion to make a fight for reduction of the work week for road drivers to forty-eight hours (which, as we shall see later, proved to be too ambitious a goal at that stage).

The wage demand was changed to provide that line drivers receive a minimum of either seventy cents an hour or three cents a mile. This was done because experience was teaching us that under certain conditions there were advantages for the workers in the mileage rate. Where that method of com-putation was used, however, we still demanded that at least seventy cents an hour be received for all work other than driv-ing.

A new provision was added that individual owner-operators must receive the cost of operating their equipment, plus its re-placement value, plus the union scale as drivers.

Our action at Sioux City on the proposals for area contract

demands proved to be most timely. The Wisconsin locals had been successful in their efforts to arrange for an expanded over-the-road conference in Chicago. And we could now go there with a well-rounded program, ready in all its essentials to be submitted for implementation.

The Chicago gathering convened on March 2, 1938, and lasted four days. It was attended by local union representatives from eight states: Illinois, Wisconsin, Minnesota, Iowa, Missouri, North Dakota, South Dakota, and Nebraska. Also present were three of Tobin's general organizers: Henry Berger, John Geary, and John Picago.

Among those on hand were two officials of Chicago Local 710, Mike Healy and Frank Brown. They announced that they had come simply as observers, pending the outcome of their efforts to get jurisdiction over Chicago-based long distance hauling. They added that the main officer of their local, John T. (Sandy) O'Brien, was in Indianapolis at the moment discussing the matter with the International officers, and his return was expected before the conference ended.

At the outset Henry Berger sought to dominate the proceedings, or to put it more precisely, he tried to prevent any serious discussion. Whenever one of us from the former NCDDC took the floor, he would reply in a taunting way: "Just you wait until O'Brien gets here." The implication was clear. He confidently expected that he was about to get important help in putting us in our place. We decided to let it pass, however, because Healy had informed us privately during a recess that Local 710 was in favor of what we were trying to accomplish.

Sandy O'Brien, who was to loom large in the campaign that followed this gathering, appeared to be in his forties. He had come up the hard way through the tough school of IBT politics in gangster-ridden Chicago. For some time he had been the unchallenged head of Local 710, a narrow craft setup based on drivers who delivered meat around the city.

Being capable of thinking ahead, he could sense the potential in the over-the-road project. Unlike the Trotskyists, though, he did not view it primarily as a means to advance the class struggle. He seemed to look upon the development more as an opportunity to broaden his base in Local 710 and strengthen his position as its central leader.

Whatever his exact motivations may have been, O'Brien perceived the strategic importance of Chicago as the hub of long distance trucking operations in the area. He also saw the need to end the parceling out of road drivers to various locals in the city. Therefore he set out to bring these workers together within Local 710, and he induced locals whose members hauled freight within the city to accept that arrangement. Two factors were basic to the latter achievement: he assured these locals full cooperation in their own spheres; and he had a well-deserved reputation as a person whose word was good.

With the groundwork thus laid, O'Brien had gone to Indianapolis to seek formal approval of the desired jurisdiction. In this connection he had more going for him than did the average local union representative. He was, himself, a member of the International Executive Board. Moreover, he was a close friend of Thomas L. Hughes, a former Chicagoan who had become general secretary-treasurer of the IBT. Thanks to this weight, Sandy got the green light from Tobin, and a basis was established for solid organization of the road drivers at the Chicago terminal.

Another problem facing Local 710 was the limited knowledge its leaders had of the long distance freight industry. We learned later that this had led O'Brien to sound out L. A. Murphy about the possibility of getting reliable help from the leaders of Local 544. Murphy assured him that we had organizational experience in the industry and that we dealt openly and above board with our collaborators. Thus we had quite good credentials with Local 710 from the start.

For us, in turn, there was much to gain from such collaboration. It represented another big opportunity of the kind that we had twice before been able to capitalize on. The first had been Bill Brown's cooperation in making the original breakthrough in Local 574. Then Pat Corcoran had served as a key figure in launching the NCDDC. Now Sandy O'Brien was about to help us expand the area campaign.

Our relationship with him was two-sided from the start. We had the program and the organizational know-how needed for the task at hand. He carried vital weight in the Chicago Teamsters Joint Council and at the IBT headquarters. Together we would be able to infuse new content into some old Teamster forms, making them vehicles for progress.

The first step toward that end took place when O'Brien arrived back in Chicago and joined in the conference we were holding there. He reported the favorable prospects resulting from his trip to Indianapolis and put Local 710 on record in full support of the over-the-road project. After that Henry Berger ceased his interference in the meeting. We got down to serious business and things began to move.

With minor changes, the contract demands we had prepared

at the Sioux City session were approved. There was only one
significant addition. At the request of the Illinois and Wisconsin locals a provision was included requiring the bosses to
employ only union members, a form of closed shop. A decision
was then made to send copies of the demands to all General
Drivers Unions in the area. These locals were asked to hold
up the renewal of any existing contracts with long distance
companies, pending the negotiation of a uniform, area-wide
agreement. Each employer was also served with a copy of
the demands, along with a request for negotiations.

A North Central Area Committee was elected to guide the
union campaign. Its members included: Mike Healy for Illinois (with O'Brien participating whenever needed); Joseph
F. Scislowski (of Milwaukee) for Wisconsin; Farrell Dobbs for
Minnesota (assisted by Harry DeBoer); Carl Keul and Jack
Maloney for Iowa; T. T. (Ted) Neal (of Kansas City) for Missouri; Jack Wirth for North Dakota; Happy Holstein for South
Dakota; and Thomas V. Smith for Nebraska. As its officers
the committee made Scislowski chairman, and I was designated
secretary.

The delegates also voted to launch an intensive membership
drive along the main trunk lines and in the terminals. In addition the committee was instructed to probe the possibility
of expanding the area beyond the eight states then participating in the campaign.

Ted Neal and I took responsibility for the probe in the southwestern region. With help from Floyd Webb of the Joplin Teamsters, we arranged conferences of local unions in western Missouri, Kansas, Oklahoma, and northern Arkansas. These
sessions revealed that a firm basis existed for including all
of Missouri in our campaign. In the other three states, however, we found that the IBT locals were still rather weak and
could not yet be considered effective battle forces.

Meantime, Sandy O'Brien and Mike Healy had undertaken
to reach eastward in the area. Their efforts were crowned by
the appearance of delegates from Indiana, Michigan, and Ohio
at the next general over-the-road conference, which took place
in Chicago on March 24.

At this enlarged gathering the decisions made earlier in March
were unanimously reaffirmed. This enabled us to go forward
in the common cause with added strength contributed by some
relatively big local unions in the eastern region. It also meant
that we could now set our sights on a single area-wide contract
to cover all long distance hauling on an eleven-state basis.

In conformity with this territorial expansion, additions were

made to the area committee. These included: J. M. (Red)
O'Laughlin of Detroit Local 299 for Michigan; B. V. Griff
of Cleveland Local 407 for Ohio; E. J. Williams of Indianapolis Local 135 for Indiana. (After a time Thomas E. Flynn
of South Bend, who was later to become general secretary-
treasurer of the IBT, was included in the Indiana representation.) Missouri's delegation was also increased by the addition of William Ryan of St. Louis Local 600, with John A. Ray
serving as his alternate.

After Red O'Laughlin joined the committee he decided to contribute his efforts on an area scale. To help make this possible, direction of organizing activity in and around the
Michigan district was assigned to James R. Hoffa (who was
later to become general president of the IBT). On both counts
the arrangement worked out well.

Hoffa already had some experience in over-the-road organization work. He also had the qualities of being eager to learn
and quick to absorb new ideas. This enabled him to make
important contributions to the collective effort through which
all were striving to achieve our campaign goals.

O'Laughlin, who had once been a sparring partner for Jack
Dempsey, was a fighter in every respect. Having come into the
over-the-road movement, he was ready to go all the way. Not
once did he show any hesitations or reservations. No matter
where a serious problem developed in the area, or how long
it took to get the thing straightened out, he could always be
counted on to lend a direct hand wherever and whenever his
help was needed.

Taken as a whole, the area committee was a remarkable
formation. Among its members were older union officers,
schooled in traditional IBT methods, who faced serious problems of readjustment in the changed situation. Alongside them
were young leaders with limited organizational experience,
some of whom had recently been over-the-road drivers themselves. Due to these contrasting backgrounds, there were several implicit contradictions within the committee. These were
offset, however, by a number of positive factors.

There was ample room for contributions from all committee
members. Due to their standing within the IBT, older heads
could win us allies elsewhere in the movement; they were also
able to give practical assistance by drawing upon useful aspects of their past experience. The younger leaders, in turn,
compensated for their inexperience in several ways: they contributed energy and militancy to the campaign; they knew the
industry and the tricks used by the bosses; and they were close

to the union rank and file. In addition, the committee was cemented together by common acceptance of mutually determined objectives, a factor serving to generate a spirit of good will.

These circumstances enabled revolutionists in the structure—who had both class political consciousness and trade union experience—to help overcome frictions that arose from time to time. We were aided in this by the fact that the campaign goals fully reflected the desires of the workers in the industry. Thus it was possible, where necessary, to bring rank-and-file pressure on the committee to halt meaningless squabbles and to overcome any tendency to deviate from effective policies.

All in all, the North Central Area Committee had developed into a competent leadership team. It stood at the head of a rapidly growing army of over-the-road workers. And dangers of adverse intervention from the IBT headquarters had been minimized. These achievements led to one conclusion: *we were ready to take on the bosses.*

Shortly after the second Chicago meeting our army got a chance to flex its muscles. Holdcroft Transportation, the largest company operating out of Sioux City, began firing drivers who joined the union. Local 383 struck the firm on March 29. Other IBT locals tied up its facilities in Marshalltown, Omaha, and Sioux Falls. Des Moines Local 90 patrolled the Lincoln Highway to halt Holdcroft's operations along that main artery, and Local 710 barred entry into Chicago.

After a shut down of eighteen hours the company gave in. The victimized drivers were reinstated with pay for time lost. Seniority rules were firmly established and workers employed there, who had previously been holding back from joining, flocked into the union.

About a week later Brady Transfer of Fort Dodge was struck by Local 844 over the discharge of union members. Its operations were quickly brought to a halt throughout the region, thanks to the help of IBT locals in Des Moines, Sioux City, Omaha, Mason City, Waterloo, and the Twin Cities. A tie-up of twenty-two hours forced reinstatement of the discharged workers, with back pay, and the institution of seniority rules. Since this company had some of the lousiest working conditions in the area, demands were made on this issue as well. It was compelled, for example, to pay the drivers for loading time and layover time, also to pay their expenses while on the road. No action was taken on rates of pay, because these were matters to be settled on an area basis.

These lightning blows against two notoriously anti-union

firms had dual effects. The workers were shown that the area committee meant business and that it had the power to protect their jobs. This gave a new spurt to our recruitment drive. At the same time the bosses were made to realize that they now had to take the IBT seriously. This was a gain, but a big problem remained. We still had to find a way to get a representative committee of bosses together for centralized negotiations. That wasn't going to be easy.

Taken on an area scale, long distance hauling was in the hands of a motley collection of firms. For every big outfit there were dozens of smaller ones. They fought each other for business on a dog-eat-dog basis. In order to shave their rates for bidding purposes — and still make a handsome profit — they competed to see who could gouge the most from labor. These factors, plus IBT neglect of the workers involved, resulted in the absence of any employer setup to deal with the union along broad geographic lines.

The only medium in sight through which centralized bargaining might be initiated was the American Trucking Association (ATA), a national employers' organization. This outfit did have a Labor Relations Committee. In fact Sandy O'Brien had just learned from Tom Hughes that IBT officials were to meet with this committee to discuss problems of union jurisdiction in motor transport. Seizing upon this opening, we sent a direct request to the ATA for action in arranging area negotiations with the employers. John Lawrence, its general manager, replied that the organization had no authority to negotiate labor contracts, leaving us to deal with the employers locally.

We responded with a telegram to V. Rogers, the ATA president. It was addressed to him in St. Louis, where the organization's board of directors was in session. Our message, dated April 21, read:

"We can only construe Mr. Lawrence's letter as a polite way of saying the employers refuse to deal with the unions on an area basis. We emphatically state to you that the unions insist on a uniform area contract and will not submit to your ridiculous program of sidetracking negotiations into a maze of sub-district and individual city conferences. We know what this would mean and why you want it. . . . If you persist in your present policy we cannot assume responsibility for any drastic action which the unions we represent might feel compelled to take."

As an indirect form of reply to our protest, the ATA board of directors dissolved their Labor Relations Committee. This

left us only one alternative: we would have to force the area
bosses to create their own central bargaining agency.

Our first step was to send an ultimatum to over 1,200 employers in the eleven states. As had been done with the ATA,
we stated our refusal "to be sidetracked into a maze of regional
and individual city negotiations." Such a course, we asserted,
would only "perpetuate the present chaotic conditions." Each
individual firm was called upon to state its intentions concerning the union's demand that a uniform area contract be negotiated. The implication was plain enough. If we didn't get a
satisfactory answer, a strike was in the offing.

Mobilization of the union forces for battle began through a
series of regional gatherings. This procedure helped to assure
maximum attendance in every quarter of the area. At these
sessions reports were given to local union representatives of
the problems we faced in forcing through area negotiations.
The locals were also alerted to prepare for strike action, if
needed, to get the desired settlement with the bosses.

At the regional meeting held in Kansas City an unusual
thing happened. Sandy O'Brien and Mike Healy went out
of their way to be present, mainly as a demonstration of solidarity. This had a good effect on the local unions in that
region. They had been accustomed to having their members
get nothing but lumps in Chicago, when working on runs into
that city. Now the leaders of the Chicago over-the-road local
had come to their territory, ready to stand shoulder-to-shoulder
with them in a progressive union struggle. This was a mark
of the way our forces were becoming knit together as comrades in arms.

These preliminary rallies were followed by a general conference on May 8 in Chicago. Attendance was heavy. It included for the first time the presence of a General Drivers Union
official from Louisville, Kentucky — Pat Ansbury, a Trotskyist
sympathizer. The delegates reaffirmed their stand for area
negotiations. All over-the-road locals were again urged to sign
no agreements with employers until uniform terms could be
established. In addition, the area committee was empowered
to consult with the IBT's general officers in the name of the
locals involved in the eleven-state campaign. The purpose was
to secure the International's cooperation in the fight for an
area contract.

A week later our committee met with Tobin at Indianapolis.
Faced by the formidable combination we now represented,
he dropped his usual pompous attitude and listened attentively to our report. Then he asked several questions, plainly
intended to get a clearer picture of the situation. In answering

him we repeatedly stressed a new, favorable development that was beginning to take form.

Our ultimatum to the bosses had thrown a scare into those who operated out of IBT strongholds like Chicago, Minneapolis, etc. They were now showing readiness to help get some form of area negotiations started. This new trend enabled us to assure Tobin that there were prospects of reaching a settlement with at least part of the employers in the area. Our attitude appeared to satisfy him that we would act "responsibly" and he promised to cooperate with us against employers who refused to negotiate.

The IBT head also approved steps to intensify the mobilization of our forces. He agreed that the area committee could arrange meetings involving the executive boards of all over-the-road locals in the eleven states. We were authorized to inform these gatherings of his promise to support us against recalcitrant employers.

Just at this point though, when the campaign was rapidly gaining momentum, a new blow fell in Minneapolis. It was a tragic and senseless one.

18. Another Killing

"Around nine o'clock Wednesday night, Arnold Johnson walked into Friedlund's cafe, on the corner of Plymouth and Washington, where Miles Dunne was sitting at a table. . . . Johnson called Miles Dunne outside and after a moment said: 'I've just killed a man. I put two slugs in him.'

"Dunne, assuming as a matter of course that Johnson was joking, in a spirit of mock seriousness asked him the name of the victim.

"'Bill Brown,' said Johnson.

"Not for a moment believing the story, Dunne asked Johnson to come in and have a drink. Johnson insisted that he was serious. 'You don't believe me, but I did it,' he said.

"After a few minutes Miles began to take Johnson more seriously. He saw that Johnson was in a strange mood and was not his usual self. When Jack Smith entered the cafe, Miles asked him, at the insistence of Johnson, to get Grant Dunne.

"When Grant appeared, Johnson took him aside and repeated his story.

"Still no one believed him, for the story didn't make sense. Johnson was on the most friendly terms with Bill Brown and the other drivers' officials.

"They decided to tell Vincent [Ray] Dunne about Johnson's behavior. Vincent, they knew, had planned to attend the regular meeting of the Central Labor Union.

"Jack Smith volunteered to drive Johnson to the Central Labor Union. There, Johnson repeated his story to Vincent.

"According to V. R. Dunne, Johnson had a wild, strained look on his face. Vincent expressed disbelief. He advised that they all return to the cafe.

"Back at Friedlund's they sat down with Johnson and asked him for details. His story was incoherent, and he refused to tell exactly where Brown was. Pressed for details, he would merely wave his hand vaguely. After an hour's questioning,

Workers filling the street outside Teamster headquarters during funeral services for William S. Brown.

Picketing a stingy Minneapolis preacher during the 1937 campaign to organize private chauffeurs.

John T. O'Brien, leader of Teamster Local 710, Chicago, Illinois.

he finally said Brown's body was in his car and that the car was parked out on Washington Avenue.

"Vincent and Miles Dunne promptly walked down Washington Avenue. A half-block away they saw Brown's auto. Someone was slumped over in the seat.

"The two immediately went to the Northside police station and reported what they had seen. A police car was sent to investigate, where patrolmen found Brown's body. An ambulance was called. The ambulance surgeon reported Brown dead.

"Police then picked up Johnson at the cafe and took him to police headquarters, where he admitted killing Brown. Johnson was then placed in a cell."

As the foregoing report in the *Northwest Organizer* showed, the first reaction to the murder of Local 544's president on May 25, 1938, was one of stunned disbelief. It seemed so unreal, so utterly lacking in motive, that the details were hard to credit. Yet he was gone. We had suffered a staggering blow, one that struck especially hard within the union staff because of our close and long comradeship with him in battle.

No matter how each of us felt personally, however, it was still our collective responsibility to react as leaders. Above all we had to remain alert to the danger of the ruling class using the tragedy against the union. For that reason we quickly issued a public statement in the name of Local 544's executive board. It said in part:

"The General Drivers Union has suffered an irremediable loss. Bill Brown, although only 43 years old, had been a leading spirit of our movement almost from its inception. . . .

"For most of the years since 1916, he was a working member in the trade, a transfer truckman. Flesh and blood of the men he led, he had their love and affection as no other union member. . . .

"The buzzards are already circling over Bill Brown's body. The enemies of labor and their press are attempting to smear him and the union he built. Union men and friends of labor will treat these enemies with the contempt they deserve.

"The death of Bill Brown must be placed in an entirely different category than the slaying of Patrick Corcoran last year. The two tragedies have nothing in common, and we warn the labor movement against the attempts which enemies are making to 'link' the two together. Pat Corcoran died at the hands of mortal enemies of labor; it is evident that Bill Brown was the victim of a friend and trade union brother in a fit of temporary insanity."

Funeral services for Bill were held at the Teamsters' hall.

At ten o'clock that morning the large auditorium, where his body lay in state, was opened to the public. Job stewards, wearing identifying armbands, served as ushers.

For the next five hours an endless line of working men and women, from all sections of the labor movement, filed past the flower-banked coffin to pay the fallen leader their last respects. Among them were delegations from Teamster locals elsewhere in the North Central area. In addition there were messages of sympathy from trade unionists in all parts of the United States.

When the last rites got under way at 3:00 P.M., all the halls in the building were filled, and many stood bareheaded on the streets outside. Loudspeakers were used to carry the proceedings in the main auditorium to the other halls and to the streets.

The relatives had agreed that Miles and Ray Dunne should participate in the speaking program on behalf of the union, but there was another factor that caused a problem. They desired that the family minister, Reverend Franklin Marlatte of the Lutheran church, handle a religious portion of the ceremony for them. We, of course, respected their request, but we also kept in mind that Bill Brown was not a religious person. It didn't seem right to have a preacher setting a tone of "repent ye sinners" at a time when we were saying our last good-by to him. So we arranged the program in a way that met the family's wishes and still set an overall tone of the kind Bill deserved.

Miles Dunne spoke first. As reported in the *Northwest Organizer*, he said in the course of his remarks:

"In this life there are people who walk through it and see the hard life of the workers. Some there are who see the truth and are resentful; but they take out their resentment in muttering in darkened rooms. A minority of those who see, have courage and a divine spark and principles. Instead of shedding tears, they deem it their task to go out in the arena of struggle and right the wrongs they see about them. There is a tiny minority of men like this, and Bill Brown was such a man. . . .

"He did the things he wanted to do. He brought a measure of comfort and security to thousands of workers. Were there a Valhalla, where the great champions of the working class gathered, there Bill would occupy one of the highest seats among those who have fought for the cause."

Reverend Marlatte then officiated at the religious service. It should be said to his credit that he seemed to sense the unusual nature of the occasion, for he spoke and prayed in low key and made it relatively brief.

Ray Dunne gave the concluding talk.

"Bill is attending with us today his last union meeting with his brothers and sisters," he said, "with the people he lived for and fought for. . . .

"He understood the working class had to be organized on a world scale. . . . He saw the necessity of applying the theories of the great working class leaders of the world to present-day conditions.

"Bill had his own vigorous ways of applying these theories. He saw in the labor movement the instrument that was going to make out of this world something better than a starvation house or a concentration camp, the instrument that would take hold of the economies of this life and weave a beautiful life for all who toil.

"Bill did not try to force his ideas on those whom he was chosen to lead. . . . He did insist that if men would be leaders they must give their lives to the labor movement. . . . His understanding and his attitude towards life should be the spirit that inspires every man and woman who comes here today."

After the ceremony was over a procession of cars more than two miles long accompanied the union president to the Crystal Lake Cemetery. There another huge throng had been gathering to give him a final salute.

Among those who came to town for the funeral was Jim Cannon, the national Trotskyist leader, who shared our fondness for Bill. Afterward he met with the party's Teamster fraction to help us shape Local 544's defense against the new attacks which were now to be expected from its enemies. In this case he didn't need to bring along a party journalist to help us. Felix Morrow was still in the city, and he had been on top of the publicity aspects of our problem from the moment we learned of Bill's murder.

One of the first steps taken after the party fraction meeting was to send an official report to Tobin. As secretary-treasurer of Local 544, I wrote the letter. It gave the facts concerning Bill's death and outlined other aspects of the situation as follows:

"Johnson joined the Local at the time of the strikes in 1934, while employed as a driver for a wholesale plumbing company. For the past two years he had been employed off and on by the Union when additional organizational forces were required and had been employed steadily as an Organizer for almost the past year. He had been a very close friend of Bill Brown's. They had worked together a good deal of the time and were known to have been in one another's company frequently after business hours.

"There is evidence that they had been drinking on the evening the tragedy occurred; however, it does not seem that this alone could be responsible for the happening. We are at a loss to find any other reason than one of temporary insanity. The police also indicate that they believe this to be the case. We had noticed that Johnson at times appeared terribly depressed but attributed this to nervous strain from overwork, as he was a very hard worker. . . .

"The Union membership seems to understand that this is just one of those unexpected things which could not have been anticipated or prevented by anyone, and they are not permitting the Union's enemies to use this to tear down the morale of the Union.

"The Union is defending Arnold Johnson, not with the intention of fighting to exonerate and free him, but first of all because he has been a loyal Union member, and secondly, because if he were to fall into the hands of an ambulance chaser controlled by the Police Department, his defense would be conducted in such a way as to damage the good name of the Union. . . .

"The Executive Board is recommending to the membership that a special election be held to replace Brother Brown so that no one can charge that there was a political motive behind his slaying."

Shortly after this letter was written a general membership meeting of Local 544 voted to hold the recommended special election to choose a new president. Four candidates were nominated at the meeting: Carl Skoglund, then a trustee; also Thomas McCue, Frank E. McArdle and Peter Harris, all rank-and-file members of the local. About a month was allowed for campaigning. Then the polls were kept open at the union hall for two days, on July 8 and 9, for the casting of secret ballots.

Skoglund was elected to the presidency, receiving a majority of all votes cast.

It was then necessary to replace him in his former post as a trustee. Because of the short interval remaining until the next regular union elections, the membership authorized the executive board to appoint someone to complete Skoglund's unexpired term in that post. Kelly Postal received the appointment to the trusteeship.

The union membership also voted an assessment to raise a fund on behalf of Agnes Brown, Bill's wife, and their two young sons, Raymond and Richard.

While these measures were being carried out, the expected assault on the union had developed. Mayor Leach took the initiative in launching a slander campaign against us. It was then systematically developed by the boss press. A preacher, Reverend George Mecklenburg, also got into the act. And the local Communist Party clique, pretending to speak in the name of the CIO, sharpened their factional hatchets to join the onslaught.

From all these quarters came a clamor to rid the labor movement of "gangsters and racketeers." Their central target was the executive board of Local 544, and as the smear attack on us gained momentum, it became increasingly vile.

The *Minneapolis Star*, for example, reprinted a vicious article from the *New York Daily News*. It was signed by one "Jerry Vessels." Although "Vessels" dated the article from Minneapolis, he was unknown in town and no trace of him could be found. His central theme was that the city had become a "terror spot" due to union "racketeering." To prove the point he manufactured his own evidence.

According to the "Vessels" account, Johnson had defiantly snarled he killed Brown because of an unfair split of money which Johnson, as an organizer, helped collect."

Since the day Johnson gave himself up and confessed to the murder of Brown, page after page in the local capitalist press had been filled with virtually every word he spoke. Not a single one of these utterances had even remotely resembled the "Vessels" quotation attributed to Johnson. There was good reason for this. The alleged quotation was a complete fabrication.

When the union movement confronted the editor of the *Star* with this fact, he tried to wiggle out with the alibi that his paper took no responsibility for the *Daily News* article. It had simply been reprinted, he claimed, "for the information of Minneapolis readers."

With smears of this kind as a backdrop for its proceedings, a grand jury began an investigation of Bill Brown's murder. Agents of the employers on the jury quickly steered it into a fishing expedition. People who had been only remotely connected with Brown and Johnson were called in, as were many who had not even had remote contact with the two. Questions asked of the witnesses roamed far afield, demonstrating that Local 544 itself was being made the jury's target. This process was dragged out across a period of weeks in an effort to create an impression that there were mysterious aspects of the case which required looking into.

In the end, however, this frame-up attempt blew up in the faces of the conspirators. They were unable to engineer an indictment of the leaders of Local 544.

On September 9 the grand jury issued a report in which it conceded that "a persistent search . . . failed to bring forth evidence to substantiate charges of labor racketeering."

Concerning the Brown case, the report stated: "After a four-weeks investigation into the murder and its background, the Grand Jury, on the basis of a mass of evidence and testimony, had no alternative save to indict Arnold Johnson as being responsible for the murder."

Johnson was then brought to trial. Again the proceedings were marked by vicious attempts to throw suspicion on the leaders of Local 544. Repeated insinuations were made that we had not told the truth about the circumstances surrounding Brown's death. Before the trial ended considerable effort had been expended to create an impression that the union's executive board, not Johnson, should be in the prisoner's dock.

On November 1, after about seventeen hours of deliberation, the trial jury found Johnson not guilty of the murder of Brown.

A report about the jurors' attitude was printed in the *Northwest Organizer*: "Concensus of jury opinion, explaining the verdict afterward, was that the state had not presented sufficient evidence to warrant a conviction. Jurors indicated they were particularly impressed with the defense plea that Johnson was in a mental fog from the morning of May 25 — the day of the murder — until three days afterward."

Following the release of Johnson, the chief of police announced: "Unless there is some new development . . . the case appears to be closed so far as the police are concerned."

Closed it proved to be. To this day Brown's murder remains officially unsolved.

In any case, we had ridden out another severe storm. The combined employer-preacher-Stalinist attack had been beaten off. Local 544 had recovered from the shock of Bill's tragic death. It remained stable internally and in full possession of its fighting powers.

There was also evidence that our newly established working relations with Tobin remained unimpaired.

Our action in providing him with a written account of the murder had been only a first step. Soon afterward the local's executive board sent me to Indianapolis to make a further report in person. In our talk Tobin listened closely to what I had to say. After that he spoke mainly about the fact that such things sometimes happen and that a leader has to get on with the union work in spite of everything.

He then described somewhat comparable problems the International had experienced a few years earlier when gangsters were trying to take over IBT locals in Chicago. The very headquarters where we were meeting bore evidence of that period. A metal grill closed off the office space used by Tobin, Hughes, and their staffs. A visitor could not get beyond the foyer, which served as an entrance area, until the electric lock controlling the grill door was released from the inside.

To have the IBT head thus exchanging experiences with me came as quite a surprise, considering what our past relations had been. For the first time since pre-1934 days, he was addressing an officer of former Local 574 in a friendly manner, offering encouragement in the organizing activities we were undertaking. It was a hopeful sign that advances registered in the over-the-road campaign were beginning to make a significant impression on Tobin.

19. First Area Contract

Around mid-June 1938 the North Central Area Committee fought a brief skirmish with long distance trucking firms operating out of Omaha, Nebraska. The clash was only a prelude to a long, bitter struggle that was to erupt there a bit later. To explain why this situation developed, a short sketch of the background is needed.

Omaha lies on the west bank of the Missouri river, opposite Council Bluffs, Iowa. It is the industrial and commerical center of Nebraska. As a transportation hub for the surrounding region, the city is also an operational base for several railroads and truck lines.

In the 1930s Omaha had a population of around 200,000. Of its 17,000-odd industrial workers, about 6,000 were employed in packinghouses and some 4,000 in trucking. The conditions under which they toiled were exemplified by a Chamber of Commerce boast that capitalists could operate with "low labor costs."

To have cheap labor it was necessary to maintain open-shop standards. This required an unremitting anti-union campaign, which was carried out by the Omaha Business Men's Association (a counterpart of the Minneapolis Citizens Alliance). In 1919, for example, the Association had been instrumental in viciously smashing a packinghouse strike, and as recently as 1935 it had broken a strike of streetcar workers. A general anti-union weapon had been devised for such purposes in the form of a state-enacted anti-picketing law, which declared in its key provision:

"It shall be unlawful . . . to loiter about, beset, patrol or picket in any manner the place of business . . . or any street, alley, road, highway or other place in the vicinity . . . for the purposes of inducing . . . others not to trade with, buy from, work for, or have business dealings with [any firm or corporation]."

These brutal policies had long held the Omaha labor movement down to little more than a few small craft unions of skilled workers. Previous attempts to organize truck drivers in 1929, in 1931, and again in 1933, had been defeated. As a result the average wage in trucking was twenty-five cents an hour. The usual work week was eighty hours.

Although a charter existed for General Drivers Local 554, it had remained more or less a paper union, dominated by right-wing officials in the Omaha Central Labor Union (AFL), and utterly lacking in organizational initiative. This was criminal neglect. Conditions were rotten ripe for a membership campaign in the industry, as the workers themselves demonstrated in the spring of 1937. One day they simply launched a spontaneous strike against Watson Brothers Transportation Company, headquartered in Omaha. Long after the event Louis Miller, who emerged as one of the Local 554 leaders, wrote a letter to me describing how their first walkout began.

"I recall the first meeting we had among ourselves to discuss how we should go about joining the union," Lou wrote. "There were only a few there: John, Fritz and Lee Jeffries, Tom Smith, Earl Carpenter, myself and maybe one or two others that I don't remember.

"We came to an agreement that the best way to get our fight going was to tie up Watson's, where we worked. Tom would get the men lined up on the Chicago end of Watson's runs. Lee and Fritz would take care of Lincoln. John, Earl and I would tie up the company's Kansas City terminal.

"The night we tied up Watson in Kansas City, the first driver who had been called for a run was Bert [Albert S.] Parker. He had a hot-freight load of bakery goods that was supposed to be in Omaha by 3 A.M. When we told him about the strike he refused to pull out the rig and everyone else on the dock also quit work.

"That's the kind of guts the men had, with no union behind us.

"Tom Watson, who had charge there, told us we couldn't do that to him. We answered: 'They ain't rolling, Watson.' Then we held a meeting on the street to decide what to do next.

"We called Omaha to report that the Kansas City terminal was shut down. Then we called the Teamster business agent at our end, O. B. Enloe of Local 41. The first thing he said when he came down was: 'I have been waiting for this for over a year.'

"About 3 A.M. Mace Brown, president of the Omaha Central Labor Union, called and I talked to him. He said we should bring the trucks to Omaha and join Local 554, which he called 'his union.' I didn't know Brown from Adam's green fox, so I asked to talk to one of the Watson drivers. I don't recall who it was I talked to, but he said it was okay to come on in because they had Omaha tied up and were about to join Local 554."

Developments similar to those described by Miller had also been taking place at other Watson terminals. Once the Omaha road drivers were all back in town, they marched in a body to the Labor Temple. There they joined Local 554 and Mace Brown helped to arrange a meeting at which they elected new local officers. After that Watson and the other trucking employers agreed to negotiate with the union, so the strikers returned to their jobs.

In the talks that followed the bosses offered little and stalled a lot. Things dragged along until the angry workers again launched a spontaneous walkout, this time at several trucking companies. The new tie-up, which lasted about two weeks, was conducted in defiance of the state's anti-picketing law, and it was very effective. Finally, on June 16, 1937, the bosses gave in. They signed a contract providing a minimum wage of forty-five cents an hour, well above the previous average rate for the city, along with other concessions. They also agreed to reinstate eleven workers who had been fired for union activity.

It was the first strike victory in the recollection of the oldest Omaha union worker.

A bit later the new leaders of Local 554 learned about the activity of the North Central District Drivers Council. Being interested, they sent a delegation to the January 1938 conference of the NCDDC in St. Paul. There was a comment on this in Miller's later letter to me:

"I was one of the delegates to the St. Paul conference," Lou wrote. "While we were there Jack Maloney showed us around the Twin Cities. I liked what I saw and found out what it meant to have a strong union."

During their visit the delegation also asked if Minneapolis Local 544 could send them some help. We responded by transferring Alfred Russell to Omaha. He was a young Trotskyist militant, who had been active in Local 544's Federal Workers Section. In Omaha he was soon put on the union's organizational staff, where he was able to give considerable help, thanks to his political training and the practical experience he had gained in Minneapolis.

Such was the setting in which a new conflict broke out in Omaha during 1938. It started in the spring of the year, when

Local 554 served the area contract demands upon the Nebraska Commercial Truckers Association. The bosses pretended to negotiate with the union, but the proceedings were a farce. The Association's lawyer, David Swarr, tried to talk Local 554's representatives to death, fogging every issue with a lot of legal lingo. Meanwhile, the bosses ran paid ads in the daily papers attacking the North Central Area Committee as "outside agitators" scheming to upset the "harmonious relations" between the local trucking firms and their employees.

As these developments showed, the Omaha companies were determined to prevent inclusion of their territory in any area-wide contract the IBT might be able to establish for over-the-road drivers. So they had set out to force Local 554 into a premature fight. They hoped thereby to split the local from the area formation and impose downgraded contract terms upon it; these terms would be decided through a strictly local battle. In the given relationship of class forces within the city, they expected to have a big edge in such a localized test of strength.

When their existing contract with Local 554 expired on May 31, 1938, the trucking bosses launched an offensive. Wherever possible they began to postpone shipments of freight for the deliberate purpose of causing unemployment in the industry. Union members were discriminated against through wage cuts and seniority violations. When the workers protested, the employers baited them on the job, daring them to go on strike.

These efforts to create confusion and turmoil in the union ranks were accompanied by another ploy. Swarr continued to stall in the negotiations with Local 554. And Mayor Butler, fronting for the bosses, used his position as the city's chief executive to promote a "public" clamor for arbitration of the issues in dispute.

Confronted with this challenge, the area committee held an emergency session in Omaha, which most of its members were able to attend despite the short notice they received. A discussion was first held with the officers of Local 554 to determine our strategy. It was agreed that we should try to avoid a showdown fight with the Omaha bosses for the time being. Chicago was a far superior battle ground on which to open our struggle for an area contract. The IBT was much stronger there than in Omaha, and a victory in Chicago would give us the most effective leverage with which to force all the trucking companies in the eleven-state area into line. Therefore temporary delay of the inevitable conflict in Omaha, while we carried through the Chicago fight, would best serve to assure a complete victory for Local 554 later on.

Having reached this understanding, a negotiating session with the Nebraska Commercial Truckers Association was arranged on June 16. It turned out to be a small mass meeting. Most of the trucking bosses attended, as did the officers of Local 554. In addition, all the area committee members who had come to town sat in, doing so to give the bosses a visual reminder that there were strong unions at the other end of their runs.

We proposed to the bosses that they make a temporary agreement with Local 554. As immediate steps, they were asked only to resume normal operations and settle outstanding grievances involving union members. With an eye to the propaganda value of our position, we contended that this was the proper way to restore a normal atmosphere within the industry. Only then could negotiations for the full terms of a contract renewal be carried on in a reasonable manner, we said, both to the bosses and in a public statement.

With Swarr speaking for them, the employers flatly rejected our proposal. So we decided to subject them to a limited squeeze by striking one firm only. Watson Brothers, which had the most extensive line operations, was chosen as our target. As a preparatory step, a telegram was sent to Tobin explaining that the bosses refused to negotiate in good faith. In keeping with his promise to cooperate with us in such cases, he gave tacit approval of the action we took.

Watson's was struck immediately after the June 16 negotiating session. The local facilities were shut down, the union defying the anti-picketing law. Simultaneously the company's terminals were tied up in Lincoln and Norfolk, Nebraska; also in Chicago, Des Moines, Sioux City, St. Joseph, and Kansas City. Although they were not part of our area formation, the Teamsters in Denver, Colorado, helped us by stopping Watson's operations at that terminal as well. This highly effective action was further reinforced by union drivers for other lines, who refused to handle feeder shipments to the struck company.

A day later the rest of the Omaha trucking firms locked out their employees. We noted, however, that they hesitated to admit publicly that it was an act of solidarity with Watson. Instead, they made the lame argument that they were afraid of the "risk" to their employees and customers, if they tried to operate under existing strike conditions. It was evident that our propaganda about trying to create a "normal atmosphere" for "reasonable negotiations" was causing the employers' association a problem.

We had no intention of allowing the bosses to entrap us

in an extension of the walkout. So Local 554 issued a public denial that there was a strike at any firm other than Watson's, and it repeated our proposal for a temporary agreement with the truck operators. Each day the workers who had been locked out reported to their jobs, and each day the union issued a public statement that they had done so.

After four days the employers backed off. They accepted temporary reinstatement of the expired contract. It was to continue in full force for another thirty days, after which either side could reopen it on forty-eight hours notice. They agreed to resume normal operations and restore employment to previous levels. In addition the temporary settlement included specific provisions for the payment of back wages involved in workers' grievances.

Although this termination of the four-day conflict represented only a lull before the coming storm, it marked an important gain for the union forces. The members of Local 554 had been inspired by the power the area committee showed in backing their cause. At the meeting where they ratified the temporary settlement there had been a discussion of the area committee's strategy in the coming contract fight. Recognizing the merit of the course we were following, the workers authorized and instructed the local's officers to act in full accordance with the area plans. As matters now stood we were in a position to launch the key fight for uniform contract terms at the time and in the place that we thought best.

To further assure that this would be the case, the area committee issued a directive which all local unions in the eleven states were asked to follow. It contained several provisions: no fights with the bosses were to be opened outside of Chicago without a decision of the area committee; during the battle in Chicago for a pilot contract no other local union was to tie up a company in support of Local 710, unless requested to do so; Local 710 was to serve notice on the Chicago employers that contract negotiations were desired forthwith; the area committee was to use its best discretion in the Chicago negotiations, and all local unions involved in the general campaign were to be kept informed of developments.

A letter was then sent in the name of Local 710 to all trucking firms operating into and out of Chicago. They were asked to meet with officers of the union for the purpose of arranging contract talks. The preliminary session we requested was held toward the end of June. Sandy O'Brien, Mike Healy, and Frank Brown spoke for Local 710; Joe Scislowski and I sat in as officers of the area committee. But only some 10 percent of the bosses turned up and they were rather vague about their intentions.

Quite obviously, the trucking employers needed a demonstration that we meant business. So Local 710 set a mid-June strike deadline for them to think about. At the same time O'Brien used his influence to secure pledges of support from both the Teamsters Joint Council and the Chicago Federation of Labor, the latter body representing all AFL unions in the city. These actions got results.

Just before the strike deadline a small committee of bosses asked for another meeting with us. When we got together they gave us a list of operators for whom they sought to speak. Some of these firms were headquartered outside Chicago, they said, and a little time was needed to get negotiating authority from the home offices. We granted them an extension of one week.

At the next meeting an employers' committee of significant weight appeared, consisting of representatives from over a dozen of the biggest outfits in the business. Jack Keeshin, of Keeshin Motor Express, served as its chairman. This committee now spoke for about 300 truck lines, including all the major firms based in Chicago. They hoped to represent even wider strata of firms, Keeshin said — if the union would press employers operating into Chicago from elsewhere in the area to come into the negotiations.

We had good reason to assume that this was not a stalling tactic. If employers find themselves compelled to deal with a union and grant concessions to the workers, they usually want to see their competitors put into the same fix. This attitude, of course, served our aim of establishing a pilot contract on the broadest possible area scale. So we gladly proffered the desired cooperation.

Finally, toward mid-August, actual contract talks got under way at the Merchandise Mart in Chicago. By this time the operators' committee was speaking for additional hundreds of employers. Keeshin assured the IBT area committee — whose entire membership had now joined in the deliberations — that all these participating companies would accept the outcome of the negotiations.

There was a catch in the matter of authoritative employer representation, however, right within the operators' committee. A couple of the bosses involved tried to send in lawyers to speak for them. This procedure met with objection from the union committee.

Either the company heads themselves must sit in on the

contract talks, we insisted, or their representatives must be given decision-making authority. Our primary object in this was to be in a position to force these key operators to sign the agreement the moment it could be successfully negotiated with them. In that way they could be prevented from reneging on their commitments, even if other bosses for whom they spoke objected to the outcome of our deliberations. Whatever might then happen on the latter score, the IBT would already have a firm base from which to battle for area-wide acceptance of the contract. For these reasons we hung tough on the point, and the bosses were forced to comply with our demand.

As it turned out, the absence of lawyers from the negotiations had another salutary effect. The final contract language was free of double-talk. It said exactly what was meant and meant exactly what was said. This made it hard for legal sharpies to twist formulations or try to represent them as the opposite of what the bosses had agreed to.

Our refusal to let powerless substitutes stand in for company heads was met by a counter demand upon us. Some operators questioned the union's right to represent their employees, and they wanted Labor Board elections to determine whether they had to bargain with us. As spokesman for our side, I proceeded to argue against the notion. Then one or two members of the union committee, long schooled in traditional IBT methods, interposed comments to the effect that they could see no harm in such elections. At that point I requested a recess so that we could consider the matter in private.

Arrangements for recesses of the kind had been made in advance. Besides the facilities for joint meetings, separate rooms had been provided for the two committees to hold caucuses. Whenever either side wanted to think out loud about a question, the joint talks could readily be interrupted for the purpose without any serious loss of time. This gave needed flexibility to the complex negotiating process, which went on day after day for well over a week.

At this particular caucus of the union committee two matters were taken up. One was the issue of Labor Board elections. The other had to do with our method of procedure when we were meeting with the operators' committee. A bit of discussion on the latter point brought full understanding that we couldn't afford to be contradicting one another in the presence of the bosses. It was agreed that we would always present a solid front in the joint sessions; at the same time any committee member, who wished to be heard on one or another point, would be free to request a recess for a private meeting. After that procedure was established the union's negotiating team functioned like a well-oiled machine.

Concerning the question of union representation elections, our ability to win such a vote was not the key point. The whole thing was simply a disruptive ploy. It was intended to stall the contract talks and throw into confusion our efforts to establish uniform wages and conditions on an area-wide scale. Consideration of the matter along these lines in our caucus discussion brought agreement that the union power should be used to establish our bargaining rights. We decided to return to the joint session and answer the bosses accordingly. If you doubt that we represent your employees, they were told, we will call a strike and you can count them on the picket lines. The operators' committee decided to drop the issue.

Making a 180 degree turn in line, the bosses not only recognized the IBT as sole representative of their over-the-road employees; they agreed that all these workers had to be members of the union. Their reasoning was not hard to fathom. Most of them were accustomed to dealing with union officials whose primary concern was to have dues-paying members. Once given some form of closed shop, such officials were usually lenient in contract negotiations and in the enforcement of settlement terms. The bosses thought this would still be the situation, not yet being fully aware that they were up against something entirely new.

As it turned out in this case, they were to be proven wrong on both counts. We fought hard on every issue, beginning with the question of wages on which we made quite an advance.

For through runs, from one terminal city to another, a minimum rate of two and three-quarters cents per mile was established for road drivers. This was only one-quarter of a cent below our original demand and it meant a significant gain in pay for most of them. Time spent on pickups and deliveries was to be computed at seventy-five cents an hour. This figure, five cents above the union demand, was granted as partial compensation for our concession of one-quarter of a cent on the mileage rate. A minimum of six hours pay at seventy-five cents was guaranteed on through runs.

A special category of local runs was established. These were to remain within a 75 mile radius of the terminal city and were not to exceed a round trip of 150 miles. The latter, seemingly obvious figure was set to prevent various forms of chiseling by the bosses. Drivers on these runs were to get no less than sixty cents an hour, with a minimum guarantee of five hours pay at that rate. Although this scale was lower than the pay on through runs, it signified a jump ahead for the drivers involved, in some cases a big one.

Up to six hours pay in each twenty-four hour period was required when equipment broke down on the road. The same guarantee was stipulated for layovers away from the home terminal, and the bosses had to provide comfortable, sanitary lodging. When deadheading (moving a tractor without a trailer, for example) drivers were to receive two-thirds of the regular scale. Previously they had often been called upon to deadhead equipment simply as a favor to the boss. It was further provided that in all operations the equipment had to be safe mechanically.

Quite an argument developed when we came to the question of impassable highways. The bosses contended that such things were in the "act of God" category and they could not be held responsible. Not wishing to offend anyone's religious sensibilities, we didn't quarrel about God's part in the matter. We simply insisted that the drivers shouldn't take the whole rap. In the end a compromise favorable to the workers was reached. When held up by impassable highways, drivers were to receive five hours pay in each twenty-four hour period, plus meals and comfortable, sanitary lodging.

Because the work week had previously been so insufferably long in most cases, we had to settle for a maximum of sixty hours in the first area contract. But at the same time, we got a commitment that wage negotiations could be reopened if the hourly maximum was reduced by legislative act.

Concerning individual owner-operators, we won the most complete coverage ever put into a union contract as of that date. Workers in this category were to have the same wages and conditions as all other drivers, and their wages had to be paid separate and apart from money they received for equipment rental. Mileage rates for equipment were set up according to the type involved. The leasing company had to pay all taxes and insurance premiums. There was to be no interest or handling charge, as in the past, on earned money advanced to owner-operators before the regular pay day; and they could not be forced to buy gas, oil, tires, etc. from the leasing company.

Full seniority rights were established to protect all union members on the job. Formal recognition was given of the IBT's right to set up job steward systems at all companies.

To handle matters of contract interpretation and enforcement, both the operators and the union were to create permanent area committees. These bodies were to help adjust

disputes which could not be settled directly between an operator and a local union. The joint committees were also to
formulate supplementary rules concerning labor conditions,
as the need arose through practical application of the agreement.

Most important of all, the union retained the right to strike
over enforcement of the contract. Besides that, it was stipulated that the companies could not try to send drivers through
the picket lines of any striking union.

The pact was to be in full force and effect from October 1,
1938 to October 31, 1939. This short delay in the initial effective date was intended to give the operators' committee an
opportunity to secure in advance the maximum number of
signatories among the trucking companies generally. So far
as the union was concerned, we had no doubts about general acceptance of the agreement by IBT locals in the area,
because we had kept in close consultation with them throughout the negotiations.

All the foregoing contract provisions were to apply uniform-
ly in an area defined as follows: Michigan, Ohio, Indiana,
Illinois, Wisconsin, Minnesota, Iowa, Missouri, North Dakota,
South Dakota, Nebraska, Kansas City, Kansas, and the south
bank of the Ohio river between Portsmouth, Ohio and Paducah,
Kentucky.

The negotiating committees arrived at the final terms of
agreement on August 23, 1938. We then insisted that both the
negotiating parties immediately sign the understanding that
had been reached. That was done the same day.

Operators who put their names on the dotted line included:
J. L. Keeshin, Carl Marinello, B. Cushman, H. H. Hiland,
John Gottlieb, E. C. Lacey, P. M. Greenberg, H. J. Lee, E. W.
Murphy, C. H. Ozee, W. F. Mullady, Walter Eden, M. A. Rid-
dle, Morris Tucker, Ray Schergert and F. A. Crowe, Sr.

Those signing for the union committee were: John T. O'Brien,
J. F. Scislowski, Carl Keul, E. J. Williams, T. T. Neal, J. M.
O'Laughlin, John A. Ray, Jack Maloney, Mike Healy, Frank
Brown, T. V. Smith, John Wirth, and Farrell Dobbs.

Also present on the final day of negotiations was Thomas L.
Hughes, general secretary-treasurer of the IBT. He, too, signed
the area pact, doing so in the name of the International as
a whole.

This was the biggest contract ever negotiated by the International Brotherhood of Teamsters up to that time. Directly
and indirectly, it stood to benefit an estimated 125,000 workers. Most would receive immediate raises in pay under the

uniform minimum rates that were to apply throughout the eleven states. They would also enjoy qualitative improvement in their working conditions.

In a minority of cases local unions had established wage rates slightly above the minimum set for the area. Their position was also protected in the broad agreement. It provided that wages, hours, and working conditions were to be maintained at the highest standards then in effect.

Definition of the area in which the contract would apply had been determined by the scope of the union power, not by the extent of operator representation in the Chicago negotiations. This left us with a two-fold task. First we needed to get voluntary acceptance of the pact by as many operators as possible. Then, using that achievement as one of the means, we had to knock the rest of them into line.

We began the new task by pressuring the trucking employers of the area to attend a conference in Chicago on August 31, which was called by the operators' negotiating committee. As a result of this gathering over 1,700 companies signed the agreement. Some firms in Ohio and Michigan held out for a time, but it didn't take long for them to capitulate. Large-scale resistance to the pact developed only in the southwestern part of the area. It was concentrated among trucking outfits in Iowa, Missouri, South Dakota and, of course, Nebraska.

With respect to IBT acceptance, the contract became official when it was unanimously ratified at a conference of 175 local unions, held in Indianapolis on September 7. The gathering also voted to make the area committee a permanent body. Only one change was made in its composition. Kenneth McCreery of Sioux Falls replaced Happy Holstein as the representative for South Dakota. The committee again designated Scislowski and me as its chairman and secretary.

The Indianapolis conference instructed all over-the-road locals to demand that the remaining operators sign the agreement at once. Wherever a local met with a refusal, all the circumstances were to be reported immediately to the area committee. Tom Hughes, who addressed the delegates, promised them support from the International against firms that tried to hold out against the union. His attitude reflected the favorable impression made on Tobin and himself by our success in getting the key bosses lined up without having to take strike action against them.

It wasn't to take long for a real free-for-all to break out. As would be expected, it began in Omaha.

IBT area committee members present at emergency conference in Omaha, June 1938. Facing page, l. to r.: (top) Jack Wirth, Farrell Dobbs; (middle) John Ray, William Ryan; (bottom) T. V. Smith, T. T. Neal; (this page, top) Happy Holstein, Red O'Laughlin; (middle) Mike Healy, Carl Keul; (bottom) Jack Maloney.

20. Siege of Nebraska

Soon after signing the temporary agreement with General Drivers Local 554 the previous June, the Omaha bosses resumed their offensive against the workers. Red-baiting was used as an opening gambit.

One day police detectives barged into the union hall and arrested Alfred Russell, who had been sent from Minneapolis to serve on the Local 554 staff. He was held in jail and told that a promise to go elsewhere would bring his immediate release. After three days he was taken into court and given ninety days for "vagrancy." In passing sentence the judge said it would be suspended if Al left town.

A paid union organizer receiving the average wage for truck drivers in the city had been convicted as a "vagrant." By implication all the drivers were being stigmatized as "bums." The union membership reacted angrily to this outrageous boss attack and voted to support an appeal of the sentence.

Dewey Hanson, a local attorney, had been retained by the union to defend Russell. At my request Albert Goldman, a prominent Chicago lawyer and a leading Trotskyist, rushed to Omaha to help on the appeal. Cooperation was also received from the American Civil Liberties Union.

When Russell was arrested the police had searched his apartment without a warrant, taking copies of radical literature and private letters. This material was used in an attempt to blackmail the union. If he didn't leave town, the cops warned, all of it would be turned over to the newspapers. But the union brushed aside the threat to intensify the red-baiting smear, which had already begun in the capitalist press when the arrest was first made.

The defense attorneys were authorized to initiate replevin proceedings to regain the illegally seized property. This action soon led to the return of the victimized union organizer's personal files.

When the "vagrancy" case again came up a bit later, the prosecutor argued that there was nothing to be appealed to a higher court because the suspended sentence Russell had been offered was in reality "no sentence at all." The judge agreed and dismissed the charge, thus ending the case. Like the rest of the capitalist stooges in government, he hesitated to let the odor of the stinking plot get beyond the confines of Omaha.

Local 554 had beaten off a frame-up attempt, and in the process the membership had been inoculated against red-baiting.

It was not long after this episode that the area contract negotiations opened in Chicago. While they were going on, representatives of the Omaha trucking firms sat in from time to time, simply to keep abreast of developments. They had no intention whatever of accepting the agreement that was reached, as they were now to demonstrate.

The day following ratification of the area pact by the IBT at its Indianapolis conference, Local 554 presented the agreement to the Nebraska Commercial Truckers Association with a request that it be signed. Demands were also submitted for renewal of the expired contract covering local transfer operations, with improvements in wages and working conditions.

Both the highway operators and the city trucking companies, acting in collusion with the upper echelons of the state's ruling class, responded with a concerted attempt to smash the union. No chances were taken of allowing the IBT to force the capitulation of major firms one at a time. The Truckers Association precipitated a general lockout of Omaha employees in the industry on September 9, 1938, not even waiting for expiration of the forty-eight-hour notice required under the temporary agreement then in effect.

A simultaneous lockout took place in Sioux City, Iowa, where over-the-road operators functioned largely as a satellite of the Omaha terminal. Local 383, whose contract with the Sioux City firms had expired on June 25, had also demanded acceptance of the new area pact.

This employer offensive put the IBT to a decisive test. We had to crush the capitalist resistance that was being generated around the Omaha strong point. If we failed to do so, the gains already registered elsewhere would begin to slip through our fingers; the relationship of class forces would be reversed to our disadvantage. If we won the fight, on the other hand, the union's eleven-state power could be fully consolidated, and still further advances could be achieved.

The chips were down—and the North Central Area Committee swiftly went into action. The lockout was turned into a strike, and the action was extended beyond the points of origin in Omaha and Sioux City. Every terminal of the Omaha-based operators was shut down. This spread the pressure on them to Grand Island, Lincoln, Norfolk, and Fremont, Nebraska; Mason City, Marshalltown, Cedar Rapids, Ottumwa, Burlington, Clinton, and Des Moines, Iowa; Chicago, Peoria, and Rock Island, Illinois; St. Joseph and Kansas City, Missouri; Minneapolis and St. Paul, Minnesota. Once again the Denver Teamsters, along with the IBT local in Cheyenne, Wyoming, pitched in to help us from outside the eleven-state area.

All told, over 3,000 workers were now involved in the struggle.

Despite Nebraska's anti-picketing law, companies throughout the state that refused to sign the area contract were tied up. In Omaha itself all local transfer concerns were also closed down. To back up these actions pickets from Local 554 constantly patrolled the highways leading into the city, allowing only firms that had signed with the union to operate. In doing so, care was taken to assure that farmers bringing produce to market, who were generally in sympathy with the union, would not be interfered with.

To all intents and purposes, we had laid siege to Omaha and the state of Nebraska, like Grant did to Vicksburg. Our task was now to hold firm in the established positions and to steadily intensify use of the union power against the class enemy. The latter aim required action against trucking employers in South Dakota, Iowa, and Missouri who had not signed the area contract. As we moved against them the siege lines around Nebraska would gradually be tightened. In the end this would force the Omaha bosses to capitulate.

At this critical point I became ill and had to leave the scene of action. Upon returning to Minneapolis I was hospitalized for about three weeks; and after that the doctor prescribed extended bed rest at home. In this situation the value of having shaped the area committee as a leadership team was fully demonstrated.

Red O'Laughlin stepped into the gap, assuming my function as spokesman for the committee. In fact he virtually settled down in Omaha to give direct support to Local 554 on a day-by-day basis, as did Mike Healy and Joe Scislowski. Harry De-Boer and Ray Rainbolt made frequent trips there from Minneapolis to lend the embattled workers a hand. O'Laughlin also called in Jimmy Hoffa at various times to help out on one or another task in the strike. In addition Jack Maloney shuttled back and forth between Sioux City and the Nebraska terminals, helping to coordinate the overall struggle.

O'Laughlin and Maloney kept in touch with me through a telephone in my hospital room. At one stage each of them came to Minneapolis for extended discussion of some of the main problems. All in all, our teamwork was continuing as usual and with the necessary effectiveness.

There was even a touching demonstration on the human side, which reflected the comradeship that had developed among us. Healy, a tough guy with a big heart, called Marvel Scholl to ask if we needed any financial aid in handling family problems caused by my illness. Thanking Mike for his thoughtfulness, Marvel assured him that we could rely on Minneapolis Local 544 to see us through any economic difficulties that might arise.

In the strike itself the functioning leaders faced two key problems. These were to prevent scab trucking operations and to see that the bosses were unable to starve out the workers in the long struggle that was beginning to unfold. Negotiations were not yet a factor at that juncture. No new developments were to be expected in that quarter until there had been a further test of strength.

All the area leaders present in Omaha were old hands at maintaining effective picket lines. Besides that, the young, less experienced militants of Local 554 were learning these arts swiftly in the course of struggle, as were the Local 383 members in Sioux City. As a result the strike was keeping operations halted. Random attempts by trucking firms to move equipment with scabs were quickly scotched by the union forces.

Several measures were instituted to meet imperative needs of the strikers and their families. A commissary was set up at union headquarters. It served six hot meals in every twenty-four hour period to the pickets, who maintained their lines round-the-clock on twelve-hour shifts. Strikers and their wives staffed the kitchen. The families of union members were welcome to join them at meals there.

After a time arrangements were made to distribute groceries to the homes of strikers and to give enough help on house rent to ward off evictions.

Ed Palmquist of Local 544's Federal Workers Section came in from Minneapolis to help organize a fight to get city relief for needy families involved in the walkout. Mace Brown of the Omaha Central Labor Union cooperated in the effort.

Immediately, the bosses launched a big campaign against this demand, and the authorities consistently held such aid down to a bare minimum of cases.

As a consequence, the union faced a big financial burden. Help was, therefore, urgently needed from elsewhere in the IBT and it was quickly forthcoming. Some ninety Teamster locals in the area made substantial contributions. Then, in the third week of the strike, the area committee sent a delegation to Indianapolis to request direct aid from the International.

Tobin now found himself caught in a contradiction. Formally, he didn't have to pay benefits in this situation, the strike having been called without observing IBT constitutional procedures. Yet he had already given tacit approval of the action by his earlier promise to support the area committee against employers who refused to negotiate in good faith.

There was still another factor involved. The IBT head was intrigued by the major gains we had registered through the Chicago negotiations. New members were pouring into the union at an increasing rate. Per capita payments to the International were rapidly growing in volume. This implied unprecedented growth in the power and status of the organization over which he presided, which gave added incentive for him to help in the struggle.

So Tobin decided to get around the formal matter of IBT "law" by making lump sum contributions periodically. The strikers' most urgent needs could thus be met, enabling them to hang tough against the bosses. At the same time he remained free to cut off such support whenever he might choose. And to doubly protect his control over the money situation, Tobin put Edward F. Murphy of Cleveland, an IBT vice president, in charge of doling out aid to the members of Locals 554 and 383.

Murphy arrived in Omaha with the first strike benefits toward the end of September. By then the bosses were preparing a series of strikebreaking moves, beginning with an attempt to incite farmers against the union. Agents provocateurs stoned trucks bringing produce to market. Lurid tales were then spread blaming strikers for the attacks in an effort to incite the farmers, the aim being to use them as a front for sending armed convoys through picket lines. But effective union publicity spiked the scheme.

In an effort to hold small operators around Nebraska in line, the big Omaha firms spread lies about the terms of the area contract negotiated in Chicago. Attempts were then made to get their help in mobilizing vigilante assaults on workers picketing the highways. Local 554 got wind of the maneuver and arranged a meeting with a committee of small operators. They were given a true picture of the contract demands and assured that immediate acceptance would not disqualify them from any modifications downward in the final terms of the Omaha settlement. As a result about sixty small outfits signed the agreement.

On September 29 Mike Sherman, a U. S. labor conciliator, arranged a negotiating session between the union and the employers. Nothing came of it. The operators' committee would do no more than promise to give Sherman an explanation later as to why they rejected the workers' demands.

Shortly after this session the Omaha police began a campaign of mass arrests. Chief Pszanowski told the cops: "If you suspect anybody is going to start trouble, throw them in jail."

Carload after carload of cruising pickets were then picked up, wherever they were found on the streets. In a few days over sixty were arrested. Then the judges cooperated with Pszanowski to hold them in jail as long as possible without bail.

A united labor movement came to the strikers' defense, both the Omaha Central Labor Union and the Nebraska State Federation of Labor joining in the effort. Public clamor raised by union officials was reinforced by the victimized pickets themselves. They threw the slop fed to them into the jail corridors, banged tin cups on the bars and generally raised hell. This united effort forced their release on bail, usually at fifty dollars each. When they were brought to trial all but seven were freed. Those convicted were found guilty of charges so minor that only small fines could be levied against them.

At the same time the union movement prepared to challenge the constitutionality of the state's anti-picketing law. Although there was little or no chance of getting results in the Nebraska courts, the action helped the strikers in a propaganda sense.

In the meantime, the bosses had begun to send trucks onto the streets, the fink drivers armed with tear-gas guns and revolvers. Acts of violence against the strikers soon resulted. John Bigley had a six-shooter emptied at him. He was then set upon by a gang of strikebreakers, but fellow unionists rescued him. Another picket, Carl Paulson, was deliberately run over by a scab truck, receiving injuries serious enough to require hospital treatment.

These acts of violence against the workers were then cynically used by the bosses to demand that the governor send in the National Guard. That was a bit too raw, though, and the attempt fizzled.

Next the employers tried to split the union ranks by promoting a "back-to-work" movement. Through a ruse the finks involved were able to schedule a meeting one Sunday at the Labor Temple. Several loyal unionists attended, thinking it was an official affair. When they saw the score, however, a call was made to strike headquarters and reinforcements rushed to the scene. In the flare-up that followed, a number of finks got banged up; Malcolm G. Love, a union officer, sprained his arm; and Tom Smith, the secretary-treasurer, got his hand cut by a razor. After it was over the victorious strikers adjourned to their headquarters for a Sunday chicken dinner.

During this period comparable strikebreaking efforts also developed in Sioux City. As in Omaha, the capitalist press was hostile to the Teamsters; efforts were made to incite the farmers against the union; and public relief was denied to strikers.

Numbers of Local 383 members were arrested on trumped-up charges. These included unlawful assembly, rioting, assault and battery, breaking and entering, arson, and other allegations dreamed up by the prosecutors. Cash bond was demanded for those jailed, usually set at $1,000.

Despite the harassment to which they were thus subjected, the strikers held firm in both Sioux City and Omaha. So far as the ranks were concerned, seasoning in the struggle had, if anything, given them greater collective strength.

Within the area committee, on the other hand, some difficulties had developed. Ed Murphy seemed to think that his assignment from Tobin required him to assume central leadership authority in the conflict. There were several factors, however, that militated against his doing so. He was virtually unknown to the strikers. Because he had played no role in the earlier Omaha battles, he had only a limited grasp of the situation. Similarly, he lacked a complete feel of nuances involved in the area contract terms, since he had not participated in the Chicago negotiations. On top of that, the Ohio locals, which Murphy represented, had tended to give little more than token support to the broad over-the-road campaign. In these circumstances the area committee members present in Omaha were reluctant to entrust him with the authority he sought to assume. Friction resulted that could endanger the embattled local unions.

Parallel with this development still another problem had arisen. Provincial-minded heads of some Teamsters Joint Councils began to intensify their opposition to the area campaign. Over-the-road locals within these bodies were urged to have nothing further to do with the drive for an eleven-state contract. To reinforce the pressure, gossip was peddled about impending doom in the Omaha-Sioux City strike.

At this juncture a special area committee meeting was called in Chicago to review the general situation and chart a further course of action. Both O'Laughlin and Maloney telephoned me to report what was happening, and it was clear that a critical stage had been reached in our struggle. So I cut short my convalescence and flew to Chicago to participate in the session there.

In the discussion that took place we managed to put the real picture of the situation back into perspective. Actually the strike remained solid, the prospects of ultimate victory excellent. The seeming difficulties were of an internal union nature and largely artificial; they could be overcome through judicious effort on the part of the area committee.

As a first step we agreed that the International should be provided with a full account of the way things stood in our fight against the bosses. Shortly after the meeting I prepared such a report in Omaha and sent it to Indianapolis. This action soon paid off handsomely.

One day Tobin sent word that it was urgently necessary for me to be in his office the following morning. When I got there he took me into a room where a delegation was waiting to see him. Among those present were Henry Berger of Chicago, E. M. Eslinger of Kansas City, and L. Camie of St. Louis, the latter two being heads of the Teamsters Joint Councils in their respective cities. When they saw me their faces fell.

Tobin opened the session by remarking that — since he understood the delegation had some complaints to make about the area committee — he had called me in to give the necessary explanations. Our critics had nothing to offer but erroneous notions about the state of the over-the-road strike, along with bits of gossip that were patently untrue. This led the IBT head to tell them, in effect, that he was competent to supervise the eleven-state campaign and that they should confine their attention to the duties of their specific posts in the union.

Plainly enough, the International officers had shifted from their earlier position of putting concern for the wishes of the

Joint Council heads above the needs of the over-the-road campaign. They were now ready to give the area committee a
degree of priority that would tip the scales in our favor. Any
doubts on this score were demonstratively removed when a
statement concerning a later, broader conference at Indianapolis was issued over the signatures of Tobin and Hughes.
It said:

"Meeting held in the Headquarters of the International Union
November 2, 1938. Present at said meeting:

"E. M. Eslinger, Local 541, Kansas City. William Ryan,
Local 600, St. Louis. T. T. Neal, Local 41, Kansas City.
O. B. Enloe, Local 41, Kansas City. Mike Healy, Local 710,
Chicago. J. M. O'Laughlin, Local 299, Detroit. Jos. F. Scislow-
ski, Local 200, Milwaukee. John T. O'Brien, Local 710, Chi-
cago. Emmet J. Williams, Local 135, Indianapolis. Jack Ma-
loney, Local 383, Sioux City. Frank Brown, Local 710,
Chicago. Ray E. Rainbolt, Local 221, Minneapolis. Miles B.
Dunne, Joint Council 32, Minneapolis. Farrell Dobbs, Local
544, Minneapolis. Carl Keul, Local 90, Des Moines. Thomas V.
Smith, Local 554, Omaha.

"Also present were General President Daniel J. Tobin, Gen-
eral Secretary-Treasurer Thomas L. Hughes, Assistant to the
General President, John M. Gillespie, General Organizers Henry
G. Berger, Edward Murphy and F. D. Brown. . . .

"It was decided . . . that the International Union was absolutely in sympathy with the [over-the-road] strike and was
rendering every possible help it could under its laws toward
the winning of the strike. . . .

"It was decided by the conference to continue the strike indefinitely if necessary, and to put forth greater efforts toward
the winning of the strike. . . .

"It was decided to appoint a committee of four to act with
a General Organizer, said committee to have full power of
settling all questions where any misunderstanding arose in the
several local unions involved in the strike, and that when
a majority of this committee decided a certain policy was right
or wrong, or made any other decision pertaining to any local
in any district, that said local must abide by the decision
of the majority of the committee; that on the failure of any
officer or local to comply with the decision of said committee, the International President would be notified and he would
immediately suspend either the officer or the local union for
their refusal to carry out the decision of the committee. . . .

"The General President appointed on the committee: Edward
Murphy, General Organizer, to represent the International
Union and to act as Chairman of the Committee; Farrell Dobbs

of Local 544, Minneapolis, Minnesota; John O'Brien of Local 710, Chicago, Illinois; Jos. F. Scislowski of Local 200, Milwaukee; and J. M. O'Laughlin of Local 299, Detroit, Michigan.

"It was understood that if Brother O'Brien of Chicago could not serve he would appoint to act for him, Mike Healy of Local 710."

It appeared that Ed Murphy had been named chairman of the special committee primarily to assure his continued supervision of the distribution of benefits to the strikers. In any case he no longer undertook to assume leadership of the struggle itself. That function was now completely in the hands of the North Central Area Committee. And internal union opponents of our campaign had been effectively warned off.

Word of the Tobin-Hughes action got around swiftly and it had considerable impact on the bosses. Within a week the largest firms operating out of Sioux Falls, South Dakota, signed the area contract. Soon after that the union also broke through in Des Moines, Iowa.

In the latter city, Local 90 had struck both the long distance operators and the local transfer outfits early in October. On November 13 negotiations took place with these companies. It quickly became apparent that they were ready to come to terms, so word was sent to the union hall that the membership should gather there in the evening for a report. About 1:00 A.M. on November 14 the union committee arrived at the hall to give the strikers an account of the proposed settlement.

The Des Moines operators had accepted the area agreement in its entirety. On local transfer work drivers got a 5¢ raise, bringing their hourly wage to 57 1/2¢. Dockers and warehouse workers got a 7 1/2¢ hike, giving them an hourly rate of 55¢. Working conditions were also improved. A delighted membership unanimously accepted these terms.

While these union conquests were in the making, the Omaha bosses had launched another frame-up attack on Local 554. Their action was intended to offset locally the impact of our victories in Des Moines and Sioux Falls. It stemmed from growing desperation over the way we were steadily narrowing the Nebraska operators' sphere of influence.

During the night of November 8-9, unknown assailants fired on a rig belonging to the Wilson Trucking Co. of Kearny, Nebraska. The driver, who was a union member, received a flesh wound in the leg. He was on the job because the company had signed the area contract and was free to operate into Omaha.

An IBT member operating a truck under the terms of the over-the-road agreement had been shot. Yet the city police

responded with a raid on the union hall the following morning. There were sixty-two members there at the time. All were
jailed and ordered held "for investigation." But it was such
a crude act of provocation that the cops had to release the
victims almost immediately.

The employers had seemed to hope that this caper would
enable them to stall further contract talks. Instead they now
found that position untenable. So they agreed to resume negotiations with the union on November 15.

During the talks Fay Watson, head of the largest Omaha
truck line, tried a bit of cute red-baiting. "You should be able
to understand our situation, Mr. Dobbs," he said. "Even your
man Marx talked about the falling rate of profit."

Watson appeared only to be repeating a rumor he had heard
about what Marx wrote. Besides, his crack was intended to
divert attention from the concrete issues in dispute. So I let
it pass with this curt reply: "Since you are quoting Marx,
Mr. Watson, let me remind you that he also said a capitalist
who can't pay a living wage should go out of business."

Other members of the union committee began to chuckle,
and with that the particular exchange ended.

The "falling rate of profit" remark had been injected in the
course of employer arguments in support of their counterpro-
posals for a working agreement. They pressed for a mileage
rate 1/2¢ below the area scale, with the drivers paying their
own expenses on the road. Payment on a hundredweight basis
for pickups and deliveries was demanded, instead of by the
hour. A cut-rate scale of 47 1/2¢ an hour was called for on
local runs. In addition they wanted an unlimited work week;
a three-year agreement; arbitration of grievances; and a no-
strike pledge for the entire contract period.

It was clear that the screws would have to be tightened further before these bosses would be ready to talk sense. That
meant we had to turn to the next place where added pressure
could be put upon them. So we shifted our attention to Kansas
City. The operators there had not yet signed with the IBT,
and they were helping the Omaha truckers bootleg some freight
through roundabout connections. We had to force Kansas
City into line, even if it took a strike to do so. However, as
matters stood that perspective entailed some immediate problems for us.

Tobin had agreed to help us in Omaha and Sioux City
on the condition that we would not broaden the strike. Moreover, if we crossed him up, it would enable our opponents
in the Kansas City Joint Council to make trouble for us. For
these reasons it was advisable to get International approval
before taking the proposed new step. We needed first to go to

Indianapolis for that purpose and then move in on the Kansas City bosses. To do so, however, the area leaders involved in the Omaha negotiations had to get loose without appearing to be breaking off contract talks. Otherwise the operators could put the union in a bad propaganda light.

We solved the Omaha part of the difficulty through a statement made tongue in cheek. The bosses were told that we could make no concessions on the area contract terms without Tobin's permission. For that reason a temporary postponement of negotiations was needed so we could go to consult him. The operators went for this pretext, thinking that we were about to give in to them, and they issued an optimistic public statement in that vein.

In preparation for the talk with Tobin we marked up a map. It gave a graphic picture of the manner in which Kansas City operators were helping Omaha firms transport freight. Then Jack Maloney, Red O'Laughlin, and I headed for Indianapolis on November 23. Ted Neal of Local 41 met us there.

The map turned the trick for us. Tobin studied the situation it depicted and then said admiringly: "Just like a general."

We had expected at best to get his informal agreement to shut down the Kansas City firms. But he had become inspired enough to go all the way. A careful briefing followed on the procedure to get official strike approval and maximum financial support.

Our demands were to be presented to the Kansas City operators. If they refused to discuss them seriously, we were to call Tobin and report the situation. He would poll the International Executive Board members by telephone, recommending that the International support a strike against them. Official approval would then be rushed to us in a telegram that could be shown to the bosses.

Apparently the IBT head considered us rather quick on the trigger when it came to launching walkouts. His parting words were: "Remember now, I want to help you, so don't call a strike until you get my wire."

During our flight to Kansas City I reflected on the discussion with him. An analogy soon came to mind. His guidance in getting strike authorization had been akin to charting a course for a friendly vessel through the mine fields of a wartime harbor.

Upon our arrival in the Missouri town we checked into Hotel Muehlebach, where negotiations with the operators were to take place. Sandy O'Brien, who had been informed of the out-

come of the talk with Tobin, joined us there. His presence
was especially important, since it constituted a visible threat
to trucking companies operating into Chicago.

We met the over-the-road bosses on the morning of November 28. Many were present. They had come from various parts
of Missouri and Kansas, also from as far into the southwest
as Texas. Feeling that they had important friends in the Kansas City and St. Louis Joint Councils of the Teamsters, they
assumed a cocky attitude toward us. Under no circumstances,
we were told, would they sign the area contract. Nor would
there be any negotiations at all, except on the basis of proposals they had drafted.

After a short discussion we asked for a recess until about
4:00 P.M., so that we might study their proposals. Then I
telephoned Tobin and reported what had happened. Again
he warned: "Remember, don't act until you hear from me.
I expect to get a wire to you before the afternoon is over."

He was as good as his word. A telegram arrived a few hours
later, giving official strike approval and guaranteeing payment of benefits to the workers involved.

We then went back into session with the operators. As an
opener Tobin's message was handed to them. Upon reading
it their cockiness suddenly vanished, and this time they asked
for a recess. Later in the evening we received word that they
were ready to resume discussion. A sub-committee had been
chosen with full power to act, we were told. Its members would
be ready to meet with us the following morning and to continue negotiations until a settlement was reached.

In the bargaining that followed, the bosses fully accepted the
standard contract on long hauls into the rest of the eleven-
state area, as our perspectives required. On that basis we
agreed to some modifications concerning through operations
that did not touch the other ten states and on local runs in
the immediate vicinity of a given Missouri terminal.

The changes, which were specified in a rider attached to the
standard agreement, involved secondary limitations on certain
forms of wage increases. For example, fifty-five cents an hour
was called for on local runs (five cents below the area scale).
Pay for pickup and delivery time was set at fifty-five cents
an hour (twenty cents under the area rate) on trips wholly
within Missouri, also on runs between Missouri and Kansas,
Oklahoma, Texas, and Colorado. A few other minor adjustments were included concerning operations entirely within
the state.

From a union viewpoint this arrangement was advisable

in the given circumstances. Drivers' earnings, as a whole, on runs of the kind had previously been well below the standards that we were able to set for comparable operations in most of the other ten states. It was unwise, therefore, to lead the workers into a strike, merely to bring these secondary provisions up to full area standards in a single leap. Had we tried to do so, the workers' reaction generally would most likely have been unfavorable, since the bosses' offer did provide them with a substantial raise as it was.

Moreover, these modifications in no way impaired the overall force and effect of the area agreement. In fact, the way had been prepared for the Denver Teamsters to successfully impose the full area terms on all eastbound operations from that terminal when their existing contract with the employers expired about four months later. And a basis had been laid for later expansion of the over-the-road drive further into the southwest.

In a separate pact, improvements were won for Kansas City workers engaged in local transfer services. Pay increases of from 5¢ to 7 1/2¢ an hour were gained. Advances were also registered in working conditions.

On December 14, 1938, these contracts were signed by the employers, after having been approved by the memberships of the Missouri Teamster locals involved and the ranks of Local 498 in Kansas City, Kansas. The Denver union had also been consulted.

A major victory had been won without having to take strike action. This achievement helped our relations with Tobin, who noted that we had not recklessly abused his trust. As a result he became more willing than ever to help defeat the remaining holdouts in the area, a goal that we were now in an excellent position to attain.

With Kansas City brought under union control, the last significant gap had been closed in our siege lines around Nebraska. This gave us a firm stranglehold on both the Omaha trucking employers and their satellites in Sioux City.

21. An Unprecedented Triumph

Chills must have gone through the Omaha bosses when news reached them of our attack on their southern flank. They knew that a union breakthrough in Missouri would leave them completely isolated, standing alone against the concentrated power of the IBT. Only local strikebreaking could then prevent their defeat, and it had to be accomplished soon. So, without awaiting the outcome of the Kansas City negotiations, they moved to intensify the repressive measures against Local 554.

In their campaign the trucking employers were backed up by the city's entire ruling class. Meetings of various business groups were held to plan specific measures. Although the sessions took place behind closed doors, it didn't take long for the capitalists' decisions to come to light.

Landlords demanded that the strikers immediately pay their back rent or face eviction. Finance companies pressed for repayment of loans and took steps to seize whatever collateral had been put up. Bill collectors hounded the workers for installment payments on automobiles, clothing, furniture, washing machines, and other items. Hundreds of union members were subjected to these extreme pressures; and they naturally turned to the organization for aid in keeping a roof over their heads and in preventing loss of their few possessions.

An appeal was made to the International officers for help and they sent a $3,500 cashier's check. Then, when Local 554 presented it at the Omaha National Bank, the officials refused to cash it. One of them, a Mr. Flowers, brazenly asserted that honoring a draft intended for use by strikers was "not in accord with good banking practices." It proved to be an ineffective move, however; the union simply got the check cashed in Kansas City.

One worker commented about these experiences: "I thought we were striking against the truck operators. It seems we've taken on the *Omaha World-Herald*, the national bank, the relief office, the police, and most every other boss in town."

Despite these new, heavy pressures, the union ranks continued to hold firm. Only a few small shipments got by the pickets. As a result the bosses became even more desperate.

Hired thugs were turned loose against the strikers. When a few of them chanced to be arrested for illegally carrying weapons, the judges let them off with one dollar fines and saw to it that they were issued gun permits. Thus free to roam the streets at will, these hoodlums attacked both pickets and trucks operated by firms that had signed with the union.

In one case the thugs riddled a picket car with shotgun pellets. The three strikers riding in it — Lard Ryan, Peck Alderman, and Ralph Gilson — received minor wounds. Then the police arrested the victims on frame-up charges from earlier in the struggle, and the union had to put up fifty-dollar cash bonds for their release. Later the charges were dismissed for lack of evidence. Meanwhile the bosses' gunmen, who had attacked the strikers, went scot free.

In Omaha and Sioux City alike, truck drivers were jailed in large numbers. The immediate aim was to weaken union morale and lay the groundwork to resume freight runs between the two terminals on a scab basis. Although they failed in this objective, the cops were doing their best to help the bosses.

Pickets were harassed day after day with "nuisance" arrests. First they would be held "for investigation." Then phony charges would be placed against them, usually for something like "malicious mischief." It got so bad for outstanding militants that, when released from jail, they virtually met themselves going back in. As this process continued the city authorities began to raise the ante, moving directly against union leaders. A typical episode of the latter kind occurred in Sioux City.

One day a fink truck was deliberately parked across the street from the Local 383 hall. Provocateurs then tipped it over. Shortly thereafter a police detail stormed into the union headquarters, claiming that pickets had damaged the scab rig. Then they undertook to arrest two strike leaders, Jack Maloney and Ralph Johnson. The intended victims demanded that the cops produce warrants. Since they couldn't do so, other workers present also took a hand in trying to fight them off. Quite a scuffle followed before the arrests were made.

Maloney and Johnson were charged with "malicious mischief" and "resisting and assaulting an officer." Cash bonds of $2,000 each had to be posted to get them out of jail. As in this case, stiff bail generally was being imposed on strikers, which made it necessary for Local 383 to put up a total of over $50,000 during this period alone.

By this time the Kansas City operators had capitulated to

the North Central Area Committee. The Omaha bosses reacted to the development by trying a new pitch, aimed at
Tobin. A meeting was requested with him on the grounds
that it was the best way to straighten things out in the local
dispute. Tobin replied that any settlement would have to be
negotiated by the special union committee consisting of O'Brien,
Scislowski, O'Laughlin, and Dobbs.

After that David Swarr, speaking for the Nebraska Commercial Truckers Association, made a direct demand upon
the officers of Local 554. He insisted that the operators' proposal for a cut-rate contract again be submitted to a membership vote. Although the workers had previously rejected
the proposed terms, the bosses seemed to hope that their will
would have been weakened by the pounding they had been
getting from all sections of the ruling class. It was a vain hope.

The union meeting was held as requested, and the operators' proposals were resubmitted with appropriate comments.
A suggestion was then made from the floor to burn the operators' document. Several workers immediately tossed packs
of matches onto the speakers' platform. After the laughter
subsided a voice vote was taken. The windows of the hall
rattled as the membership uttered a thunderous "No!"

After fifteen weeks of grueling struggle, the Omaha strikers
remained as determined as ever to win their battle against
the employers. And the mood was the same in Sioux City.
These heroic rank-and-file fighters had become the backbone
of the entire area campaign. In the given circumstances, of
course, they needed outside help to achieve victory. But without their firm stand at the scene of action, the rest of the IBT
forces would have had no base from which to contend against
the employers' Omaha-Sioux City axis. The territory involved
would have had to be written out of the area, and the broad
campaign would have suffered a setback accordingly.

As it was, thanks to the workers' fighting qualities, the
union's position was steadily improving. The bosses, on the
other hand, were now in a hopeless bind. It could no longer
do them any good to lash out viciously at the strikers, but
they tried it anyway.

Two officers of Local 554, Malcolm G. Love and Walker
K. Stultz, were arrested at Columbus, Nebraska, while picketing. The action taken against them in this out-of-the-way place
was part of a plot that was carefully cooked up by the bosses.
Jailing strike leaders away from the main arena of the struggle made it harder to arrange their defense. In this way, our
enemies hoped, the union could be subjected to double handicaps. It would be weakened at the top, and the blows thus

dealt would have a more lasting effect. At least that seemed to be the way the script read, even though matters didn't work out as the bosses had expected.

David Weinberg, who had been serving as counsel for Local 554 ever since the hard fighting began, rushed to Columbus to handle the defense. Because of the seriousness of the case, Albert Goldman once again made a special trip from Chicago to aid him.

At first Love and Stultz were charged simply with violation of the state's anti-picketing law. Then the frame-up was compounded by accusing them of carrying concealed weapons. Property was refused as security for bond and cash bail of $2,100 was set. This failed, however, to present as big a problem as the authorities had thought it would. Between the Minneapolis Teamsters Joint Council and a friendly Omaha merchant the money was quickly raised.

Love was then released, but it took a bit more effort to free Stultz, because a charge of kidnapping had also been cooked up against him. As it turned out the bosses had gained nothing. The two officers were soon available for union duty, and part of any strike settlement would have to be the dropping of such charges against the workers.

Using the Columbus frame-up as a springboard, the strikers picketed the Nebraska legislature at Lincoln. Support was received from other trade unionists. Banners were carried protesting police harassment and demanding repeal of the state's anti-picketing law. The legislators themselves were denounced for their servile role as agents of the Omaha Business Men's Association. Although the action did not bring repeal of the anti-democratic statute, it did give new impetus to the growing popular support of the Teamsters' struggle.

The latter trend was further helped along when Local 554 finally managed to establish regular publication of a strike bulletin. Late in December the *Farmer-Labor Press* of Council Bluffs printed a special edition for the purpose, sponsored and edited by the union. Carlos Hudson of the *Northwest Organizer* staff made several trips to Omaha to assist in this project.

On December 24 truck drivers took to the streets with 30,000 copies of the first issue of their bulletin. At one busy intersection in downtown Omaha over 5,000 copies were sold in less than an hour. The paper was also distributed in Sioux City, as well as in Nebraska and western Iowa towns generally, and copies were sent to IBT locals throughout the area. Several more issues of the bulletin were gotten out in rapid succession. Then the publishers turned the *Farmer-*

Labor Press over to the union, and it appeared thereafter as the official organ of Local 554. At that point Tom Gaddis, who later became a well-known biographer, was sent from Minneapolis to edit the Omaha Teamsters' paper on a regular basis.

Headlines in the first bulletin read: "Nebraska only state to refuse pact"—"Omaha boss group has 35-year record of anti-labor terror"—"Truth about 'offer' made by the operators"—"Farmer's wife refuses to shop in Omaha today"—"Omaha workers, the fight of the drivers' is your fight."

In the issues that followed the bulletin continued to hammer away at the bosses. It exposed the lies in the capitalist press, told the union's side of the story and pinpointed the actual issues in dispute. As a result popular support of the strike continued to mount.

The propaganda offensive against the truck owners was accompanied by intensified picketing, which had become quite sophisticated because of the complications raised by the anti-picketing law. The union lookouts had to be on the alert because the operators had ceased to pretend that they could use regular equipment. Normally their rigs had a map of the U.S. painted on the sides, with a large white dot where Omaha is situated. An accompanying slogan declared: "White spot of the nation. Our workers are satisfied." As matters stood, though, the long struggle had raised a reasonable doubt as to the truth of the bosses' claim.

Tacitly admitting that fact, the Omaha firms now tried to move freight by various undercover means. Wide-ranging union action was required to cope with such tactics. In Chicago, for example, a concern named "Western Car-Loading" was created. Teamster Local 710 quickly discovered that this was a dummy company set up by a pool of Omaha truckers. It was struck at once. Through comparable efforts, at all terminals and on the highways, tight IBT control prevented scab operations of any kind.

Squirming under the heavy strike pressures, individual operators began to clamor for their committee to open meaningful negotiations with the Teamsters. This led to the resumption of contract talks on January 23.

The trucking bosses wanted to begin with bargaining over wage rates. But their attorney and spokesman, David Swarr, who appeared to be an agent of the Omaha Business Men's Association, had other ideas. He insisted that the first topic be the form of union recognition. We stood firm on the closed-shop provisions of the area contract, and Swarr used the issue to again break off relations. This action clearly showed that the top leadership of the city's ruling class was ready to fight to the last drop of the operators' blood to prevent any kind of a union victory. It also marked the beginning of the end of the conflict.

After a few days several trucking firms began to negotiate directly with the union entirely on their own. Then one of the major lines, On Time Transfer, signed a temporary agreement with Local 554. It provided that operations would be resumed immediately under the terms of the area contract. An understanding was also included that, if any modifications were made during subsequent talks with other companies, these would be accorded to On Time as well. This accomplishment gave us the last lever needed to force a general capitulation in the industry.

On January 30 representatives of four big truck lines met with the union committee, ready to talk turkey. Three were based in Omaha: Watson Brothers Transportation; Union Transfer; and Red Ball Transfer. The fourth, Daugherty Van and Storage, operated out of Sioux City; its action showed that we were now on the way to a breakthrough in that terminal as well.

Several days of hard bargaining followed. Apparently welcoming sanctuary against pressures from the Omaha Business Men's Association, the bosses accepted a suggestion that the sessions be held in my room at the Rome Hotel. Fay Watson and Mickey Krapinski spoke for the operators. Tom Smith and I represented the Teamsters, and from time to time, rank-and-file militants were brought in to participate in the discussion of terms concerning types of work in which they were normally involved.

This time the closed-shop clause was accepted without quibbling; the truck owners knew that they had to recognize the full union power on whatever terms we wanted. Agreement was also reached on full application of the key provisions in the area contract. As in the case of the Kansas City rider, minor adjustments were made only on secondary matters and for similar reasons.

Standard mileage rates were to be in effect on runs to points outside Nebraska. Pickup and delivery pay on these operations was to be the full seventy-five cents an hour, except on the Kansas City leg, where the rate would be fifty-five cents. Pay on trips entirely within Nebraska, also between Omaha and Sioux City, was to be sixty cents an hour. A scale of fifty-five cents was set on runs within a seventy-five mile radius of Nebraska terminals.

Because of the long strike after the area agreement first went into effect, the union found it advisable to compromise on the tenure of the settlement now being negotiated. The standard pact expired October 31, 1939. It was agreed that the Omaha contract would run an additional year to October 31, 1940. At the same time, it was understood that any improvements established in renewing the area provisions would automatically be accepted by the Omaha firms. The bosses were saying, in effect, that they would take the next area settlement, sight unseen, because they didn't want to be hit soon by another strike. This was agreeable to the union, since the workers themselves also needed a breathing spell to recuperate from their exhausting struggle.

Renewal terms were also negotiated for the contract involving city trucking companies. An across-the-board increase of 7 1/2¢ an hour was provided, bringing the scale up to 52 1/2¢. Comparable gains were registered concerning overtime and job conditions.

On February 15, 1939, the jubilant membership of General Drivers Local 554 accepted the proposed settlement. With that the strike ended in Omaha. Soon afterward Local 383 ratified similar terms for over-the-road and local operations of firms based in Sioux City, also bringing the walkout there to a close. Smaller companies in the region that were still holding out against the IBT were then quickly forced into line. At long last the fight was entirely over.

After nearly six months of fierce conflict, the embattled workers had emerged victorious. In the process, their union had given a most impressive demonstration of its power.

For the first time the Omaha Business Men's Association had received a thorough whipping. The myth had been shattered that Nebraska was an impregnable haven for open-shop employers. With the long record of labor defeats there finally reversed, the ground had been laid for a general labor upsurge. Every worker militant in the city and state now understood that the bosses could be beaten.

Equally important, the over-the-road contract had now been planted firmly in the trucking industry all up and down the Missouri river valley. Defeat of the Omaha-Sioux City employers gave final assurance that uniformity of basic wages and conditions on an eleven-state basis had become a reality. Most of the trucking operators in the area now realized as much; and the union forces were ready to make short shrift of any who might still entertain doubts.

For the Teamsters International, it was an unprecedented triumph.

22. A Transformed International

Among those deeply impressed by the union's success was Daniel J. Tobin. In the May 1939 issue of the IBT's official magazine, he said of the Omaha-Sioux City settlement: ". . . another great victory has obtained for the officers and the unions that participated in this strike. . . . Most of the men on strike had not been members of our union more than a year, but in all my time and my years of service I have never known a better conducted strike or better union men than those that were engaged in this conflict."

Not long after the battle ended the IBT head asked me to join his staff of general organizers. As far as local union officers and members were concerned, formal authority of that kind was not needed for me to play a leading role. Yet it would help in confounding oppositional elements within the Teamsters Joint Councils. So we decided in the party fraction that I should accept the post.

Such action required my resignation as secretary-treasurer of Minneapolis Local 544. Kelly Postal, who had held the office of trustee in the local, was selected by the membership to complete my term as secretary-treasurer. Curt Zander was named to fill the post vacated by Kelly.

On May 1, 1939, I was accredited to the new position over the signatures of Tobin and Hughes. Their authorization stated: "This is to certify that the bearer of this credential, Mr. Farrell Dobbs, is a direct, salaried officer, organizer and representative of the International Brotherhood of Teamsters. . . . Wherever Organizer Dobbs is directed to work local unions and officers must extend to him all the helpfulness and. information desired by him or that may be useful to him in his work."

It was understood that I would be assigned the special task of supervising over-the-road organizing in the central states. Agreement was also reached that I should set up my headquarters in Omaha, so as to help the relatively new local unions in that region and to let the bosses know that they would be kept under surveillance.

Without awaiting such formal authorization, the necessary post-strike activities had already been set into motion. Action on grievances in the eastern part of the area stood at the top of the agenda. Numerous contract violations had been occurring in that region. The operators involved seemed to bank on the union losing the fight in the west, which would have weakened our position. Even if we won, they had come to expect that the agreement would not be tightly enforced. That assumption had arisen due to laxness exhibited by local union officials at a few terminals. It gained further credence because of inadequate attention to matters in the east on the part of the area leaders, who had been compelled to concentrate almost entirely on the battle along the Missouri river. The time had now come, however, for these bosses to learn that they were gravely mistaken.

The union had emerged from the western conflict stronger than ever. Problems in the east, which had temporarily been put aside, could now be dealt with effectively, and they were. We decided to make an example of a major chiseler, so as to teach every boss a meaningful lesson. TransAmerican Freight Lines, a big outfit based in Detroit, was chosen as the target. It had extensive operations, reaching from the east well into the southwest.

A meeting was held with the operators' area committee. There we presented grievances against TransAmerican involving thousands of dollars in back pay. After a week went by without any action, the union committee took matters into its own hands. At a fixed hour the company's entire system was struck. Not a wheel was allowed to turn until the employees had received the money due them.

The bosses got the point.

To the union's area committee in those days, all operators looked alike. None were subjected to special demands; none were granted special favors. Full compliance with the contract was required and nothing less was tolerated. Grievances were not allowed to pile up without decisive union action. As the TransAmerican example showed, employers who got out of line risked having their operations closed down.

Advantage was next taken of a special clause in the area pact. It provided that the union and employer committees would jointly formulate supplementary rules concerning labor conditions as need arose through practical application of the agreement. Using this mechanism for the purpose, we raised the issue of sleeper-cab operations, which had not been specifically covered in the area negotiations. Terms established in the 1937 Twin Cities contract were used as a precedent.

In the latter document, sleeper-cab runs out of the Twin Cities had been explicitly banned. Relay operations had to be set up wherever a through run could not be completed in a normal driving span within a twenty-four hour period. On Minneapolis-Chicago trips, for example, a division point was established half way between the two cities.

Applying this concept, we set out to eliminate other sleeper-cab operations. Considerable progress was made over a period of time. An outstanding accomplishment of the kind involved runs between Denver and Chicago. With help from Local 13 in Denver, we forced the employers involved to shift over from sleeper-cabs to a relay system.

A fight was also launched against use of independent owner-operator status as a means to evade payment of union wages. Viewed in its purest form, this category involved drivers who were required to furnish their own tools as a condition of employment. Workers caught in that situation got all the protection that the area committee could give them.

Even within this group inclinations to expand the holdings existed. If additional units of equipment could be acquired, other workers were hired to do the extra driving. Types thus appeared in the industry which were known variously as gypsies, skimmers, wildcatters, etc. They were found hauling for one company today, another tomorrow, and the next day trying to drum up business entirely on their own.

Individuals, who had once been simple owner-drivers, thus became transformed into owner-driver-employers. As the process developed further, the reality became one in such cases of a single owner and several hired drivers. Efforts were then made through use of paper titles for equipment, issued under the guise of deferred payment plans, to conceal the real status of the hired drivers. When the pressures of economic depression upon the worker-victims who took such employment is added to the picture, a diabolical scheme for the payment of scab wages comes to light.

Digging into this mess was no small chore, but the area leaders did the best they could. Gradual headway was made toward preparation of explicit prohibitions in this sphere, which could then be included in future working agreements.

On every issue the IBT forces stood in full solidarity against the bosses and their stooges. Locals throughout the area had learned the value of using their collective strength in defending the workers' interests. As a result, fair and equitable internal relations prevailed in the union's over-the-road activities. Those involved tended to deal with one another in an open and above-board manner.

In this democratic atmosphere the union fighters became increasingly responsive to a class-struggle outlook. To help this trend along, I often used the parting injunction, "Don't arbitrate," when we separated after a meeting. It was intended to drill into them an instinct to cling tenaciously to their freedom of decision, never letting it be taken from the union's hands by a so-called "neutral party."

Another slogan was envoked when a local leader asked if the union could do one or another thing. My opening reply was usually: "You can do anything you're big enough to do." Then we would discuss more concretely just how strong the union's position was in the given situation. This helped to instill in the workers a reflex tendency to think always in terms of using their class power.

An incident in Sioux City illustrated the attitude that now prevailed among IBT militants. Sid Jarrett of Local 383, a strike veteran and job steward, had a grievance to handle at the Watson Brothers terminal in that city.

"Fay," he firmly informed the head boss, "it don't stand nowhere in the text that you can bring your kinfolk in from the hills and work them out of seniority."

Sid made his ruling stick, as was becoming more and more the case with job stewards throughout the area. They militantly applied the concepts of union control on the job.

While enforcing the contract where it had been signed, other steps were also taken. We sought to saturate the eleven states with its coverage and to expand the area as a whole. Methods first developed in Minneapolis two years earlier were used. During the interim, however, these had been improved as we profited from new experiences.

At the outset the over-the-road campaign had focused primarily on the main terminals in the area. Radiating outward from Chicago, conquests in other cities were used each time to bring other, more remote, major terminals under union control. Advances previously made in that way now enabled us to concentrate on localities between these points that had at first been by-passed.

Line drivers and dock workers at organized terminals provided the initial IBT muscle. In various ways they blocked the flow of freight to and from nonunion outfits. This pressure was reinforced by a recruitment campaign among employees of the open-shop firms. Caught in this pincers movement, the bosses involved had to sign the area contract.

Union forces in the newly penetrated towns could then use these successes as a means to establish control over local cartage operations. After that, organizational activity could be extended into other spheres of general trucking. Open-end prospects were thus created for continuous union growth.

Similar methods were used in a drive to extend the area deeper into the southwest. In this case organized terminals in Missouri served as jumping-off points. Daily guidance of the activity was undertaken by Ted Neal of Kansas City, with able backing from Floyd Webb of Joplin and Gordon Shryock of Tulsa.

We first took on Yellow Transit, based in Oklahoma City. This firm had other terminals in Tulsa, Oklahoma; Dallas and Houston, Texas; and Wichita, Kansas. Of central importance was the fact that it also operated into Kansas City, St. Louis, Joplin, and Springfield, Missouri; there, especially, maximum union pressure could be brought to bear. Using its strength to the full, the IBT tied up the whole Yellow Transit system. Within twenty-four hours the company signed the area contract on the basis of the Kansas City rider negotiated earlier.

This advance laid the basis for creation of a southwest organizing committee. It embraced Teamster locals in Kansas, Oklahoma, Arkansas, Texas, and Colorado. Work to further extend the over-the-road drive was then carried forward by that body.

One day a problem arose involving contract violations by a truck line operating out of Fort Smith, Arkansas. It required direct action, so Neal and I decided to go down there. Suddenly I recalled that Ray Dunne had once been sentenced to an Arkansas chain gang during his IWW days. This, it seemed, would be an appropriate occasion for him to pay his first return visit to the state since that time.

We arranged for him to meet Ted and me in Kansas City. Then the three of us headed south in Neal's car. On the way we stopped at a beautiful spot in the Ozarks to enjoy a few sips of liquid corn and a delicious chicken dinner.

Upon arriving in Fort Smith we checked in at a hotel. Neal then called the company head, asking him to come over for a talk. He soon showed up, and as we had agreed in advance, Ray Dunne laid down the law to the exploiter of labor. It seemed fitting that he should be the one to do so.

During this period we sought to develop even closer relations with IBT forces in the Rocky Mountain and West Coast states. An area structure had also come into being there, more or less parallel with the rise of the Central States body. It was led by Dave Beck of Seattle, who later became general president of the IBT for a time.

Beck appeared to have watched Minneapolis developments rather closely since 1934. At first he sought to emulate our aggressiveness, using tactics of his own kind. Then, when Local 574's charter was revoked, he slowed the tempo of his expansion program. Only after Tobin was forced to reinstate us into the IBT did Beck seriously embark on the building of an area formation in the west. In both his case and ours, such efforts began to gain momentum in 1937.

These rough parallels related only to shaping some kind of broad organizational structure. They did not extend to matters of basic policy. In keeping with Trotskyist concepts, we put forward a class-struggle outlook; Beck adhered to the class-collaborationist norms of business unionism. We advocated the industrial form of organization; Beck was essentially a craft unionist. We defended and sought to advance trade union democracy; Beck used bureaucratic methods, ruling those he led with an iron hand.

There was yet another difference, related directly to over-the-road contract policy. We bargained on an area-wide basis to establish uniform wages and conditions for all the workers involved. Beck allowed considerable variation in contract terms, according to each operator's so-called "ability to pay."

Despite these conflicting outlooks, we were able to establish practical cooperation in organizing and strike activities. In fact it had begun when Pat Corcoran visited Seattle toward the end of 1936. At that time he and Beck exchanged pledges of mutual support in area terms. Since then we had worked closely with the Denver and Cheyenne locals at the eastern edge of the Beck-led formation. Ray Keigley and Homer (Dutch) Woxburg, Teamster leaders in that region, were frequent visitors at our area committee meetings. These relations were broadened some when I, in turn, attended a 1939 conference of the western locals in San Francisco.

On the whole, such cooperation would continue to be helpful as we now prepared to negotiate renewal of the Central States over-the-road contract, which was soon to expire.

Preparations for this step began with regional consultations among the local unions involved. An area-wide conference was then held to ratify the workers' demands. It took place at the end of July in Cincinnati, Ohio. Delegates came from locals throughout the eleven states; also from Kentucky, Tennessee, Kansas, Arkansas, Oklahoma, and Texas. All were in a confident, enthusiastic mood.

Observers were present from the western states and from New York and Pennsylvania. Tobin, who had just returned from abroad, went directly from the boat to the gathering.

Unanimous agreement was reached on proposed renewal terms, and talks with the operators' representatives soon followed. This time their committee spoke for companies throughout the eleven states. Among its members were bosses from Iowa, Missouri, Nebraska, and South Dakota. For the first time they were participating seriously in the centralized bargaining sessions, which were again held in Chicago.

In the talks that followed, significant new concessions were won by the union committee. Wage raises were to be received in two separate annual installments. This was arranged within the framework of a two-year extension of the agreement, which was to expire on November 15, 1941. The time period involved was agreeable to the union under the given conditions. We still needed a breathing spell to recover from the 1938-39 battle, also to further consolidate and expand the area.

On through runs, mileage rates were to be increased to three cents and hourly allowances in all categories to eighty cents in the second year. Guaranteed minimums on daily hours of work — also minimum compensation related to layovers, breakdowns, etc. — were to be hiked at once. New clauses setting higher pay rates for driving special types of equipment were added. Concerning local runs, an immediate raise of five cents an hour was provided, with a second five-cent jump a year later.

A carefully-worded clause on dock-to-dock operations was included for the first time, so as to knock out certain types of chiseling. Various adjustments for the better were made on matters involving working conditions.

In overall terms, the workers would get an immediate boost in earnings of about 15 percent, with another 10 percent to come the second year. They would have more congenial job conditions generally. And they would face fewer occupational hazards. Besides that, no chances were being taken as to whether these advances would materialize in practice.

As before, the agreement left the union free to strike over any grievance that could not be settled to the satisfaction of its area committee.

Definition of the contract's scope was expanded to include Kansas, giving us a twelve-state structure. The "contiguous territory" clause was broadened to reach indefinitely beyond the southern, southwestern, and western boundaries of the area. This aided our efforts to break into new regions. It also benefited the Colorado, Montana, New Mexico, and Wyoming locals concerning runs to the east from those states in the Beck-led territory.

The new pact was signed by the negotiating committee for the two sides on October 6, 1939. It was then ratified by some 350 local unions in the twelve states and approved by Tobin. Regional meetings of the operators also brought acceptance from about 2,500 companies throughout the area. By this time close to 200,000 workers would be favorably affected by the contract, either directly or indirectly.

So great had the union power become that all this was accomplished without having to take major strike action. Nothing more was required than a few minor skirmishes with random bosses.

An instructive balance sheet could now be drawn.

With Trotskyist militants playing a key leadership role, the policies needed to build a potent International had been demonstrated in living terms. The necessary course had first been put into practice during the 1934 Minneapolis strikes. A means of projecting effective union-building measures onto a larger arena had then been exemplified through the North Central District Drivers Council, as it was initially conceived. Its successes proved the value of broad union cooperation developed with unfettered aims and limitless forms of action.

Examples had also been provided of ways to overcome obstacles created by the Tobin machine. The IBT head had been defeated in his attempt to read the Minneapolis Teamster militants out of the union movement. After that his objections to the NCDDC were sufficiently overcome to enable us to launch the over-the-road campaign.

Still another gain was made later through our perception of changing reality, combined with use of flexible tactics and the ability to maintain the necessary patience. Tobin himself was drawn into support of the eleven-state project.

The latter development had significant effects. Former IBT concepts of maintaining a loose federation of insular baronies were definitively fractured. As a corollary, the old-line craft structure began to crack wide open. The movement was no longer rooted primarily among relatively privileged driving crafts in exclusive sections of the industry. It was beginning to embrace workers in a much broader range of occupations.

A modified social composition resulted that implied new class-struggle potential.

Advances in organizational structure were also occurring. New patterns had been set for broader, more sophisticated methods of area-wide cooperation between local unions in pursuit of uniform goals. New examples of leadership guidance had been introduced in shaping the necessary strategy, tactics, and functional norms to achieve union objectives.

In the course of their struggles the workers had acquired increased awareness of their strength as a class. They had grasped the importance of bringing their collective weight to bear against the bosses on the necessary scale. And they had come more and more to identify themselves with militant union policies.

Full use of the Teamster power along the foregoing lines had brought the workers victory in the over-the-road conflict. The dramatic gains registered in that struggle had, in turn, inspired truck drivers generally. As a result the way had been opened for unprecedented union growth in all quarters of the industry.

In fact, new members were already pouring into the International Brotherhood of Teamsters at an accelerated rate. In both 1938 and 1939 it reported the biggest recruitment gains of any national organization in the AFL. By the fall of 1939 this added up to a total membership nearing 500,000, which represented quite a jump for the International from the 1933 figure of about 80,000. The IBT was well on the way to attaining its later standing as the largest single union in the country.

With competent leadership, the rapidly growing Teamsters union would have been capable of wielding great power in the service of the working class.

23. My Change of Activity

Back in 1937 a conflict had developed within the Socialist Party. It stemmed from actions taken by the Norman Thomas wing, which had a majority in the organization. The Thomasites were playing fast and loose with socialist principles. At that stage their domestic deviations centered on the crossing of class lines in politics. In New York, to cite an example, they withdrew the SP's mayoralty candidate in favor of the Republican Fiorello La Guardia, a capitalist politician running on a fusion ticket.

When the Trotskyists and other left wingers in the party opposed majority policies of this kind, objective discussion of the differences was evaded. Instead the dissidents were subjected to bureaucratic harassment. What amounted to a loyalty oath was demanded of party branches. Those refusing to comply had their charters suspended, and even state units were reorganized.

Such tactics caused a deep-going split in the SP. The entire left wing assembled in a special convention of its own at the beginning of 1938, the delegates representing both Trotskyists and other revolutionary militants. The rebel gathering voted to form the Socialist Workers Party, which has existed since then as this country's revolutionary-socialist movement.

During informal discussions at this founding convention of the SWP, new plans were projected concerning my activities. I was to withdraw from the Teamsters as soon as practical. When that could be done, I was to take up new duties at the party's national center in New York, functioning as its labor secretary. This step was intended, among other things, to implement party work in the trade unions generally. There were grounds for optimism about future progress along those lines, since workers now constituted a majority in the party. Moreover, a good many of them were seasoned trade unionists with considerable experience in the class struggle.

Soon after the convention, however, a new development had

taken place in the IBT. We had overcome Tobin's objections to the over-the-road campaign in which I was playing a large part. It thus became necessary to postpone indefinitely the contemplated shift in my activities. As a corollary, though, the new situation enabled us to broaden party recruitment of truck drivers.

Revolutionists always strive to win supporters among those with whom they are associated, wherever that may be. In broad organizations such as trade unions, their efforts assume dual forms. On the one side, socialist militants involve themselves as fighters in support of the immediate aims of the masses. On the other, they also approach such activity as political work, using the lessons of the conflict to recruit new members into the revolutionary party. This duality, in turn, serves to strengthen class-struggle influences among the masses generally, as conditioned by the given objective trends.

These concepts were, of course, applied by Trotskyist militants engaged in the over-the-road campaign. Acting through the indicated divisions of labor, every comrade in the Teamsters made contributions to the effort. We also got help from the party nationally through both leadership consultations and direct forms of support. Functioning as a combination along these lines, the comrades were able to make significant gains for the SWP.

In doing so we took full advantage of the changing situation within the IBT. It was generally recognized, for example, that key leaders in the over-the-road struggle were "some kind of socialists." This circumstance was taken simply as an accepted fact, even by old-line officials who were part of the action. Interest tended to center on how well we fought, not on our politics. This attitude, generated under conditions of intense struggle against the trucking bosses, tended to promote a democratic political climate in the union.

In some cases officials of long-established local unions went a bit further. A few were willing to do occasional favors for "your party," as they put it. This, too, gave a boost to our political work.

Most important, though, we found considerable interest in revolutionary ideas among militant young workers. This trend arose mainly in the western part of the area where the most intense battles occurred. As a first step toward advancing their political education, we got interested workers to read the *Northwest Organizer* regularly. Those ready to go further were introduced to the paper fully reflecting the views of the Socialist Workers Party, then the *Socialist Appeal*. These efforts led to recruitment of party members by ones and twos in a few places.

Our biggest gains of the kind were made in Omaha, where the conflict in the west centered. There the situation was somewhat like it had been in Minneapolis during 1934. The workers were engaged in a life and death struggle. Ruling class attacks on their union had immunized them against red-baiting. And Trotskyists in the IBT stood foremost among their acknowledged leaders. As a consequence of these combined factors, some of them showed lively interest in our political ideas.

These circumstances enabled us to establish a branch of the SWP in Omaha. It began to take form during the strike there and developed more fully after the union victory. The unit was composed almost entirely of truck drivers, reinforced by a couple of more experienced party comrades sent from Minneapolis to help them. Al Russell, who had become well integrated into the Omaha union, was elected branch organizer. He, in turn, used methods learned in Minneapolis to intensify political education among the new party members.

Such gains would have brightened the outlook for the years immediately ahead, if objective conditions had remained favorable. Injection of class-struggle perspectives into the IBT, which had proceeded apace ever since 1936, could have been further extended and deepened. In the process, party recruitment would have been advanced to new heights.

By mid-1939, however, profound changes were developing in the international and national situations. World War II was about to begin. Evidence was mounting of preparations by the capitalist ruling class to plunge this country into the bloodbath. At the same time, conservative union bureaucrats were beginning to voice their readiness to climb onto the war bandwagon. Under these conditions new trends, adverse to revolutionists, were bound to arise in the trade unions, at least during the first stages of the world conflict.

An unusual circular Tobin sent to his general organizers on August 3, 1939, constituted the first warning signal.

"I am enclosing herewith copy of the August issue of our Journal," he wrote, "which contains an article on the situation in Europe today. I am also enclosing copy of a letter from the President of the United States regarding this article. Kindly regard the President's letter as confidential."

In the appended article, written by Tobin, the key passages stated:

"Well if war comes, you ask, how long will it last? What

will be the results? My judgement, as a layman, is that it may last two years and that eventually the British-French forces will win. They must win, or else the result would be too terrible to contemplate. . . .

"You think we can keep out; you listen to those self-protection patriots in the Senate of the United States. Don't make me laugh. We will be in the struggle in one way or another in one year after it starts. Of course I want no war. . . . But who can stand aside and see a madman beating up the innocent, defenseless, peaceful citizen that has done no wrong. . . .

"Some of our Senators believe we should be neutral; in other words, close our eyes to the destruction of civilization. They quote the words of Washington, 'European entanglements, etc.' It can't be done. Washington lived in a different age. Washington was no coward. If he lived today he would fight for justice. It's hard for me to say we will be in it. It's hard to order a strike. But sometimes we are forced to do unpleasant things. . . .

"Thank God that the Stars and Stripes still wave over your roof at night and that your Union can function freely and your voice and protest can and will be heard; and vow again to preserve that Flag and that Union, and swear once more that you will help to defeat by your voice and vote, inside and outside of your Union, anyone who advocates the destruction of this free land of ours by substituting some other form of government such as now prevails in many countries in Europe, where men of Labor are destroyed and where no Labor Unions are allowed to prevail. Happy we should be, even in our troubles, to have this land of liberty as our land, our country."

President Roosevelt's letter to the IBT head said:

"Dear Dan: That is a grand article and I am glad that it is going to get such wide distribution. Somebody ought to go on the air and deliver, with very few changes, what you have written. Be sure to get in touch with General Watson when you are in Washington next week, as I do want to see you."

If ever there was a clear portent of coming times, this was it. Tobin was serving notice that he would back Roosevelt in taking the country into war. He was also setting the line for a witch-hunt inside the IBT against opponents of that course.

This posed a question of principle. In our view as socialists there could be no compromise on such a vital issue. We had to oppose the imperialist warmakers, no matter what the consequences might be within the union. That being the case, it would soon become impossible for me to serve on Tobin's organizational staff. Hence, concerning my future role, the time had come to subordinate union work to direct party activity, the perspective outlined at the beginning of 1938.

During August I made a special trip east to discuss the matter with Jim Cannon, then national secretary of the Socialist Workers Party. We found ourselves agreed that I should leave the IBT post with no unnecessary delay. The matter was next taken up with the party's Teamster fraction. A general understanding was reached that my resignation should be submitted after renewal of the over-the-road contract had been negotiated and the bosses had signed the changed terms. These matters were taken care of by mid-December and an appointment was arranged with Tobin to inform him of the action I intended.

About a week before our talk, he had sent me a complaint that my expenses for telephone calls and telegrams were "more than the bill for the International President, International Secretary and General Organizer combined." This immediately came to his mind upon being told that I was resigning. He assumed that my action was caused by dissatisfaction over matters of salary and expenses. Considerable effort followed to placate me on this point.

Perhaps enough consideration hadn't been given, he said, to the unusual expenses entailed in far-flung over-the-road activities. In any case, there would be no repetition of such complaints. More than that, I would soon be getting a big raise in pay. In fact, he added, I would reach the top salary for general organizers of $15,000 a year (in 1939 dollars) faster than anyone before me ever had, and there were no limits to how high I might rise in the organization.

Money was not the issue, I replied. My action had its roots in a basic disagreement with him over the war question. He had, to all practical intents and purposes, spoken in favor of U.S. entry into the world conflict (which had begun by that time). I, on the other hand, was against it. That was bound to make it increasingly difficult for me to work with him as a union organizer.

Tobin bridled at these remarks. I was calling him a warmonger and it was not true, he protested. Considerable argument followed about our respective positions on the war question. Then, tacitly agreeing to disagree on the issue, we turned to another subject.

"What plans do you have for the future, Farrell?" he asked in his distinct Irish brogue. I informed him of my intention to go to New York and devote full time to the political work of the SWP. This would center on two issues: opposition to the war; and advocacy of a labor party to contend for public office against both the Republican and Democratic parties. It was high time, I added, that steps were taken to prevent the capitalists from using their control of the government to undermine gains won by the workers on picket lines.

My ideas about a labor party were not realistic, the IBT head contended. He argued as follows: few, if any, union officials would listen to such notions. They knew that it was necessary to be practical about politics, finding a way to work, here and now, within the existing structure. He, for instance, had gained important favors for the IBT through his connections in high Democratic Party circles. The best course for me was to follow the road he had taken. Trade unions were the place for a labor leader to devote time and effort. It was there that the most good could be done. As matters stood, he stressed, I had already accomplished a good deal in the IBT and there would be bigger things to follow.

When these arguments failed to sway me, a new tack was tried. He, too, once thought of himself as a socialist, Tobin said, when he was an inexperienced and impressionable youth. As time went by, though, he found it necessary to shed such concepts. One must learn to live in the world as it is. As I grew older, he predicted, these facts would come home to me, and youthful inclinations toward socialism would be forgotten.

Next he asked about the future of my three daughters. What about their college education? Would "those people in New York" see to it that they were able to get full schooling? Would all of my family's needs be met by them, as would surely be the case if I remained with the Teamsters?

Seeing that the father-to-father approach was getting nowhere, the IBT head then tried a father-to-son angle. He told about one of his children who had developed "impractical" notions in choosing a career. After a time the lad was talked out of it, and through the father's connections, placed in a well-paying job. That episode, it appeared, was supposed to prove the father's superior wisdom.

Continuing in that paternal vein, he asked me to give further thought to my proposed action in the light of the discussion with him. Then I was to inform him in writing of my final decision. A suggestion was added that, if I remained determined to quit, my formal membership in Minneapolis

Local 544 should be kept up through regular dues payments. He explained that this would facilitate my return to IBT activity, if I changed my mind later on.

Matters involved in choosing my successor were then discussed. There was no point in nominating another party comrade for the post, and I made no recommendations. As for Tobin, he merely noted that, when word of my action got out, there would be a flood of applicants for the vacated job; few of whom would be qualified. He then asked my help in buying some time in order to make a deliberate choice of my replacement. We agreed that, for the time being, a simple announcement should be made that I was taking an extended vacation.

As the discussion in its entirety revealed, the IBT head did not contemplate indefinite retention on his staff of an organizer who was a revolutionary-socialist. He obviously relied on the corrupting effects that he assumed high wages and soft living would have upon me. With the passage of time, he expected that I would become just another business unionist. For a period he would have tolerated my continued radicalism, because of my special knowledge about the union's newly developed activities in the long distance trucking industry; but only as part of a transitional process. In the end, either I would have allowed my principles to become compromised, or moves would have been undertaken to oust me from the staff. With the country soon to enter World War II, there could be no question that these were the alternatives.

Toward the end of the month I submitted my written resignation from the position of general organizer, effective January 1, 1940. As had been agreed, letters were sent to all members of the union's area committee informing them that I was taking a temporary leave of absence for personal reasons. They were advised to assume the initiative in handling workers' grievances through established area procedures. Similar notification was sent to John Bridge, who was then chairman of the operators' area committee.

On January 5, 1940, Tobin asked my opinion about a choice between Carl Keul and T. T. Neal to replace me in union office. He wrote: ". . . if you had to make an appointment, on the question of ability, loyalty, and an understanding of the Labor Movement, and especially of the intricate questions that arise in the district in which you have been working, who would you choose, Keul or Neal?"

In response I recommended Neal, giving the following reasons:

"You already know the odds he has worked against in Kansas City and that he has come through successfully despite the fact that he was frequently fighting almost single-handed for a correct program. I have seen him operate in communities that are bitterly anti-labor and he does very well in combining the qualities of courage and discretion in just the degree necessary in such a situation. He has learned to hear all sides of a story before making a decision. He is very conscientious in carrying out assignments and remembers to keep the interested parties informed of developments in any given situation without having to be prodded for reports. He does not place personal considerations above the interests of the movement. . . .

"I would also choose Neal from an entirely different point of view. You mention the intricate questions which arise in the district in which I have been working. I believe that the ripest fields for organization in the western district lie in Missouri, Kansas, Oklahoma, Arkansas and eastern Texas. . . . The ground work for this has already been laid. Neal has participated directly in this foundation work, knows all the problems, has many contacts and is probably in the best position of any one man I might name to get this job done in the most efficient manner.

"As for the question of the Area Committee, it is not, in my opinion, mandatory that my successor fulfill entirely the functions which I performed. We have today an Area Committee of 14 men, everyone of whom is more or less an expert in his own right on over-the-road matters. They have learned to function as an organized group, and of no less importance, a systematic method for dealing with the employers has been developed and is working out very well in practice. I believe that by holding a consultation with the Area Committee you can work out a very satisfactory solution of existing problems in that department of the work."

By this time, Marvel Scholl, the children, and I had left Omaha to return temporarily to Minneapolis. There the girls stayed with their grandparents, enabling Marvel and me to set out on an auto trip to Mexico. Our purpose was to visit Leon Trotsky and his companion, Natalia Sedova, who were residing in that country.

During the time we were in Mexico City, Sandy O'Brien reached me by telephone. It appeared that Tom Hughes had informed him of my departure from the Teamsters and he expressed concern about the action. He wanted very much to see me, he said, but was about to depart from Chicago for an extended stay in Miami, Florida. So when Marvel and I left Mexico, we decided to drive back to Minneapolis by way of Miami.

When we got there, Sandy's first question was: "What did that old bastard do that made you quit?"

Not waiting for an answer, he then asked me to go to work for Chicago Local 710, adding that I could continue to concentrate entirely on over-the-road matters, naming my own salary.

Having developed great respect for Sandy, I tried hard to explain why I had left the Teamsters and the reasons for devoting myself in the future to party activities. He listened attentively. But it seemed incomprehensible to him that anyone would voluntarily walk away from a well-paid, promising career in the Teamsters.

There being nothing further to say, we bid each other a friendly good-bye. Marvel and I then resumed our journey back to Minneapolis. When we got there, another letter from Tobin awaited me.

"I am writing to advise you," he said, "that Brother T. T. Neal of Kansas City, is going on as General Organizer for the International Union beginning March 1, 1940. If at any time you can give him any information or assistance that will help him in the district in which he will work, I am sure that it will be very much appreciated by Brother Neal and our International Union."

In February I went to New York to take up my new duties as labor secretary of the Socialist Workers Party. Later on Marvel and the children joined me there.

Then, during the spring of 1940, Sandy O'Brien telephoned me at the party office. Several operators were claiming that I had granted them special exemptions from various terms in the union contract, he said, and the area committee needed my help in putting an end to such crap. He asked me to come to Chicago to attend a joint session of the union and employer area bodies. I did so, denouncing the bosses making such assertions as liars.

It was my last involvement in official business of the International Brotherhood of Teamsters.

When I returned again to trade union activity, it would be to help Minneapolis Local 544 in yet another fight with Tobin, which arose over the issues of war and union democracy. The course of that struggle, from its inception to the climax in 1941, merits extensive description. This will be undertaken in the third and concluding volume of these reminiscences of a participant in the labor upsurge of the 1930s.

Index